Nation,
Governance,
and Modernity in China:
Canton, 1900-1927

Studies of the East Asian Institute, Columbia University

The East Asian Institute is Columbia University's center for research, publication, and teaching on modern East Asia. The Studies of the East Asian Institute were inaugurated in 1962 to bring to a wider public the results of significant new research on Japan, China, and Korea.

Nation, Governance, and Modernity in China: Canton, 1900-1927

Michael Tsin

STANFORD UNIVERSITY PRESS

STANFORD, CALIFORNIA

Stanford University Press
Stanford, California
© 1999 by the Board of Trustees of the
Leland Stanford Junior University

Photographs courtesy of the Hoover Institution,
Stanford, California
Printed in the United States of America
CIP data appear at the end of the book

To Judith and in memory of my mother, Lau Tak-kit

Acknowledgments

Research for this book started in Princeton, where Marius Jansen afforded me both intellectual space and unfailing support to conduct my work. Encouragement from the other members of my dissertation committee—the late C. Martin Wilbur, Gilbert Rozman, and Arthur Waldron—gave me the confidence to pursue the project further. I owe a special debt, however, to Joseph Esherick, who over the years has generously donated his time and energy as reader and critic of my work, and kept me on course with his insight and guidance.

Had I not met Daniel Kwan in London, my initial research in the PRC would have suffered from a lot more blunders and obstacles. Dr. John Wong of the University of Sydney also kindly provided letters of introduction. In the PRC, the hospitality of Huang Yan, Ye Xian'en, Qiu Jie, and Ni Junming ensured that I not only got some work done, but also had a chance to learn about contemporary Guangzhou and its people. Financial support from the Program in East Asian Studies and the department of history at Princeton as well as the Councils for Research in the Humanities and the Social Sciences at Columbia made my research trips possible. Photographs in this book appear by courtesy of the Hoover Institution.

Professors Prasenjit Duara, John Fitzgerald, and R. Bin Wong read the manuscript in the last stages of the revision, and I am very grateful for their helpful comments and suggestions. My intellectual debt to the pioneering works of Arif Dirlik and Martin Wilbur should be obvious to every student of Chinese history. In the last several years I have been fortunate to be in the company of a stimulating and diverse group of scholars and students at Columbia. Andy Nathan has been the exemplary senior colleague. He also graciously took on the task of critiquing an earlier draft on short notice.

Matti Zelin offers wise counsel, and Haruo Shirane has been generous with both his time and advice. The many students who passed through my classes have taught me more than they probably realized. Timely assistance in preparing the manuscript came from Rebecca Nedostup. At Stanford University Press, Muriel Bell and Stacey Lynn ensured a smooth publication process, and Holly Caldwell was meticulous in her editing.

This work has been subjected to Judith's critical scrutiny since its inception, but her role goes far beyond that. Without my family, all of this would have simply been impossible.

M.T.

Contents

Nation,
Governance,
and Modernity in China:
Canton, 1900-1927

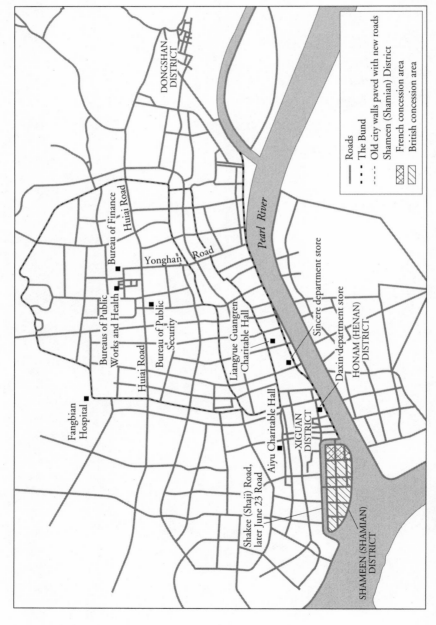

Canton in the mid-1920s

DONGSHAN DISTRICT

Bureau of Finance
Huiai Road

Yonghan Road

Bureaus of Public
Works and Health

Bureau of Public
Security

Huiai Road

Fangbian
Hospital

Liangyue Guangren
Charitable Hall

Sincere department store

Daxin department store

HONAM (HENAN)
DISTRICT

Pearl River

Aiyu Charitable Hall

XIGUAN
DISTRICT

Shakee (Shaji) Road,
later June 23 Road

SHAMEEN (SHAMIAN)
DISTRICT

Roads
The Bund
Old city walls paved with new roads
Shameen (Shamian) District
French concession area
British concession area

Social Unity and Modern Governance

> What is society? Where is society? Can't find God, so I
> cannot believe in God. Can't identify society, so I cannot
> follow society. Yet there are many who, though not know-
> ing what society is, nonetheless recognize its representa-
> tives. What are the latter? Those who are now on top,
> occupying positions of privilege and power. . . . Worship
> of the national flag; worship of genitalia; worship of God
> . . . now that we obey society, will we not also obey those
> things?
>
> —ZHANG SONGNIAN, 1921[1]

A common feature of modern polities, as Benjamin Schwartz once pointed out, is their claim that they "derive their sovereignty from the people."[2] They also invariably subscribe to the notion that "the people" are best represented as a cohesive social body. Even in a liberal democracy such as the United States, where conflict of interest has arguably become part of the political structure, the issue of whether the people can remain bound together as a putatively unified body has animated the debate on multiculturalism in recent years. Indeed, the idea that the people within a given polity can be seen as an organic unit, that is, as a discrete and ordered social body or "society," has often been taken for granted. In the case of China, for example, it has become a truism, as the twentieth century draws to a close, that the raison d'être of its government is no longer the quest for a communist utopia. It is rather the guarding of what the government repeatedly declares to be the sacrosanct unity of the Chinese "nation." And national unity, in the eyes of the Chinese political leaders, is not merely a matter of territorial integrity but also one of social cohesion.[3]

As the constitution of the People's Republic reminds us, the duty of the Republic's citizens is not only "to safeguard the unity of the country" (Article 52), but to accept that "their freedom and rights may not infringe upon the interests of the state, of society and of the collective" (Article 51).[4] In a similar vein, residents of the newly established Special Administrative Region of Hong Kong have been pointedly and repeatedly told that they will be free to carry on their business as long as they work within the parameter of national unity. If the Chinese regime seems extreme in its privileging of the collective, the apparent striving for a cohesive national/social body is by no means unique to China. It is hence presumptuous to dismiss, as some observers are prone to do, the Chinese leadership's emphasis on unity as little more than the last-ditch rhetoric of a weakened government which can no longer draw on the authority of Marxism-Leninism and Mao Zedong Thought.

Such obsession with unity does not, in fact, simply stem from the heads of a Chinese Communist old guard trying to hold on to power. Rather, it has always nourished a powerful current within the political culture of twentieth-century China. Students of China, however, have a strong tendency to reduce summarily such preoccupations with unity to the abstract label of "nationalism," a term which is routinely and readily invoked as a major explanatory factor for the course of modern Chinese history. Despite the voluminous literature on the subject, the question of how nationalism actually works in practice, that is, how it actually exercises its force beyond the realm of consciousness, remains something of a mystery, as it is rarely explored as a substantive problem. This is true not only in Chinese studies.[5] To many scholars, for instance, it has become almost obligatory, particularly in the wake of the seminal works of Benedict Anderson, to emphasize the constructed nature or the imagined quality of the nation.[6] Much attention has thus been paid in the last decade to the role of symbols, the medium of ritualistic performance, or the formation of elaborate pageantries in providing the cultural fabric for the construction of a nation.[7] Yet these approaches, innovative as they are, do not quite solve the puzzle of this persistent impulse to create discrete and unified national/social bodies in modern times. More important, they have relatively little to say about its material impact on the actual lives of the people themselves.

An account of the virulence of such obsession with unity which attributes the phenomenon entirely to the organizing system of nation-states is insufficient, moreover, because it does not explain the mechanism through which the system is sustained.[8] Instead, some clues might be found, I will suggest, in the inherent logic of the political culture of modernity, in particular the symbiotic relationship between the discursive premise of modern government and its actual effort to constitute a unitary social body to be placed under its jurisdiction. Unlike ancien régimes, which tended to enlist the divine to provide sanction for their rule, modern governments claim to derive their legitimacy from this constructed social body. The privileging of this unified body thus not only works at the level of the imagination or the symbolic, but is sustained by direct and specific mechanisms made possible by the power of government. The effects can be seen in the new ways in which the government seeks to interact with all those who come under its purview. Little wonder that John Fitzgerald recently suggested that one can hardly come to grips with the history of twentieth-century China without first exploring the genealogy of this relentless pursuit for unity.[9]

THE ADVENT OF SOCIETY

The belief in the actual possibility of creating a unitary and cohesive social body can be traced to tenets of modernist political thought first formulated in nineteenth-century Europe. As delineated by Alain Touraine, the quest to turn "the people" into a rationally organized body, which could be imagined as "an order or an architecture based upon computation," lies very much at the core of the culture of modernity.[10] In his discussion of sociology as an academic discipline, Eric Hobsbawm suggests that it "was probably the most original product of the social sciences" at the turn of the century. "For the fundamental problems which preoccupied its most notable exponents were political. How did societies cohere, when no longer held together by custom and the traditional acceptance of cosmic order, generally sanctioned by religion, which once justified subordination and rule? How did societies function as political systems under such conditions?"[11]

Fearing that their own country might disintegrate in the face of a collapsing dynasty and foreign encroachment, many members of the Chinese elites of the late Qing and the early Republic turned to new channels of knowledge such as sociology for guidance and inspiration. In fact, one of the most enduring images bequeathed to us by these elites is that of the people of China as "a heap of sand,"[12] even though the various dynastic regimes of the past had obviously been able to keep their subjects in order. But to these modernist elites,* China's survival in the world demanded the creation of a new kind of social body, and the allegedly loose sand must somehow be metamorphosed into concrete blocks to be cemented together. They believed that the key to China's weakness lay squarely in the lack of cohesion among its constituents. Much ink and, indeed, blood have been spilled in twentieth-century China to determine the best means to modernize the country: how to reorganize the institutions and the economy, advance technological production, and so on. Yet, despite their differences, most members of the elite—monarchists, republicans, Guomindang (Nationalists), Communists—shared an affinity for a new modernist temporal and spatial consciousness, the ultimate embodiment of which was to be found in a newly unified national/social body.

In their writings, the elites often described their endeavor in terms of the construction of a "society-and-nation" (*shehui guojia*). In his recent study on Liang Qichao's historical thinking, for example, Xiaobing Tang notes how Liang (1873–1929), writing at the dawn of the twentieth century, offered a narrative of history that equated the evolutionary development of society with that of the nation.[13] However, there was, as Alexander Woodside reminds us, originally no equivalent concept to the Western notion of society (as evolved since the eighteenth century) in the Chinese, Japanese, or Vietnamese languages. It was the Meiji Japanese philosopher Nishi Amane who appropriated the classical Chinese term *shehui* (*shakai* in Japanese), which usually meant communal gathering of some kind, and arbitrarily as-

---

*The term "modernist" is used here to denote a set of discursive and material practices that stemmed from a particular worldview: a specific constellation of ideas associated with European thought since about the eighteenth century, usually referred to as the Enlightenment. Central to this worldview are the notions of the power of reason inherent in each individual subject, the unlimited possibilities of scientific knowledge, man as an active and rational agent in the making of the world and its future, the cult of progress, and the ultimate knowability of all the intricate processes at work in both the human and the physical worlds. In terms of political practice, it signifies the belief in human mastery and in the power of human reason and capacity to order the world.

cribed to it the Western meaning of society—a body social—in the late nine-teenth century. The "new" term was then reincorporated into the Chinese language.[14] Indeed, acknowledging the alien origin of the contemporary term *shehui*, the distinguished Chinese historian Qian Mu could only sug-gest that its Chinese equivalent was *xiang,* which, interestingly enough, means the place to which one belongs and in which one's identity is lodged.[15]

Yet, despite its rather recent vintage, the term "society" quickly gained a pivotal place in the lexicon of the intelligentsia in early-twentieth-century China. The popularization of the concept is usually traced back to the pio-neering works of the late Qing intellectual Yan Fu (1854–1921). Yan has often been credited with introducing sociology, which he rendered in Chinese as *qunxue*—the study of the logic of grouping—to China. The term *qunxue,* however, was first coined by Kang Youwei who, in Canton in 1891, also be-came the first known teacher of *qunxue* as an academic subject in China.[16] His most famous student was his fellow native of the Canton region, Liang Qichao. The first full Chinese text on sociology was, moreover, translated from Japanese by Zhang Binglin in 1902. Sociology then appeared as a course in government institutions of higher education in 1906, and became a part of the curriculum of the National University of Peking four years later.[17] By 1917, as one critic wryly observed, the neologism *shehui* had "lately become the most fashionable of platitudes [*zuishimao zhi koutouchan*], which is being used to explain every phenomenon."[18] Not surprisingly, Wen-hsin Yeh finds that in Shanghai University, which was established in 1922 with close ties to the Guomindang, the sociology department was "the stronghold of radical thinking to which the university owed much of its reputation."[19]

The burgeoning interest in sociology, however, was about more than just the transmission of ideas. The process through which knowledge is produced is often also instrumental in the creation of the very entity it claims to ana-lyze.[20] By subscribing to the idea that the web of human relations can be framed within a finite structure of meanings, and that its working can be scientifically and systematically analyzed as an organic whole, sociology in effect served as a medium through which the notion of society was at once legitimized and objectified as an anterior structure. It also instituted the idea that the construction of society as a cohesive body was both possible and natural.

The key question for most elites of early-twentieth-century China, then, was how to turn this idea of society into reality. This was to be achieved through political means: the establishment of a new mode of governance with very specific means of organizing and mobilizing its constituents. This modern government would operate on the basis that the masses of people under its jurisdiction, however diverse, were nonetheless a knowable entity, a potentially ordered society of citizens that could be rationally arranged and organized as a discrete collective through governmental means.[21] It was hence no accident that in republican China social surveys (*shehui diaocha*) designed to collect detailed information about people's living conditions, some of which were used as sources for this study, were relentlessly churned out by government agencies and the new universities. The objective was to inscribe the realm not as some "imagined community" but as a real social body, whose web of human and material resources could then be harnessed by the government.

The modus operandi of such a government differed significantly from that of the dynastic regimes. To be sure, over the centuries dynasties had developed a sophisticated repertoire of mechanisms to sustain their own rule, to safeguard their notion of a proper order, and to collect revenues. Subjects of the dynasty were recorded as taxpaying units and as providers of labor service. They were exhorted to dress, behave, and worship according to their station, and to refrain from heterodox activities. It was thus imperative for governmental power to be perceived as awesome and encompassing, capable of granting rewards and inflicting punishment. It did not need, however, to penetrate to the level of everyday local domains. Above all, subjects of the dynasties were not assumed to be the constituent parts of a discrete aggregate body that would exhibit, under methodical dissection, its own internal relations and dynamics. Indeed, it is a signal feature of the political culture of modernity that government is deemed capable of shaping, arranging, and reconfiguring, by overt force if necessary, the constitution of this aggregate body, and of subjecting it to discipline and direction.

The point is that obsession with a cohesive social body or a well-ordered society as the necessary basis of a modern nation does not operate only at the discursive level. Rather, concrete political mechanisms are employed to create this organic entity, however elusive the objective might prove. For the government, the construction of this organic entity serves a dual purpose:

defining the organizational patterns of its body of constituents and providing it with the source of legitimacy necessary for a modern regime. It was with such background in mind that Michel Foucault noted a transition in the technologies of rule in eighteenth-century Europe from "an art of government to a political science," a process in which the population came to represent "more the end of government than the power of the sovereign."[22]

CANTON AS A CASE STUDY

To trace the process of the Chinese elites' attempt to institute a new body social, one must bring together different fragments from the late Qing and the early republican period. That was a time of intense debates and reconceptualization of how the realm should be governed. The lives of the people were shaken by the myriad material changes as well as the discursive remapping of their world. Old practices took on new meanings. Openness to new knowledge brought the promise of a new age. It was in the shadow of these developments that the first modernist government in Chinese history—the Guomindang-led administration of Canton (Guangzhou) in the first half of the 1920s—was established. From there the Guomindang, in alliance with the Communists, engineered what came to be known as the Nationalist Revolution, with its stated objective to create a new society-and-nation. It set off a chain reaction the effects of which are felt in China till this very day.

The choice of Canton as a case study, then, is in part dictated by the fact that it was the site of this government. It is also my belief that only through the detailed and textured history of a locality can one have a sense of the life of the people, and the effects of the larger forces which shaped their milieu. This book is hence an exploration of how the lives of the inhabitants of a city intersected with the efforts of a group of modernist elites to reorder the realm. As the only port officially open to foreign trade from the mid-eighteenth century and then as one of the earliest "treaty ports" created by the Treaty of Nanjing of 1842, the city of Canton, located on the southern coast of China, is a familiar name even to the cursory reader of Chinese history.[23] For its role in the early-twentieth-century history of China, it has been variously labeled "the cradle of revolution"[24] or described as "a case of seemingly local developments affecting the revolutionary transformation of the entire nation."[25] Yet, despite or perhaps because of its centrality in the political drama of the period, surprisingly little has been written from the perspective of the city and its inhabitants. Moreover, in view of the momentous changes in the People's Republic in recent years, and the apparent increasing friction between the central government and the localities, particularly in the south, a closer look at the social history of a key southern urban center can also shed some light on the tensions inherent in the process of national construction.

Chapter 1 retraces the history of Canton in the late Qing period. It focuses on the activities of the nonofficial organizations, particularly the emergence of the Nine Charitable Halls in the local scene. The purpose here is to bring into view the often complex negotiations between the government and the nonofficial organizations and to ask whether the nature of their interaction constituted a departure from past practices, as some scholars have argued.[26] The evidence in Canton suggests that while, as in the case of previous dynasties, there was more room for the existence and the maneuvering of the nonofficial organizations in a period of weakened government, there was actually little substantive change to the relations between the two sides.[27] The significance of the nonofficial organizations was not that they became more autonomous or powerful in late Qing Canton. It was rather that they were seen, by both themselves and others, as articulating a novel position vis-à-vis the apparatus of the imperial government. They represented themselves, in short, as the embodiment of the new *qun* or society, opening up new political space though still hardly capable of mounting any material challenge to the dynastic regime. These nonofficial organizations did, however, leave an important legacy: By grafting themselves onto the movement to reorder the realm and by appropriating the language of the intelligentsia, the leaders of the nonofficial organizations undoubtedly helped to legitimize and popularize the discourse of society within the rapidly changing milieu of early-twentieth-century China.

Chapter 2 then takes us through Canton during the uncertain years of the early Republic. The failure of the parliamentary republic to create a viable new order and to inscribe China with the trappings of modernity had left the country in shambles. A new generation of elites, particularly though by no means exclusively those in the Guomindang and the Communist Party, began to perceive their mission as literally to construct from the ruins a modern, unified, and cohesive society-and-nation. Meanwhile, the physical and economic geography of Canton was transformed. The process was initially made possible by the efforts of the émigré elites in the 1910s and continued under the direction of the new Guomindang-led government. Inspired by the novel concept of urban planning, the government tried to create a new spatial structure as an integral part of its drive to reorder the realm.[28]

The new society was to be classified into different discrete "classes" (*jieji*) or "segments" (*jie*), with the industrialists and workers in particular signifying the advent of a new age. It should be noted that the notion of class put forward by many of the elites here had more in common with Durkheim's idea of "the division of labor" than with Marx's "class struggle."[29] The institution of class division, in other words, was considered a sign of modernity and a conduit through which a society established its "organic solidarity."[30] However, the industrialists of Canton, despite the strides made in what has often been referred to as "the golden age of the bourgeoisie" in the first decade of the Republic, remained a rather marginal force.[31] The local workers, rooted in their conventional mode of organization, also proved to be far from an ideal replica of the working class of the modernist imagination. Still, the success of the Hongkong Seamen's Strike (1922) against the British did impress the Guomindang, as the latter began to entertain the possibility of utilizing the workers' militancy against the imperialists as a potentially vital and leading thread to weave together a new form of social body.

Chapter 3 takes up the story around 1923–24 when the Guomindang government, now with the assistance of the Soviets and the Communists, began in earnest to implement its project to construct society-and-nation. The government would attempt to mobilize the people and to mold them into a cohesive collective. In doing so, it was inevitable that the new government would have to confront the entrenched interests of the existing order. The merchant community, for instance, proved to be difficult to deal with. Not only did it resist many of the initiatives of the government out of its own material interests, but it also posed a problem in terms of its positioning in the new society. Simply put, if the industrialists and the workers signified modernity, were the merchants an inherently recalcitrant force or a progressive segment of the new organic collectivity?

As the conflict between the two sides escalated to an armed battle in late

1924, the government responded by positing a divide between the merchants in Canton: The big merchants, allied with foreign imperialists, were on the side of reaction, while the middling and small merchants were supportive of the government project of reconstruction. This distinction by the government did not bear much relation to reality, as there was little evidence to suggest such a systematic split within the merchant community. Its significance lies instead in the revelation of the internal logic of the elites' endeavor: The construction of a cohesive body was a process of boundary-making, and the putative integrity of the organic whole could be represented only by consistently dichotomizing those who belonged and those who did not.[32] The self-assigned task of the government was to dissect systematically the makeup of the people. It was to identify, marginalize, and exclude those deemed threatening to the unity of the social body.

Chapter 4 turns to the effort of the Guomindang-led regime, in the aftermath of the Hongkong Seamen's Strike, to organize the workers as the foundational bloc or *qun* for the construction of a new society. The workers, it hoped, would lead the way in demonstrating how the people could be organized into a cohesive unit, with the different classes or segments then joining together into a unified body. Much of the organizational work was carried out, with the blessing of the government, by Communist activists or their sympathizers in Canton. In their writing on the politics of class in this period, most scholars are quick to point out the potential conflict between the interest of the nation and that of specific social classes.[33] It is also well known that many within the Guomindang, including its leader Sun Yat-sen, accepted class analysis as a modern and useful guide for their project but were nonetheless very wary of the Communist advocacy of class conflict.[34] What has often been overlooked, however, is the process of the organizational work itself, the logic of which could only lead to a failed attempt to construct a working class. By exploring in some detail three different sectors of the local labor community—the unskilled rickshaw pullers, the semi-skilled oil-processing workers, and the well-placed railroad crews—we will see quite clearly that the imposition of organizational unity did not create a new cohesiveness among the workers. It actually had precisely the opposite effect: It highlighted the heterogeneity of labor and led to further fragmentation among its ranks.

Finally, Chapter 5 focuses on the impact of the Canton-Hongkong Strike of 1925–26 on both the government and the city on the eve of the Guomindang's embarkation on its "Northern Expedition." The staging of the strike, in the aftermath of the May Thirtieth incident in Shanghai in 1925, has often been described as the apogee of the Guomindang-led government in Canton. The strike was said to have propelled the Guomindang to national power through its successful mobilization of the people, spearheaded by the workers, to form a multiclass alliance against the imperialists. Upon closer examination, however, this narrative of mobilization proves to be rather misleading. It obscures the disciplinary aspects of the mobilization process. Indeed, the strike organization turned out to be not a representative organ of the working class, still less a medium to effect the unity of the different classes, but rather a competing power structure to the government. To complicate the matter further, neither the strike organization nor the government necessarily controlled the rank and file of the mobilized, who often defied the disciplinary apparatuses of both regimes. Despite its intentions, then, the government could not harness the forces it unleashed, as it was unable to regulate and direct its constituents to form a cohesive social base.

Seen from this perspective, Chiang Kai-shek's use of force against the strikers was not simply a power play against the Communists and their Soviet patrons, as has often been alleged. Nor did it signal a wholesale retreat from the effort to seek the support of society. His objective, rather, was to reassert the authority of the government and to enforce discipline among its mobilized constituents. Chiang envisioned a clearly ordered and unitary social body, even if its construction demanded the use of extreme disciplinary measures, including overt force. The price, however, was clearly visible in Canton. Despite the effort of the government to continue the mobilizing process, the repression of the factious strikers and the Communists did not result in a rejuvenated and unified society. It simply turned Canton into a sea of passivity and apathy.

THE LOGIC OF MODERN GOVERNANCE

Both the Guomindang and the Communists, who successively ruled China for much of the twentieth century, were modernist in that they subscribed to a specific form of political rationality: the belief that a cohesive society-and-nation could be constructed through systematic analysis, mobilization, and organization of the various elements which constituted the social.[35] Both invoked "society" or "the people," while at the same time engaging in new and detailed forms of manipulation of the very group in whose name they spoke. If it is indeed true that, in the modern world, "*society* replaces God as the principle behind moral judgement and becomes, rather than an object of study, a principle that can explain and evaluate behaviour,"[36] then there is clearly every reason for government to arrogate to itself the role of both architect and representative of the collective. It was undoubtedly such concerns which prompted the philosopher Zhang Songnian to express his reservation, cited at the outset of this introduction, about the valorizing of society in early-twentieth-century China.

This is not to suggest that the discourse of society amounts to nothing more than a shibboleth. If the quest to create a cohesive social body invariably entails new disciplinary techniques of government, it also inevitably opens up new spaces and avenues for the negotiation of power, however unequally structured, between the governing elites and the governed. In Canton, for example, mobilization of the people meant that the hitherto excluded became a part of the political process, even if those mobilized were subjected to governmental intervention lest they simply turn into just another heap of loose sand. Indeed, both the Guomindang and the Communists were caught within the contradictory logic of modern governance: Society was simultaneously the organ from which their legitimacy was supposed to be derived and the subject on which they exercised their governmental power. The project to construct a cohesive society-and-nation, then, was perforce at once emancipatory and disciplinary. By privileging the social, modern governance, however unwittingly, brings into sharp relief the heterogeneity of the social realm and empowers its constituents. The empowerment, however, also produces an irreducible tension, generated by an impossible quest to repress the infinite differences within the social realm into the finite disciplinary structure of an organic body: "society-and-nation."

Induced in part by the breathtaking pace of change in China in post-Mao era and its uncertain future, scholars have recently been actively engaged in a reassessment of the history of twentieth-century China. Many old assumptions and interpretations have been subjected to critical scrutiny and reevaluation.[37] It has even been suggested that the Chinese elites' embrace of anti-imperialist nationalism has resulted in "a failed Chinese modernity."[38] The influential works of scholars such as Partha Chatterjee have, of course, long alerted us that freedom from the yoke of imperialist political domination can easily lead to the reproduction of the repressive conditions of modernity instead of liberation from them.[39] Still, one will do well to remember, at least in the political sphere, that the imposition of a modern mode of governance, in the name of "society-and-nation," was often negotiated, contested, or even subverted by the newly mobilized constituents, as the history of Canton clearly demonstrates. The point perhaps is not whether Chinese modernity is a success or a failure, but that the culture of modernity itself is riddled with ambiguities and contradictions, and is hence decidedly Janus-faced. By retrieving fragments of the history of Canton in the first quarter of this century, this study may reveal some of the logic as well as the consequences of modern governance and thus, by extension, of the culture of modernity of our time.

CHAPTER ONE

In the Name of Society

> This timely rise of society in our country was the result of
> the people's effort to carry out their unequivocal duty.
>
> —LI LIANGFU, 1912[1]

What struck most observers, particularly those from the West, about late imperial Canton was simply its physical appearance. One enthusiastic, if somewhat exasperated, late-nineteenth-century visitor described the city as "one labyrinth of lanes bordered by houses and shops running in every direction. . . . So narrow are the thoroughfares that one seems to be passing for hours through the interior of some mammoth establishment, where, in endless succession, wares of all varieties are exposed for sale, and where manufacturers and producers of the same may be seen at their work." He exclaimed, with apparent delight, that "there were shouting and calling; Laughing and scolding! What a singular Chinese Babel!!"[2] Not everyone, needless to say, viewed the seeming disorder with such fascination. Arriving at the southern metropolis in 1866, the Reverend John Turner, for example, was appalled by the "low shabby-looking houses stretching away for miles" and "the prevalence of foul odours." "The shops were mostly poor, with open fronts," he added. But even Turner conceded that "some of the richer merchants' places of business are gorgeous with fantastic designs."[3] Commerce, indeed, had always been a hallmark of Canton. A vibrant commercial life in Canton can be traced as far back as the Tang (618–907). In the words of Edward Schafer, in the city then "foreigners of every complexion, and Chinese of every province, summoned by the noon drum, thronged the great market, plotted in the warehouses, and haggled in the shops, and each day were dispersed by the sunset drum to return to their respective quarters or, on some occasions, to chaffer loudly in their outlandish accents in the night markets."[4] Canton remained one of the most important ports, if not necessarily always the premier port, of south China throughout the late imperial period.[5]

Yet commerce, significant as it might be, was just one dimension of the milieu of Qing Canton. Canton was also a seat of some political prominence. Not unlike many other urban centers in late imperial China, Qing Canton did not have any clearly defined boundaries. Nor did it constitute a single administrative entity.[6] It fell instead within the jurisdiction of two separate counties, Panyu and Nanhai, each of which claimed about a half of the city. In addition to the two magistrates, Canton also housed a prefect (of Guangzhou Prefecture), a governor (of Guangdong Province), and a governor-general (of Guangdong and Guangxi). Other officials included a provincial education commissioner, a provincial surveillance commissioner, a salt controller, and various circuit intendants. There was, in other words, a palpable presence of the world of officialdom.[7] But the strategic location of Canton at the head of the Pearl River, fed by its three major tributaries—the West, the North, and the East Rivers—meant that the city was destined to have more than just a collection of *yamen*.

The demarcation between official and mercantile activities in the metropolis, however, was often said to have been the imposing sixteen-gate city wall. Although the foundation of part of what became the wall was laid during the medieval period, the complete six-mile circumference, like so many other such structures in China, was actually not constructed until the Ming dynasty (1368–1644). The wall was extended around 1377 to connect what were then three discrete parts of the city. Then a new section of the wall was added in the year 1565, with the additional enclosed part acquiring the label of New City (*xincheng*) in contrast to the Old City (*laocheng*). Both the outer and inner walls were reportedly kept in good repair throughout the

Qing period (1644–1912).[8] The primary arena for trade and commerce, however, was always located outside the walls. While the officials inside took a keen interest in supervising the flow of tributary trade, and there were obviously shops and itinerant vendors operating inside the gates, the presence of the walls nonetheless constituted a poignant symbolic divide between the two sides.[9] To the officials, the commercial quarter might have been a source of loans, contributions, and revenues, but they were content to leave its economic processes largely to its own device.

This sense of division was perhaps further reinforced with the arrival of the bannermen under the Qing. Stationed within the walls, their distinctive large dwelling quarter placed them apart. In sharp contrast to the rest of Canton, the streets within the bannerman district were wide and the houses, mostly built of adobe, bore the distinguishing mark of broad black lines round the doorways. "The general appearance," according to an observer, "is like that of northern cities."[10] In close association with the imperial bureaucracy were, of course, members of the gentry. They generally patronized the institutions, such as the leading academies, Confucian temples, or other orthodox religious establishments, which tended to cluster around the official buildings. The fact that the mercantile quarter (outside the walls) had become a defining feature of the Nanhai section undoubtedly contributed to the views of the compilers of a Panyu gazetteer. Commenting on why there should be a separate body for each half of the city to prepare for local self-government during the last years of the Qing, the authors insisted that the people of Panyu and Nanhai, despite their common place of habitation, had nonetheless markedly different customs, values, and habits (*fengqijishu xishangyiyi*).[11]

Despite such rhetoric, the division between officials and others in late Qing Canton should not be exaggerated. There were, first of all, the so-called gentry-merchants. The more conspicuous among them, like the famous reformer Zheng Guanying, were active in the original Canton Chamber of Commerce that was established under the auspices of the Qing government in 1905. Not only were the headquarters of the chamber located in the New City within the wall, the social connections and style of the gentry-merchants also put them more in the company of the official elites. The career of Zheng was quite typical of this particular stratum. Born a native of Xiangshan county near Canton in 1842, Zheng chose to leave for Shanghai while still a teenager, worked as a comprador, purchased an official title, and developed a close working relationship with the imperial bureaucracy.[12]

The gentry-merchants were, to be sure, a rather small group. But in late Qing Canton, even the humbler merchants seemed to be making great social strides. For example, the proliferation of merchant-sponsored organizations, which engaged in activities ranging from the education of women to the promotion of local self-government, undoubtedly lent a new level of prominence to their leaders. On the other hand, one should not confuse visibility with autonomy. In his study of Ming-Qing Foshan, a commercial town near Canton, David Faure argues persuasively that a burgeoning mercantile sector does not necessarily translate into a distinct form of urban political power.[13] As will be shown, in Canton, despite their increasing assumption of extrabureaucratic functions, the merchants negotiated consistently, and not always from a position of strength, with the official elites in order to safeguard their operations. What was unprecedented in the last years of the Qing was therefore not so much the enhanced network of merchant and civic organizations which, like their predecessors, rarely posed any direct challenge to the entrenched power of officialdom. It was rather, I will argue, the introduction of a new political discourse which enabled the merchants and others to reposition and articulate themselves as representatives of a novel entity, society, the fate of which was said to be tied to the increasingly precarious state of the nation.

THE MAKING OF NINETEENTH-CENTURY CANTON

To take advantage of the waterway, the original center of commercial activities in Canton was located to the south of the city wall along the Pearl River, particularly in the area then known as Haopanjie (Moatside Street) just outside the gate. It then began to expand toward the western part of the city during the Ming-Qing period. According to the early Qing scholar Qu Dajun (1630–1696), Haopanjie, where the rich and the notable once congregated to engage in conspicuous consumption and ostentatious display, was already by his day "a far cry from what it used to be [*jinjiebukewenyi*]."[14] Such an observation, however, seems to have sprung from the pessimism caused by the political chaos in the south after the Ming-Qing transition, which resulted in the evacuation from the coast. Haopanjie, in fact, retained a strong measure of vitality throughout the "High Qing" in the eighteenth century. The area, moreover, remained the domain of powerful extraprovincial merchants, its impressive array of *huiguan* (lodges) mere affirmation of the activities of the sojourners in the commercial world of Canton.

The famous Huizhou merchants, for example, had a virtual monopoly on the supply of stationery. The Ningbo and other Zhejiang merchants specialized in luxury goods, while merchants from Sichuan and the northwest tended to concentrate on medicine and herbs. Crucial to the success of these economic enterprises were the ubiquitous Shanxi merchants, whose financial networks and resources made them indispensable partners in the transaction of capital or the remittance of profits.[15] To remind themselves of their distant homes, sojourners brought 44 theatrical troupes from their various native places to Canton in 1791.[16] Together these merchants formed part of a marketing system which stretched from one end of the empire to the other and functioned rather efficiently whenever the realm was fortunate enough to be blessed with political stability and free of natural calamities.

It was, however, the revitalization and growth of external trade which started the gradual westward drift of economic activities away from Haopanjie in the early Ming. As Canton regained its position as the principal port of south China after the fall of the Mongols, the problem of a congested waterfront, accentuated by an accumulation of silt along the moat, provided strong reasons for an expansion into other areas further along the river. An early indicator of the shift was the construction of a special facility, the *Huaiyuanyi*, in Xiguan (Western Suburb) in 1406 for the purpose of housing tributary traders. The arrangement was inherited by the early Qing, although for a time foreigners were apparently free to provide for their own accommodation, on the condition, of course, that they remain outside the wall. After the Cohong system was established in 1720, however, foreigners were increasingly restricted to the *yiguan* (foreign quarter) located in the Shisanhang (Thirteen Guilds) section in southern Xiguan, where they were supposed to deal solely with the Cohong merchants.[17]

Befitting its status as the only port open to foreign traders after 1759, Canton came increasingly to depend on external commerce for its economic life. Compared to the extraprovincial merchants of Haopanjie, Western traders were far more reliant on their local intermediaries. Their presence, therefore, generated myriad subsidiary employment opportunities, most of which were found in Xiguan.[18] By the nineteenth century, Xiguan had become a prosperous center of merchant activities that rivaled, and was soon to overshadow, the splendor of Haopanjie. The wealth of the Cohong merchants is legendary, and they adorned Xiguan with some of the most luxurious dwellings in the empire, especially along its Shibafu (Eighteenth Ward), which has been described as "the street of Canton millionaires."[19]

One of the first symbols of the merchants' venture into the respectable realm was the construction of the Wenlan Academy in Xiguan around 1810. It came into existence as part of a new *xiuhao gongsuo* (agency for moat clearance) established by the Cohong merchants. The *gongsuo* itself, in turn, was an outgrowth of an initial joint effort by several leading members of the gentry and the merchants to ease the clogging in the moat.[20] The title of "academy," however, was something of a misnomer for Wenlan. Unlike its better-known contemporary, the Xuehaitang of Canton, Wenlan actually did not accept any students. Instead, it spent most of its resources holding literary competitions, and, true to its origin, continued to be responsible for the task of moat clearance in the winter.[21] The academy was, therefore, more of a meeting place for the local notables, where young literati could gain the patronage of the rich in Xiguan. Thus throughout its history, Wenlan was identified with the very top stratum of merchants with close official connections, and as such was not entirely representative of the generation of merchants who attained prominence in late-nineteenth-century Canton.

The Treaty of Nanjing of 1842 had the ironic (albeit intended) effect of "democratizing" the merchant constituency by putting an end to the Cohong monopoly, yet at the same time opening the door to foreign domination of the treaty port economic system. By exerting their dominance in the financial and transport sectors rather than over the forces of production, Westerners controlled not so much the raw muscle as the pulse of what was principally a commercial economy in Canton.[22] Yet, although the metropolis would never regain its position as the premier port of China, its mercantile sector proved to be quick to adapt to the new economic structure. It became at once more diversified and more dependent on the services of Western banks and trading houses, the most potent symbol of the latter undoubtedly being the Hongkong and Shanghai Bank founded in the neighboring British colony of Hong Kong in 1865.

At the same time, with the instability of the late Qing empire, the old extraprovincial merchants found it increasingly difficult to maintain their networks of trade. Faced with mounting competition, they assumed a progressively reduced role in the economic life of Canton.[23] A vivid example is the growth of local native banks (*yinhao*) in the latter half of the nineteenth century. Established usually with only limited capital and hitherto existing in the shadow of the powerful Shanxi banks (*piaohao*) and often reliant on the latter for logistical support, the native banks developed a close working relationship with members of the mercantile community who were able to take advantage of the increased Western presence, such as investors in the booming silk industry or the *sanjiangbang* merchants.[24] The Western banks' reluctance to deal directly with local enterprises, together with the subsequent establishment of the Hong Kong currency as the preferred medium for settling accounts in business transactions involving foreign traders, meant that the native banks were given the opportunity to fill this valuable niche, to say nothing of cornering the foreign-exchange market.[25] They were, moreover, dominated by natives of nearby Shunde county, which was also a major center of silk production. A republican study concluded that over 55 percent of the native banks' capital and 70 to 80 percent of their staff came from Shunde.[26] Indeed, from the late nineteenth century on it was by no means uncommon to find merchants who owned both banking and silk concerns.[27] This classic combination of financial and industrial entrepreneurship enabled native bankers and silk merchants to become a commanding force in Canton.

Another significant impact of the aggressive Western presence was the recasting of Canton's economic and marketing system. The well-developed, albeit always tenuous, mercantile networks that covered disparate parts of the country during the heyday of the empire suffered severe dislocations as a result of the midcentury upheavals and the opening of the treaty ports. The opening of Fuzhou, Ningbo, and Xiamen, not to mention the emergence of Shanghai as the leading economic center, meant that Canton no longer served as the only distribution point for goods from the interior. To cite just one example, in 1860 Canton was the port for only 23 percent of the out-

going tea, although it had monopolized tea exports until 1843. The balance
was picked up by Shanghai (44 percent) and Fuzhou (33 percent).[28] Produce
that used to travel from the upper or middle Yangzi via Hunan's Xiang River
valley, then either overland or down through the West River to Foshan and
Canton, or from the lower Yangzi region to Jiangxi, and overland into northern Guangdong before following the North River to the Pearl River delta,
now headed east in unprecedented quantities.

As Canton's status as the premier port faltered, there began to develop a
regional commercial network in the south that no longer centered so much
on Canton as on the colony of Hong Kong. As Hong Kong, located about
150 kilometers south of the old metropolis, rose to dominance by virtue of
its political stability and superior harbor facilities,[29] it furthered the economic ties of the Canton area with southeast Asia and beyond, and northward with Shanghai and its surrounding areas through direct coastal trade.
In just over fifteen years toward the end of the nineteenth century, for
instance, there was a tenfold increase in the volume of imports from southeast Asia into Canton, although total foreign imports to the metropolis during the same period did not even triple.[30] But even this figure conceals the
large amount of goods that were shipped first to Hong Kong and showed up
in the statistical tables as imports from the colony. The increasing dependence of the Canton area on southeast Asian rice, for example, was often
obscured by the fact that most of the transactions were done in Hong Kong
instead of Canton.[31] Those provinces, such as Guangxi in the southwest,
which had no logical alternative to Canton and Hong Kong as their ports of
access were to become an integral part of this southern system.

Moreover, by the nineteenth century, the Pearl River delta area had
become the leading source of emigrants from China, which further strength-
ened the socioeconomic linkages of the region to the outside world. Emigré
merchants, who were involved in activities ranging from the rice trade in
Thailand to rubber production in the British Straits settlement, began in
earnest to tap the markets at home, usually through utilizing Hong Kong's
financial and transport facilities. In doing so, they weakened still further
Canton's economic connections with the inland trade.[32] Not until the completion of the whole course of the Canton-Hankou railroad in late 1936
could this trend begin to be partially reversed.

THE NINE CHARITABLE HALLS

The first example of an organized mobilization led by the local notables in nineteenth-century Canton came as a response to the midcentury upheaval caused by the combined onslaughts of internal rebellion and foreign invasion. The willful destruction of the Thirteen Guilds section by fire in 1856, for example, epitomized the kind of local disturbances that were to plague Canton periodically well into the twentieth century.[33] The motives of the mob which set the fire were less than clear. An antiforeign outburst was inextricably mixed with a revolt against the privileged, and both were made possible by the reduced capacity of the government to enforce order.[34] Voluntary organizations of the city's inhabitants, in which the merchants played a conspicuous role, were thus called upon to augment the meager resources at the government's disposal.

The first urban militia in Canton, financed and organized largely by the mercantile community, was formed in 1847. But a prototype of the famed Merchant Corps of the early Republic was actually not created until two years later, when a citywide effort was launched. Rather than relying on mercenaries, the militia required shops to provide volunteers, the number of which depended on the size of the establishment. Each shop also contributed one month's rent for the militia's maintenance.[35] The effort was short lived, however. Probably owing to the problem of organization or insufficient governmental support, most wards of the city decided against keeping a militia when the issue once again arose in 1857.[36]

It was not until the twilight years of the Qing that there was a sharp rise in the number of voluntary associations in the city. There were, of course, always the trade guilds and *huiguan*, but those were relatively restrictive in terms of their membership and activity. At the pinnacle of the group of new fin de siècle organizations stood the Nine Charitable Halls (*Jiushantang*) which, for all practical purposes, became the focal point of unofficial civic activities in late Qing Canton.

The commitment of private wealth to charitable institutions has historical precedents that can be dated back at least to the late Ming,[37] and not surprisingly such enterprises flourished particularly in the declining years of a dynasty when both the need and the tolerance of the government for such activities were greatest. Unlike state institutions, private charities tended to be more encompassing in their declared purposes and reached out generally to the "deserving poor" instead of specifically to any designated group.[38] For instance, the most prominent of the Nine Charitable Halls, the Aiyu, founded in 1871, had the avowed aims of providing schooling, medicine, and burial facilities for the needy, in addition to caring for the sick and the old.[39] Whatever else might have accounted for the interest in sponsoring charities,[40] there is little doubt that philanthropic work endowed their patrons with the kind of social respectability and influence that could hardly have been duplicated otherwise. In Canton, moreover, the charitable halls provided a vital framework through which the insular nature of the city's commercial structure could be transcended. The limitations of the guilds have already been mentioned, and the problem was, if anything, accentuated by Canton's commercial geography. "For each branch of trade has its district, and separate locality," wrote a resident in 1875, "to which, as a rule, it is restricted."[41] Even the short-lived militias were organized on the basis of individual wards and as such were little more than a symbol of the temporary coalition of the different sectors within the mercantile community.

It was perhaps a sign of how times had changed that the Aiyu was established out of the downfall of a descendant of the one-time chief of the Cohong system, Pan Zhencheng (1714–1788). Pan Shicheng, who was conferred a *juren* degree in 1832 for his contribution to a famine relief effort in Zhili and who subsequently purchased a position of bureau director, was once active within bureaucratic circles and a noted salt merchant.[42] When he was hit by hard times and unable to fulfill his obligations to the government, his properties, which included some of the most sumptuous examples of architecture in Xiguan and a rich collection of fine art works, were confiscated.[43] The founders of the Aiyu were thus able to purchase Pan's old residence, located in Shiqifu (Seventeenth Ward) at the heart of Xiguan, as the headquarters of the charitable hall.

The purchase was made possible, however, only through personal connections between high officials and a gentry-merchant involved in the project. Indeed, while the Aiyu was known as an unofficial initiative, the blessing from the government was instrumental for its launching. Even the first contribution made to its coffers was in the form of an official grant.[44] On the other hand, a principal force behind the enterprise was a nouveau riche named Zhong Jinping. Born into a poor family and with little education,

Zhong became a successful entrepreneur by dealing in cinnamon bark from Guangxi.[45] An anniversary volume published by the *Guangdong Seventy-two Guilds News* in 1931 referred to the most important of the Aiyu's founders simply as wealthy merchants (*fushang*) instead of the more exclusive gentry-merchants (*shenshang*), and it is clear that the institution was financed by annual contributions from the various trades.[46] The management was initially run by elected representatives of the various *hang* or guilds. It was subsequently replaced by a board of directors, which served to coordinate the charitable work.[47]

The real blossoming of philanthropic associations in Canton, however, did not occur until the 1890s. Like the *huiguan*, the new charitable halls were located outside the walls, mostly in Xiguan or to the south of the city. Some, like the Liangyue Guangren (founded in 1890), were supported by merchants involved in the growing trade between Guangdong and Guangxi and were designed in part to assist natives of either province to return home in times of difficulties. The Liangyue Guangren boasted a network of directors from Wuzhou and Guilin in Guangxi to the Portuguese enclave of Macao, as well as in Shanghai.[48] Others, such as the Fangbian Hospital (founded in 1894), were an outgrowth of community organizations founded initially in response to specific crises. In addition to Aiyu, Liangyue Guangren, and Fangbian, other members of what subsequently became known as the Nine Charitable Halls included the Guangji Hospital (founded in 1892), Chongzheng (founded in 1896), Shushan (founded in 1897), Mingshan (founded in 1898), and Huixing (founded in 1900). The ninth member, Runshenshe, was originally founded as a literary organization in 1869 and later became involved in charitable work. Besides this group of leading institutions, there were also a significant number of other philanthropic associations in Canton and the surrounding areas.[49]

As institutions which openly claimed to transcend trade or regional differences, the charitable halls provided an excellent, and legitimate, training ground for those who sought visibility in the public arena. For example, the native bank merchant Chen Huipu, a man of humble origin who might have purchased a minor official rank, became a leading activist in the Guangdong Merchant Self-Government Association after initially coming to public attention through his effort in saving the Fangbian Hospital. It was he who enlisted the support of the other charitable halls to put together a rescue package for the hospital, steering it from the brink of bankruptcy to become, in the words of a contemporary, "the best of the Nine Charitable Halls."[50]

According to a proclamation of the Nanhai magistrate in 1899, the petition to construct a *fangbiansuo*—a kind of shelter for the homeless and the needy—in the western part of the city was presented by a group headed by a certain local licentiate named Chen Xianzhang.[51] The protocol of communications with the bureaucracy dictated that the petitioners be headed by a degree-holder. It is interesting that, unlike the Aiyu or the Liangyue Guangren, this case involved a mere magistrate in the multitiered bureaucratic world of Canton granting sanction to an organization represented only by a member of the lower gentry. Paraphrasing the petition, the proclamation suggested that some sort of facilities were needed for the large number of single travelers (most of whom were probably itinerant merchants, casual laborers, or peddlers) who had fallen on hard times in the city, and servants who, because of illness, had been abandoned by their masters to fend for themselves. The petition stated that although a *fangbiansuo* already existed in the Panyu half of the city within the wall—and was thus presumably government-run—people in Xiguan were fearful that they were too far removed from it because of the barrier imposed by the walls (*zuge zhongcheng zhi lü*). Hence a group of "like-minded fellows," the petition declared, had pooled their resources for an extra institution to share the burden.

The initial impetus for establishing the new *fangbiansuo* was the dire and visible consequences of the plague which swept through Canton in 1894.[52] Corpses were heaped outside the city wall, as victims were left to perish. According to an informed contemporary, the conditions prompted a group of philanthropists (*shanshi*), most of whom were merchants from Xiguan, to act.[53] The fact that the group lacked the necessary connections to the elites was revealed by their initial shortage of funds. Unlike the Aiyu, the *fangbiansuo* did not have the privilege of a government subsidy to help launch the institution. The lack of a strong seal of approval from high officials also undoubtedly hampered efforts to seek further financial support from other donors. Still, the shelter's operation was timely and it quickly gained a positive reputation. Its merchant sponsors, however, soon fell into discord.

After a series of disputes in 1899 and the withdrawal of some of its patrons, the institution was on the verge of bankruptcy and had virtually closed down its facilities.[54] It was then that a merchant with business connections in Hong Kong, Chen Heyun, attempted to raise the money to continue the venture. While Chen Heyun sought donations in Hong Kong, it was Chen Huipu and his associates in Canton who carried out the significant task of coordinating the other charitable halls to provide the *fangbiansuo* with financial aid, laying the foundation for the collective which later emerged as the Nine Charitable Halls. A new charter for the institution was drawn up, as it expanded and was formally renamed the Fangbian Hospital in 1901. Donations, from both within and outside Canton, were estimated to have increased almost twentyfold between 1899 and 1906, from over C$6,000 to C$110,000.[55] By the end of the Qing, the hospital had evolved from its humble origin to become an established force in Canton.

Charitable institutions like the Fangbian Hospital or the Guangji Hospital are often described as being run by merchants from the Seventy-two Guilds (*qishierhang shang*). The term "Seventy-two Guilds" requires explanation, as there is some confusion over its exact connotation in the literature. The term was reportedly coined and popularized after a large number of merchant guilds came together to deal with the demand of the Qing government for a guaranteed submission of transit tax (*lijin*) for goods in 1899.[56] But the assembly of various trades had never evolved into a formal institution with an administrative structure, nor did it have a permanent headquarters of its own. Subsequently, in documents or in popular parlance, the name "Seventy-two Guilds" did not represent an actual organization but rather was used as a generic term in reference to the general merchant community of Canton.[57]

Thus, for example, when the price of rice rose dramatically in 1907 and riots broke out in the Dongguan area near Canton, a *pingtiao zonggongsuo*, an agency for providing relief grain, was established, according to a contemporary report, through the joint effort of the Nine Charitable Halls, the chamber of commerce, and the Seventy-two Guilds in conjunction with the Donghua Hospital—a leading charitable institution of Hong Kong.[58] But a breakdown of the donations to the operation, which was based in the Aiyu, revealed that aside from the expected funding from the charitable halls and the chamber, most of the contributions came from the imperial bureaucracy and loans from the native banks of Xiguan. There was no independent contribution from the Seventy-two Guilds, although the name was once again mentioned with regard to the administration of the collected fund.[59] Similarly, some organizations, such as the Guangdong Merchant Self-Government Association or the Guangdong Anti-Opium Association (see page 35), which were often dominated by the same core group of activists, felt little restraint in claiming to speak in the name of the Seventy-two Guilds, not as a specific institution but as their perceived constituency.

For the merchants of Xiguan, however, the label did serve a useful purpose: Prior to the fall of the Qing in 1912, they invoked it whenever they wanted to distinguish themselves from the gentry-merchants of the chamber of commerce. But with the collapse of the dynasty and the takeover of the chamber by a new generation of merchants, the need for such a distinction was no longer apparent. It is thus no accident that, save in the influential newspaper *Guangdong Seventy-two Guilds News* (*Guangdong qishierhang shangbao*) (founded in 1906), the term "Seventy-two Guilds" appeared far less frequently in documents of the early Republic pertaining to mercantile activities. For the emergent self-anointed leaders of society in Canton in the early part of this century, it was the Nine Charitable Halls, not the Seventy-two Guilds, which provided the organizational backbone for their activities.

IN SEARCH OF SOCIETY

Despite the plethora of "unofficial" charitable institutions in late-nineteenth-century Canton, there is scant evidence to suggest that their activities amounted to any form of political challenge to the hegemony of the official elites. If Frederic Wakeman's description of Hankou, another center of commerce, as "a major entrepot completely under the official thumb of the government" seems overstated,[60] there is little doubt that the merchant and civic leaders of late Qing Canton operated under the watchful gaze of the imperial bureaucracy. That does not mean, however, that there was a complete closure to new possibilities. From the turn of the century onward, for example, local civic leaders began to extend their activities beyond the philanthropic realm. The process was gradual but clearly perceptible, culminat-

ing in the founding of the Guangdong Merchant Self-Government Association (*Yueshang zizhihui*) in late 1907. Significantly, simultaneous with this
process was a discursive shift in the intellectual milieu of the time. Simply
put, to many Chinese intellectuals then, those "unofficial" organizations were
no longer regarded as mere supplements to the arms of government or as the
random assembly of select individuals. They were transformed into the signal representative of an important new entity: "society" (*shehui*).

As mentioned in the introduction, the objectification of society as a structured totality analogous to an organism or system, whose web of processes
and relations is amenable to scientific scrutiny and analysis, is a product of
the modern era. In China, Yan Fu's translation of Herbert Spencer's *Study of
Sociology*, initially two chapters in 1897 and then the full text in 1903, was
instrumental in spreading this novel concept among the elites. While Yan
called this new branch of knowledge *qunxue*, it was the term *shehuixue*,
which was first used by Tan Sitong in 1896, that was to gain currency as the
translation for "sociology" in subsequent years.[61] Yan was particularly
impressed with the Spencerian analogy of the social to biological organisms,
and he was one of the first Chinese intellectuals to draw the connection
between the body social and the health of the nation.[62] He suggested, moreover, that sociology offered insights on how people could join together to
form collectivities or *qun* with a common purpose.[63] Not surprisingly, then,
shehuixue proved to be alluring material for many contemporaries who were
frustrated by the apparent lack of unity among the Chinese people. As Liang
Qichao noted in 1901, despite the fact that there had long been various kinds
of voluntary associations in China, her people were still like "a heap of
sand."[64] The remedy, Liang insisted in his famous treatise on the "new people" (*xinmin*), was to inculcate "public morals" (*gongde*) in the people, so
that they could look beyond their parochial ties, which were based on connections made through family, occupation, or place of origin, and form
larger collectivities. Society, in Liang's analysis, represented precisely such
larger collectivities, the underdevelopment of which was a revealing sign of
the want of cohesion among the Chinese.[65]

Following Yan Fu, Liang also considered a vigorous society to be crucial
for the strength of the nation. Public morals were key to the forging of
society-and-nation and were almost utilitarian in nature. Indeed, they

seemed at times to be simply a way of codifying the needs of the collectivities: Anything beneficial to the collective was good and morally desirable and vice versa.[66] As Liang put it, those who shirked their duty to serve society and nation, disregarding their moral standing as private individuals, were "insidious pests" (*maozei*).[67] Society was thus not the product of natural affection among people nor the result of the demands of their self-interest. It sprang rather from a deliberate and willful construction of certain moral norms.[68]

In an essay on constitutionalism written in 1910, Liang suggested that if a collective were to prevail over the forces from without, it must first solidify (*jianshu*) within. In a passage with rather ominous implications for the fate of the country, Liang argued that in order for a *qun* to solidify within, it must first suppress and eliminate elements harmful to the *qun*.[69] And it was through the exercise of such force of repression and elimination (*qiangzhili*), otherwise known as the power to rule (*tongzhiquan*), that a nation came into being. Liang thus concluded that the progression from an arbitrarily or loosely formed society (*renyi jiehe zhi shehui*) to a disciplined and organized nation (*qiangzhi zuzhi zhi guojia*) was both inevitable and human.[70] The formation of society, in other words, was not so much a virtue in itself as the necessary path which gave rise to the nation.

Seen through the prism of such discourse, voluntary civic organizations took on a larger significance. They should not, and indeed must not, focus merely on their particularistic interests. Instead they should demonstrate the spirit of public morals by involving themselves in the affairs of the public arena *for the good of the collective*. In doing so, these associations would provide the building blocks for larger collectivities, or the essential fabric with which society could be woven together. More important, they would lay the vital foundation for the construction of that ultimate collective: the nation.

The significance of this discourse of society was not lost on the leaders of the civic organizations themselves. The discursive link forged between society and nation lent a new legitimacy to their role in the public arena. For example, Deng Yusheng, an active participant in the voluntary organizations of late Qing Canton, pointedly titled his chronicle of the activities of fellow philanthropists *Quanyue shehui shilu* (A veritable record of Guangdong society) in 1910. Li Liangfu, a prominent silk and fabric merchant, stated in a prologue to the membership roster of the Guangdong Merchant Association for the Maintenance of Public Order (*Yueshang weichi gonganhui*), which emerged as the most powerful civic organization in Canton in early 1912, that the fortune of the nation was directly tied to the power and influence (*shengshi*) of society. Reiterating the familiar themes put forward by many intellectuals, Li suggested that the establishment of a republican form of government had propelled China to the same rank as the Western nations and had brought benefits to every citizen. That was why those who were aware (*shizhe*) rallied and brought together different associations to safeguard the republic. It was a "timely rise of society in our country [*woguo shehui suoyou yingshi erqi*]," according to Li.[71] It is perhaps superfluous to point out that Li and company had by then arrogated to themselves the role of representatives of this emerging society.

The bold words of the Association for the Maintenance of Public Order must be read, however, within the context of the unexpectedly rapid collapse of the imperial order in 1912. While the patrons of the civic organizations must have been emboldened by the discourse of society after the turn of the century, it would be erroneous to infer that they always assumed an uncompromising attitude toward the Qing government. In Canton, as civic leaders expanded the scope of their activities following the founding of the Nine Charitable Halls, they continued to take care to cultivate and maintain their close relationships with the imperial bureaucracy. To interpret the interactions between the two sides in terms of the familiar paradigm of state versus society, then, is to miss the point. Rather, as self-proclaimed representatives of society, the civic organizations were actually complicit in a process to (re)invent the state. To the civic leaders, the idea of an omnipotent state—and that of a binary opposition between state and society—was both useful and important because it legitimized the articulation of a new space in which their role as representatives of society could be performed. They could position themselves, both literally and metaphorically, as the polar opposite of officialdom. In this sense, every society, as it were, needs its state. To explore the intricate process through which late Qing civic leaders negotiated the discursive space of state and society, then, it is instructive to retrace the career of Chen Huipu, the most visible of the civic leaders in Canton in the first decade of this century.

THE POLITICS OF SOCIAL REPRESENTATION

In many ways, Chen Huipu, also known as Chen Jijian, personified a new type of civic leader who achieved prominence in late Qing Canton. He was believed to have started his career as a shop assistant and then rose to become the manager of a native bank.[72] Owing to his visibility within the voluntary organizations, Chen was said to have aroused the wrath, and perhaps even the jealousy, of the old gentry elites of Canton. According to a letter sent by the ministry of foreign affairs to Governor-General Zhang Renjun during the *Tatsu Maru* incident of 1908, for instance, the upright gentry considered the behavior of Chen and his associates "barbaric" (*xingtonghuawai*). In typical manner, they accused Chen of having absolutely no qualifications or prestige, and of failing consistently to repay his debts. Chen's close partner, Li Jieqi, who held a licentiate degree, was derided as an "impoverished scholar" (*hanru*).[73] The self-proclaimed impartial members of the gentry reportedly insisted that people like Chen and Li should not have been allowed to hold public meetings or to express their opinions freely. Such objections were voiced, of course, during a time when the discussion for local self-government was at its height, and it was obvious that members of the gentry were seeking to protect what they considered to be their rightful domain from the potential reach of Chen and his associates. As it turned out, the concerns of the gentry were unwarranted, as they easily dominated the ranks of the Provincial Assembly subsequently established under the auspices of the Qing reform program. Nevertheless, it was clear that the presence of Chen and company was felt well beyond the realm of philanthropy in the last years of the Qing.

Yet, Chen Huipu's leap from the world of the charitable halls to the wider public arena was by no means instantaneous. As mentioned earlier, Chen's first claim to fame was his significant role in the revitalization of the Fangbian Hospital. He was also a founding patron of another of the Nine Charitable Halls, the Chongzheng. The very first line of the Chongzheng's charter, while urging its members to observe the rules of the organization, stipulated that the institution was created specifically for philanthropic purposes, and that it would not interfere in other public affairs (*difanggongshi gaibuganshe*).[74] The statement was copied almost verbatim from the charter of another major charitable hall, the Liangyue Guangren. These obligatory self-imposed restrictions were made, to be sure, to assure the always watchful government of the organizations' noble intent and were subsequently honored more often in their breach. Still, it is worth noting that, for many activists within the charitable halls, the transition from philanthropy to a more overt public role was a gradual process, which must be understood within the context of the changing political and intellectual milieu of the time. Indeed, during the famous anti-American boycott of 1905, the leadership of the boycott continued to lie firmly within the hands of the gentry-merchants of the chamber of commerce. Similarly, in the dispute over the right to operate the Guangdong Railway Company in 1907, the voice of protest, whether raised against Governor-General Cen Chunxuan or gentry leaders like the *juren* Liang Qinggui or Li Guolian, remained primarily that of the representatives from the chamber.[75]

However, if the gentry-merchants were dominant in their leadership role during those incidents, the task of organizing the community, particularly the rank and file of the mercantile sector, was left mostly to the charitable halls and the various guilds. While there is little information on the activities of Chen Huipu then, it is perhaps reasonable to assume that he participated through his position as a leader of both the Fangbian and the Chongzheng. The experience of some success in organizing merchants and others, coupled with the apparent general disenchantment with the vacillating gentry-merchant leaders, must have given the likes of Chen cause for thought. It was reported, for example, that supporters of the anti-American boycott, outraged by the betrayal of two student activists to the American consul by the leaders of the Boycott Committee, put up a poster urging those from the guilds and schools to keep the boycott alive.[76] The internecine conflict and corruption of the gentry-merchants in the management of the railroad company served only to further delegitimize their leadership.[77] Moreover, at a time when the public discourse among intellectuals increasingly emphasized the virtue of *qun*, there were clearly opportunities for those willing to step forward as organizers and representatives of society.

Chen, however, was not about to become an agitator against the imperial order. In fact, he might have even purchased a title of subprefectural magistrate to enhance his own status.[78] Using his philanthropic works as vehicles, Chen maneuvered into contact with the higher echelon of the official world.

His name, for instance, appeared prominently among the list of founder-volunteers of the *pingtiao* relief agency of 1907, an undertaking which received blessing from the highest level of the provincial government.[79] Although Chen's lack of rank still precluded him from heading the operation, it undoubtedly elevated his standing and paved the way for him to become the director of the Guangdong Anti-Opium Association (*Guangdong jieyan zonghui*).

In September 1906, the Qing government issued an edict ordering that opium use be stamped out. The Guangdong authority, however, was slow to respond. Sensing an opening for themselves, Chen Huipu and Li Jieqi held a reception at the Fangbian Hospital on July 14, 1907. Among those in attendance was the prefect Bi Changyan, who agreed to assist Chen's effort to fight opium addiction by seeking support from his superiors. A second meeting was then held at the Aiyu where the provincial surveillance commissioner Gong Xinzhan headed a long list of bureaucrats donating for the cause. Sanctioned by high officials, the Anti-Opium Association, now with the backing of the charitable halls, came into existence in an elaborate ceremony, reportedly attended by over 10,000 people, that took place at the Wenlan Academy on July 26. A delegation headed by the acting governor-general Hu Xianglin graced the occasion with its presence. As protocol demanded that such an enterprise be led by a member of the upper gentry, an honorary chair (*zhawei zongli*) was created and filled by Xu Zhixuan, a gentry-merchant from the chamber of commerce. There was, however, no question that real authority within the association lay with the director, Chen Huipu. Indeed, upon that occasion Chen must have felt that his entrance into the world of the official elites was finally secured. The association was even given an official seal (*qianji*) in order to distinguish the organization from other charities.[80]

While clause four of the charter of the Anti-Opium Association contained the obligatory statement that the organization would stay clear of matters not relating to the campaign against opium, the first clause was perhaps more faithful to the spirit of its founders. The aim of the association, it states, was "to assist the government in suppressing opium smoking and facilitating rehabilitation in order to establish the foundation for local self-government."[81] Indeed, emboldened by their success in receiving official backing for the launching of the Anti-Opium Association, Chen and his associates went on to establish the Guangdong Merchant Self-Government Association later in the same year, thereby putting themselves squarely at the center of the public arena to become, as it were, the voice of society.

Local self-government had, of course, been an officially sanctioned topic for discussion since 1906, as a result of the proposed conversion to constitutionalism by the Qing government. The establishment of the Merchant Self-Government Association, however, did present a challenge to the old gentry elites who hitherto had tended to assume a monopolistic right over public affairs, which accounted for their vitriolic attacks on Chen mentioned earlier. Even more galling to members of the gentry was the fact that the merchant association operated its own Institute for the Study of Self-Government (*Yueshang zizhi yanjiusuo*) in direct competition with the gentry-run Organization for the Study of Self-Government (*Zizhi yanjiushe*), founded in 1907. The differences between the two were revealed in their respective memberships. Of the 161 original members of the gentry organization, close to 90 percent held either official titles or degrees.[82] On the other hand the merchant institute, while not exactly open to anyone, had less stringent requirements. It required its members to be literate, sponsored by a neighborhood or a guild, and between the ages of 25 and 60. In addition, it was stipulated that members be interested in public affairs, possess good moral standards, and, as a patriotic gesture, refrain from smoking foreign cigarettes.[83] The Merchant Self-Government Association itself was open to any employed male over the age of 25 who could write his own name, address, and occupation. However, only those who owned businesses or property worth over C$2,000, or managed enterprises worth over C$5,000, and had a minimum of a primary school education or its equivalent could stand for election to hold office.[84] Thus while the main constituents of the association were clearly the operators of the 27,524 shops (*shangdian*) in Canton, the property qualification undoubtedly kept many small merchants out of the ranks of the leadership.[85]

Who then, apart from Chen Huipu, were the leaders of the Self-Government Association? Precise information is sparse. Still, one can trace the broad contours of the leadership's composition. There were, for example, two leading newspapermen of Canton, Luo Shaoao and Tan Liyuan, editors of the *Guangdong Seventy-two Guilds News* and the *Goat City Daily*

(*Yangcheng ribao*) respectively.[86] Luo, like Chen's close associate Li Jieqi, was once ridiculed by his gentry detractors as an "impoverished scholar." Tan also was known to have run into financial trouble at times.[87] If Luo and Tan helped to drum up public support for the association, others provided the wherewithal. They included Chen Zhujun, son of Chen Qiyuan of Jichanglong Silk-Reeling Factory fame, and uncle of Chen Lianbo (who was a villain, as we will see in Chapter 3, in the eyes of the Guomindang-led government of the 1920s); Hu Ruifeng, a merchant who had converted to Catholicism; Huang Huanting, a machine-tool shop owner; Zhu Boqian, a tobacco merchant who was also a shareholder of the Daxin Bank (the first privately owned, modern-style bank in Canton);[88] Tang Shiyi, a physician and drug merchant; Guo Xianzhou, a jeweler; and Li Henggao, an educator.[89] Serving in the association's Institute for the Study of Self-Government was a group of younger members, most of whom were returned students from Japan or graduates of the new Guangdong Academy of Law and Government, including, for instance, the future Guomindang luminary Zou Lu.[90]

It is evident that the composition of the leadership of the Self-Government Association defies any easy categorization. They were, perhaps, the "middling sorts"—neither patrician nor plebeian—who stood outside the gentry (or gentry-merchant) establishment of the city. But even that has to be qualified. According to Li Henggao, for example, Chen Zhujun, Tan Liyuan, and Guo Xianzhou were all once active in that bastion of the gentry-merchants, the chamber of commerce, though they did not appear to have held any major office there.[91]

Most of the leaders of the association, it seems, were beneficiaries of the recent changes in Canton induced by the Western presence. They were also keenly aware of the precarious state of their country, and considered their contributions in the public arena part of the effort for its revitalization, not to mention a means of enhancing their own status and prestige. Encouraged by the call of the intellectuals, they organized themselves as a constituent part of society and got involved in public affairs. At the same time, as men of property and wealth, they were also apprehensive of social instability. Thus while the association declared in its charter that one of its functions was to "rigorously question" (*zhiwen*) the policies of local officials, it nonetheless spoke in terms of "the bestowing of power upon the people [*shouquanyumin*]" by the government.[92] That which was given, needless to say, could also be taken away. Society might have had its self-styled representatives, but the day when it would constitute the foundation of governmental legitimacy was yet to come.

THE LIMITS OF CHANGE
UNDER THE OLD REGIME

The immediate pretext for the establishment of the Self-Government Association was the West River incident. The incident was the result of an attempt by Britain to seize the right to patrol the West River, a crucial commercial waterway for Canton, for the apparent purpose of protecting her trading and shipping interests against rampant piracy. Even before the patrol actually began in December 1907, agitation, led by Chen Huipu and Li Jieqi at the Anti-Opium Association, had already anticipated the British move, resulting in the founding of the Self-Government Association. The agitation continued with a letter dated November 20, 1907, and addressed to the chamber of commerce, sent shortly after the formation of the new association. In the letter Chen and his associates argued that if the West River fell under foreign control, the Yangzi and other internal waterways would soon follow. Messages had been delivered to the Shanghai Chamber of Commerce and others, the letter said, alerting them to the fact that this was "a matter of life or death for the people of Guangdong." The letter contrasted the response of the Foreign Ministry at Peking with that of the former governor-general Cen Chunxuan, who reportedly once rebuffed a similar demand by the British. By conceding the right of patrol, the foreign ministry was said to have "aided the tiger in committing evil [*weihuzuochang*]." Such objections to the policies of the central government in conjunction with attempts to draw on the support of local officials were to become a familiar strategy of the association. Needless to say, the association urged that the British demand be resolutely denied, and that the Canton chamber seek support from its counterparts in other provinces. An almost identical letter was sent to the Nine Charitable Halls two days later.[93]

In subsequent open letters appealing for support, the Self-Government Association proclaimed that, in its fight against piracy, it was willing to organize the policing of the areas bordering the river and actually prepared a detailed twelve-point program for the purpose. It tried, moreover, to raise the capital for a steamship company to compete with the two British boats that ran on the West River.[94] As in the case of the charitable halls, much of the donations came from the émigré communities outside China.[95] Unfortunately, these two ventures failed to yield substantial results. The proposed steamship company, for instance, never went into operation. Nevertheless, they helped to propel the Self-Government Association to a pivotal position, making it the focus of public attention in Canton.

The West River incident was merely one of a number of episodes in which the Self-Government Association was involved. It found itself, for instance, advocating an anti-Japanese boycott in early 1908 as the Japanese government demanded an apology from the Qing authorities. The dispute occurred after a Qing naval officer and his men seized a consignment of arms aboard the Japanese freighter *Tatsu Maru II* off the coast of the Portuguese enclave of Macao, just southwest of Canton, in February. Later in the same year the association led yet another protest against the British and the Portuguese authorities, as neither of them was willing to take action after a Chinese passenger was allegedly kicked to death by a Portuguese ticket collector aboard the local British steamer *Foshan*.[96] In these protests, there is no doubt that the association tapped into an acute sense of frustration felt by many with regard to the ineffectiveness of the government. And there seems to have been a genuine sense of imminent crisis permeating the correspondence of the association.

The language used in its writings was based on an eclectic mixture of old and new terms from the political lexicon. In a typical letter addressed to "fellow compatriots" regarding the West River incident, for instance, the leaders of the Merchant Self-Government Association invoked the conventional specter of the destruction of family and country as well as the decimation of the race. At the same time, they also made reference to sovereign rights (*zhuquan*), and to the fear of dismemberment (*guafen*) of the polity. Echoing the call of intellectuals such as Liang Qichao, the leaders warned gravely that the Chinese as a people might be so decimated that they could not even become the slaves (*niumanuli*) of others. Only through joining together in organized form (*lianjietuanti*), as in the case of the Self-Government Association, would they have a chance of saving themselves.[97]

With few options at their disposal, an obvious tactic employed by the Self-Government Association for their protest was the boycott. Boycotts were to become a familiar occurrence in early-twentieth-century China.[98] A conventional form of protest for the weak, boycott was by its very nature reactive and defensive. For the merchants who made up the primary constituents of the Self-Government Association, the politics of boycott were, moreover, rather ambiguous. For while the strategy undoubtedly enabled them to make their impact felt in the public realm, boycotts tended to reinforce the notion that the activities of the merchant community were to be restricted to the mercantile arena, and thus perpetuated the merchants' subordinate status to the gentry. Furthermore, although the boycott was meant to be a punitive measure, its effects were often as costly, if indeed not more so, for the boycotters as they were for its supposed victims. Although selective sectors of trade might reap benefits, it was often the remainder of the mercantile sector which bore the brunt of the losses. The association's choice of Japan rather than Britain as the target of a commercial boycott in 1908 was surely related to the Canton merchants' close ties to the British trading and financial houses.

Boycotts, usually launched when emotions ran high, were therefore difficult to sustain. They were most effective when the issues in question were sharply local and could be resolved quickly, and when group solidarity engendered by a relatively small community could to some extent be relied upon. Boycotts were less forceful when the campaign was stretched over time and place. The fact that violence and intimidation were often features of a commercial boycott after its initial enthusiastic stage spoke perhaps less to the merchants' lack of commitment than to the reality of small-scale enterprises short on both inventory and capital. Vulnerable to any prolonged cessation of trade, small owners were targets of coercive tactics to keep them from breaking ranks. At the same time, as men of property, the leaders of the Self-Government Association were also wary of the social instability which violence might bring. Thus the association urged its supporters not to resort to riots during the West River incident, and moved quickly to condemn the violent tactics used by the Boycott Committee in Hong Kong during the *Tatsu Maru* episode.[99]

Indeed, the attitudes of the leaders of the Self-Government Association toward the foreign presence were not without ambiguity. As fledgling industrialists, some of them, to be sure, used the opportunities presented by the boycotts to promote their own products. But a better glimpse of the thinking of Chen Huipu and his associates can be found in a letter dated February 16, 1908. Like some other proclamations of the Self-Government Association addressed to community leaders outside Canton (who might not have heard of Chen or of the recently formed association), this letter was sent in the more familiar name of the Seventy-two Guilds merchants. The invocation of the generic title of "Seventy-two Guilds" was meant, of course, to lend the leaders of the Self-Government Association legitimacy as the mouthpiece of the entire mercantile community. The authors stated that foreign pressure was the key for bringing about collective action on the part of the merchants. The West River incident, they said, presented a golden opportunity that must not be missed. The proposed steamship company was thus merely the first step toward the establishment of various other enterprises. Also telling was the authors' description of those who had the most capital (*dazibenjia*) in China, an oblique reference to the gentry-merchant elites who controlled the chamber of commerce. The latter were castigated as the upholders of conservatism (*baoshouzhuyi*). Not only did they not give any thought for bringing benefit to the larger collectivity (*yiqunsixiang*), the letter pointed out, they were apparently even fearful of making profits—an indictment, no doubt, of the role of the gentry-merchants during the anti-American boycott and of their management of the railroad company.

Yet, the letter continued, to enrich and strengthen the country, new sources of profit must be developed, and that required substantial capital. Since those with the most capital could not be relied upon, the authors reasoned, a group (*tuan*), such as the steamship company, should be established in order to attract the dispersed resources of the small entrepreneurs. Only through the formation of such a group could substantial capital be put together.[100] In short, Chen Huipu and his supporters sought to translate the passion generated by the West River incident into economic cooperation in order to compete and prosper. Their strategy dealt with Western pressure less as oppression than as a challenge that needed to be faced. It is interesting to note, moreover, that their proposed twelve-point program of patrolling the West River area contained clauses which clearly specified the protection of churches and missionaries.[101]

In its dealings with the government, on the other hand, the association faced issues of a different kind. In positioning itself as a representative of society and in defining itself against officialdom, it also conceded certain political space to the latter. The Self-Government Association, like other civic organizations, was thus vulnerable to the countercriticism that it stepped beyond what was legitimately within its purview. Indeed, the association did seem to concede ground to the guardians of the imperial order. During the one episode when the issue of national sovereignty was unambiguously at the forefront—the dispute with the Portuguese government over the boundary of Macao in 1909—the Self-Government Association was conspicuously restrained. Instead it was organizations headed by members of the gentry that played a leading role in whatever local agitation there was.[102] The deference shown by Chen Huipu and his associates suggests that they were willing to step back from the center of the public arena in matters of such magnitude, which they considered to be properly within the prerogative of the governing elites. This might also help to explain why the Self-Government Association, despite its earlier vociferous presence, fell so eerily silent even after the new Provincial Assembly all but excluded the association's members in 1909. It was thus through the narrow opening enabled by the discourse of society that Chen Huipu and others both found and lost their voice.

THE COLLAPSE OF THE QING

Despite their visibility, the leaders of the Self-Government Association did not find ready acceptance within the halls of power in late Qing Canton. As already mentioned, the Guangdong Provincial Assembly, a symbol of the Qing government's concession to constitutionalism, formed in October 1909, all but excluded members of the association from its ranks. It has been estimated that only 0.49 percent of the population of Guangdong were registered to participate in the election.[103] The reason for such a low level of participation goes beyond simply the restrictions imposed by the government. To be sure, the minimum age for a voter was 25, and for a candidate 30. More important, to register as a voter or to stand for election, one had to be male and either possess the necessary academic qualifications or record of public service or, alternatively, own business or property worth over C$5,000. The wording for some of the requirements, however, was rather vague and certainly left room for discretion. A person, for example, was qualified if he had "a demonstrable record of educational or other public service for at least three years in the province."[104] For many merchants, the easiest way to qualify was presumably through revealing the value of their assets. But a deeply ingrained fear, prompted by a not unjustifiable association of the exposure of wealth with taxation, understandably prevented many from stepping forward. It led to a lament by the then governor-general Zhang Renjun that "people do not know the right to elect, even the qualified are often reluctant to register."[105] The result was inevitably tilted heavily in favor of the gentry elites. Indeed, of the 94 newly elected members of the Guangdong Assembly, none qualified by virtue of his property holdings alone, while all of them held the necessary educational qualifications or official titles.[106]

It would be erroneous, however, to assume that the assembly was filled with hardened conservatives. On the contrary, many of them fit well into the group which Joseph Esherick once labeled the "urban reformist elite."[107] In both residence and orientation, it was an undeniably urban cohort. Thirty percent of the 94 members lived in Canton, while all but 5 lived in other smaller urban centers. Over twenty of the assemblymen, moreover, were engaged in the introduction of what can be called a "new culture" into China. They were, in other words, sponsors of modern schools, newspapers, and educational societies.[108]

In fact, while the vast majority of those elected had traditional degrees, many were also exposed to new intellectual currents. Out of a list of 112 elected after the first round in Guangdong, for instance, 61 (including 34 with official titles) had attended the recently established Academy of Law and Government, and an additional 14 were graduates of a special institute for the study of local self-government run by the prefectural authorities.[109] Nor was there a lack of entrepreneurship in the new assembly. In fact, at least two dozen assemblymen were engaged in commercial activities. For example, Yang Weibin, a native of Xinhui county, was a noted businessman in both Canton and Hong Kong, while Zhang Nairui of Kaiping county operated his enterprises both at home and in Canton. Also included were a director of the Canton Chamber of Commerce, Ou Zansen, and two leaders from the Shantou and Jiaying Chambers of Commerce, Xiao Yonghua and Liang Guoxuan.[110] Yet, if the new assemblymen were reformist, they also clearly did not share the same background with the likes of Chen Hupui and his associates. As far as the leaders of the Self-Government Association were concerned, organizational strength obviously did not lead to political representation.

Not only were the civic leaders excluded from the assembly, they were also rebuffed with regard to their demand for a Merchant Corps (*shangtuan*). Unlike in Shanghai, where the corps was sponsored by gentry-merchants such as Li Pingshu and Zeng Shaoqing and thus sanctioned by the government, in Canton the merchants' requests for a militia were spurned by the imperial bureaucracy as well as the newly elected Provincial Assembly.[111] Still, the problems encountered by the civic leaders in their dealings with the official elites did not necessarily turn them into advocates for the republican cause. In fact, as late as the summer of 1911, a proclamation, written by several members of the Self-Government Association, was authorized for distribution by Chen Huipu. Its purpose was to remind the people that "revolution" could lead to banditry and disorder, which would have an adverse effect on business. It ended by urging the émigré communities not to support the republicans. The statement was reportedly prepared by request of the Qing authority, and its appearance was said to have cost Chen the support he needed for a leadership role after the collapse of the dynasty.[112] Confronted with the specter of chaos, merchants and gentry closed ranks in defense of property and privilege. The primary concern of the merchant and civic leaders, including the outspoken activists such as Chen Huipu, was not to dislodge the gentry elites but to maintain order and stability in a scramble to keep pace with the course of events.

The initial reaction of the gentry in Canton to the Wuchang uprising in October 1911 was to try to keep any potential crisis away from Guangdong, and to use the opportunity to expand further their own political power in the name of reform. This line of thinking was exemplified in the speeches given by two retired officials, Deng Huaxi and Liang Dingfen, in a meeting called by the gentry elites at the Wenlan Academy on October 25, following consultation with Governor-General Zhang Mingqi. Deng announced that the purpose of the meeting was "to seek a way to maintain public order in the earnest hope that Guangdong can be free from the pain of destruction and chaos." Liang spoke about how

Guangdong belongs to the people of Guangdong, governed by officials only on behalf of the people. . . . What is being discussed today is the implementation of self-government. . . . As a result of the disorder in the neighboring provinces, our own Guangdong now has the incentive to carry out political reforms. If we can use this opportunity to get rid of all the defects of government, not only will the calamities wrought by the revolutionaries be avoided, but our Guangdong will benefit.[113]

The elites' emphasis on safeguarding the integrity of the province was reinforced by a resolution passed at the meeting stating that Guangdong could no longer take care of other provinces, and that it should retain its military forces, arms, and funds for its own use. Their position was quickly echoed by the merchant and civic leaders.[114] To highlight the close relationship between Canton and Hong Kong, six representatives were selected to go to the British colony to coordinate the maintenance of public order in the region.

The resolutions passed by the gentry at the Wenlan were endorsed by Governor-General Zhang, who was then sitting unabashedly on the fence. But the assassination of the Manchu general Feng-shan, together with rampant rumors that the so-called people's armies (*minjun*) were about to enter the city, prompted the merchant and civic leaders to hold another meeting at the Aiyu on October 29. The reasoning behind the decision on that occasion to recognize the republicans was clearly spelled out. "The old autocratic government has lost its political power, while the power of the republican government has already been established, recognized by friendly countries. To preserve perpetual peace and order, the republican government should be recognized now."[115] Fearful of an attack on Canton by the "revolutionaries," the merchants thus tried to placate the republicans by declaring their acceptance of the republican government as legitimate so that "the general situation would then be stabilized, and business could be conducted with peace of mind."[116] The motion was obviously less an unqualified vote for republicanism than a bow to the inevitable.

Nor did the merchant and civic leaders intend to chart a new course only for themselves. Representatives were dispatched immediately to the Wenlan Academy to discuss the issues with the gentry leaders and the bannermen. In fact, there were those, like the newspaperman Tan Liyuan, who attended and took an active part in both meetings. Members of the gentry proved to be more than receptive to the overtures of the merchants. Gentry leaders including Liang Dingfen reportedly gave speeches amid thunderous applause, as did Chen Huipu, who spoke about recognition of the republican government. By the day's end, a hastily produced flag proclaiming the independence (*duli*)—independence, that was, from the Qing government—of Guangdong flew outside the Wenlan Academy.[117] It was surely a sign of the changing times that it had become possible in 1911 to imagine independence from the dynasty as distinct from secession from the polity, whereas even in the recent past the dynasty *had been* the polity.[118]

This dramatic gesture of the local notables left Governor-General Zhang Mingqi with no choice but to reveal his stance. Had Zhang chosen to side with the drive for recognition of the republicans, there would probably have been a smooth and controlled transition of power in Canton. Unfortunately, Zhang bet on the wrong horse at the last minute, setting the scene for his subsequent, rather undignified exit to Hong Kong. He repudiated the initiative by the gentry and merchants, quelling "the rumor of independence." Without Zhang's collaboration, the community notables were left in limbo. After all the expectations they had generated on that eventful day of October 29, their credibility was now in jeopardy. The result was general panic in the city. The usually vibrant commercial life was grinding to a halt, and an exodus began for those who could afford to leave. The exhortations of the leaders of the charitable halls and the guilds, perhaps made under government orders, could do little to stem the tide. Two placards which appeared on November 1, supposedly written by the same Liang Dingfen, reminded the people that they were subjects of the Qing and that they should not listen to rumors; these also had apparently little effect.[119]

Zhang, of course, could not single-handedly stop the collapse of the Qing. Almost exactly a month after the Wuchang revolt, Guangdong finally became "independent" on November 9, while Zhang quietly slipped out of the city. In many ways, however, the triumphant republican government in Canton won a Pyrrhic victory. There the republicans, a motley group loosely assembled under the direction of Hu Hanmin (1879–1936), a onetime student in Japan and a stalwart in the anti-Qing movement nominally headed by the émigré Sun Yat-sen (1866–1925), had neither the organization nor the resources to run the city. At the same time, the tarnished legitimacy of the old gentry and merchant notables, which stemmed from their vacillation and inept leadership during the critical days of October, made the prospect of a modus vivendi rather difficult. As Hu himself put it, Canton was "completely devoid of officials and functionaries, which is to say that it was without any government" when he arrived on the evening of November 8.[120] To muster even a semblance of an administration, the new regime could only try to retain the remnants of the old bureaucracy, and to issue an appeal for "talent" to volunteer for service.[121]

It was said that, with the fall of the Qing, "the government of almost every city in China was for months virtually carried on by the chambers of commerce and associated guilds."[122] In Canton, a group of local leaders, most of whom were prominent merchants who had been active in the civic organizations, established the Guangdong Merchant Association for the Maintenance of Public Order in the spring of 1912. It is significant that those heading the group were less visible and vocal than the likes of Liang Dingfen and Chen Huipu during the fateful earlier months. As a result, their reputations were not compromised in quite the same way. In any event, only such a group had the organization and the resources then to perform the basic tasks of government.

As could be expected, the association was dominated by those involved in the silk and native banking businesses, who made up about 30 percent of the founding leadership.[123] With the collapse of the Qing, the tone of the new association lacked the caution and deference of its predecessors. Its leaders made it quite clear, for instance, that its formation was due to the fact that "the politics of the new government could not for the moment be well organized."[124] Indeed, in the words of the fabric merchant Liu Zhongping, one of its two assistant directors, the association "could be described as having a philanthropic nature, but it could also be said to be rich in political ideas [*fu yu zhengzhi sixiang*]."[125] As mentioned earlier, its director, the silk merchant Li Liangfu, echoing the views of many intellectuals, argued for the organic link between society and nation. The idea was further elaborated by the other assistant director, the import-export trader Xie Kunyi. "The existence of society," he wrote, "was to bring together a large collectivity (*hedaqun*) for self-government."[126] Far from posing a threat to the fledgling nation, however, this self-governing society, as represented by organizations such as the Association for the Maintenance of Public Order, would bridge the conventional gulf between official and people (*tongda guanmin gehe*). As if to emphasize the point that self-government and the construction of the nation were not mutually incompatible, Xie stated that the association promoted, inter alia, the study of Mandarin in Canton. The new Republic was depicted as a wobbly young child desperately in need of support. The ultimate purpose of the association, it was said, was thus to contribute to the strengthening of the nation and to the creation of, in Li Liangfu's felicitous phrase, "a society of citizens" (*guomin shehui*).[127]

The stridently confident rhetoric of the new association was supported by its considerable wherewithal. In Canton, the Qing administration had left behind virtually empty coffers. Officials of the old regime had reportedly converted the deposits at the treasury into notes of the Hongkong and Shanghai Bank before fleeing with the public funds.[128] Hu Hanmin maintained that the government had only C$10,000 left when he took over the city. According to Hu, the former governor-general Zhang Mingqi had predicted that even if the republicans managed to take Guangdong, they would not be able to hold it for three days, presumably due to the lack of financial resources.[129] Apparently the government even briefly entertained the radical idea of confiscating the properties of officials or the rich who opposed the new regime, but the absence of a solid base of support quickly rendered that option impracticable.[130] Yet, it faced serious problems raising revenues through conventional channels. During the initial euphoria after the establishment of the new government, the much resented miscellaneous taxes imposed by the late Qing administration were abolished. But the new regime's precarious hold on the province's hinterland meant that much of the land tax failed to come into Canton. While laden with a bloated military budget for the assorted forces assembled in the city, the income of the new government was estimated to be only about a tenth of its Qing predecessor's.[131] The republicans were thus forced to finance their administration through borrowing, selling public bonds, and the innovative but disastrous method of simply printing unconvertible paper notes.[132] All these operations, needless to say, required the contributions and support of the merchant community.

In his autobiography, Hu Hanmin remarked, somewhat sardonically, that with the change of government the merchants were just as quick to welcome the revolution as they had been to condemn it a few months earlier.[133] Still, with the dawn of a new regime there usually comes, however briefly, a general sense of renewal and unbounded possibility. It was said then, for example, that debts to foreigners could be eliminated by raising funds through public borrowing. The merchants were, at least initially, receptive to the requests of a government which at one point promised returns with as high as 100 percent annual interest.[134] The bubble, however, soon burst. Despite various government measures and appeals for confidence, the value of the paper notes remained erratic at best, putting great strains on the economy.[135] By the summer of 1912, it was clear that the commercial revival that the merchants had hoped for was simply not there.[136] By the end of the year it was evident that the government was not even in a position to repay its debts, most if not all of which were scheduled for only one to two years. When the Huizhou Chamber of Commerce, for instance, tried to collect in August, what it got was a rather nonchalant reply from Hu Hanmin which simply amounted to a request to forgive the loans.[137]

Not surprisingly, then, when President Yuan Shikai turned against Sun Yat-sen's new political party, the Guomindang, in 1913, the merchant and civic leaders in Canton did not rally behind the Guomindang's cause. Instead, as Hu Hanmin protested against Yuan's autocratic policies, handbills and flyers in favor of Yuan were reportedly distributed by the Nine Charitable Halls. In fact, not only did the merchant and civic leaders remain passive during the so-called Second Revolution launched by Sun's supporters against Yuan Shikai in the same year, they apparently gave the troops of Long Jiguang, which occupied Canton under orders from Yuan, an enthusiastic welcome.[138]

By appropriating the language of the intellectuals and positioning themselves as representatives of society, the civic leaders of late Qing Canton, to be sure, opened up new possibilities by lending substance to the suggestion that the people were more than mere subjects of the empire. Implicitly or explicitly, they made the case that the participation of society—or the people coming together as *qun*—was imperative for the revitalization of the country. Nevertheless, the modus operandi of the civic organizations, prior to the fall of the Qing, could only be characterized as consistent accommodation and negotiation with the imperial order. Their leaders might try to extend the boundary of the permissible, but they never seriously challenged their own subordination to the imperial government. Still, their endeavor proved to be a productive process which, despite all its limitations, provided the notion of society with some material content in early-twentieth-century China.

The Qing government, unlike a modern regime, did not consider a mobilized society a legitimating force for its own rule. But while the dynasty remained suspicious of any claim of large scale organization of its subjects, its successors, notably the Guomindang and the Communists, sought to reconstruct society for their own purpose. The late Qing civic leaders' idea of society as simply a large collectivity represented by themselves struck a new generation of governing elites as inadequate rather than threatening. The latter, in the spirit of the writings of Yan Fu, Liang Qichao, and others, regarded society as a potentially organic entity signifying the unity of its people. Indeed, it was their self-appointed mission to bring this society into being, in turn laying the foundation for a new political order. As the Guomindang founder Sun Yat-sen put it in a speech given shortly after the founding of the Republic, "The revolution of the political system has already been successful, but the revolution of society has not yet begun."[139] Sun and his followers might have suffered a setback at the hands of Yuan Shikai, but they were determined to create a cohesive and robust society-and-nation through the institution of a new mode of governance. And Canton was to be the first site of their experiment.

CHAPTER TWO

Toward Modernity

The objective of carrying out the revolution now is to
reconstruct the Chinese nation and society.

— DAI JITAO, 1919[1]

The construction of a rational and well-ordered society is more than a discursive exercise. Command over one's physical environment is deemed vital to the formation of the material base from which social practices can be articulated. The "conquest and rational ordering of space," to use David Harvey's words, is thus an integral part of the culture of modernity.[2] Space is "to be shaped for social purposes and therefore always subservient to the construction of a social project."[3] The past can be physically discarded, its social forms literally remade. Mona Ozouf wrote that the men of the French Revolution widely assumed that space exerted an "educative influence over people's minds," and that "a new political arrangement seemed to involve a new arrangement of urban space."[4] It was also such an impulse of "creative destruction," so critical to the understanding of modernity, which subsequently produced such landmark European enterprises as the Haussmannization of Paris in the latter half of the nineteenth century.[5]

Many members of the Chinese elite were likewise afflicted with

Dionysian impulses in the early twentieth century. Their most visible and forceful spokespersons in the post-Qing period were often found among members of Sun Yat-sen's Guomindang and, subsequently, the Communists. One of the most vocal advocates of urban reconstruction in early republican China, for instance, was none other than Sun Yat-sen's son, Sun Fo (also known as Sun Ke). The younger Sun, who studied at the University of California and Columbia University, was the first mayor of the newly created municipality of Canton in 1921 and oversaw the city's physical transformation. In an article published in late 1919, he exalted the virtue of utilizing scientific knowledge for the purpose of urban planning as a hallmark of modernity. Urban planning, Sun wrote, must be based on detailed "investigation" and "survey." It must contain all the facts which can be put in statistical form (*yi tongji de xingshi biaolie*). Data on the number of the population, their occupations, transportation facilities, trade volumes, and so on should be collected well in advance, for the purpose of creating a plan which would serve the needs of "society" and the "economy" (*jingji*).[6] The rationalization of the use of space, in other words, was aimed not only at a simple renewal of the physical infrastructure. It had a more ambitious goal: to transform the conditions in which people ordered their lives.[7] It was meant, in short, to be instrumental in the creation of a "new people." Sun Fo was particularly impressed by the urban planners in Germany, who had reportedly mapped out carefully the development of Berlin for the next hundred years.[8] As a committed planner, Sun, like his European counterparts, envisioned control over *the future* through the power of scientific prediction, which enabled "social engineering and rational planning, and the institutionalization of rational systems of social regulation and control."[9]

Although Canton had already undergone significant changes even before the reconstruction of its physical structure in the early 1920s, the impact of the renovation on the metropolis was nothing short of profound. For example, the new municipality of Canton (Guangzhoushi) featured a network of new roads which served to integrate the different parts of the city, including its new downtown, with the surrounding areas. This network not only resulted in an expansive spatial structure more amenable to the flow of capital and commodities, as demonstrated by the new nodal points of commerce and industry. Just as important, it facilitated the new government in the exercise of its authority. Indeed, Canton was to become the model for urban administration in republican China, as acknowledged by the mayor of Shanghai, Huang Fu, in 1927.[10]

The physical reconstruction, however, was ultimately meant to provide the material basis for the emergence of a new society. Indeed, disillusioned by the chaos of the early Republic, many elites felt that new initiatives had to be taken to reorder society. But what were the mechanisms or forces which drove the formation of a vigorous society? What should its morphology be? Most significant, in what specific ways could its energy be harnessed and its constituents mobilized?

As self-proclaimed modernizers, the new generation of elites believed that the people should be given a voice. Yet, given the latter's nature as "a heap of sand," they also needed to be reformed and disciplined to provide the basis for the construction of the nation.[11] In this quest for modernity, the people had to hence be treated not only as "the subject of needs, of aspirations," but also as "the object in the hands of government."[12] Discipline, however, was not to be confused with simple coercion. Rather, disciplinary power was to be used productively for the creation of a new body social.

In an essay written in 1915, Liang Qichao, for example, offered his enthusiastic endorsement of the works of the German nationalist philosopher Johann Gottlieb Fichte (1762–1814). Liang sought to bring the ideas of the author of the famous *Addresses to the German Nation* to his Chinese readers. To Liang, Fichte was one of four sagacious leaders (*zhe*) responsible for the construction of modern Germany, though Liang wrote that he had selected only those of Fichte's popular pronouncements which were best suited for application to China for discussion.[13] Elaborating on the themes of his own earlier writings, Liang, citing the authority of Fichte, emphasized that it was both the nature and the duty of man to serve society. The nation, as the highest form of society, represented the pinnacle of human ideals.[14] In a section entitled "Class and the Division of Labor" (*Jieji yu fenye*),[15] Liang suggested that the differentiation of classes, deriving from the division of labor, was not only natural and inevitable, but indeed essential for the functioning of society. Echoing Fichte's idea that individuality found its ultimate expression only in the collective, Liang put forward an organic view of society in which the role of each person was to contribute to the well-being of the whole. Constituents of society should be like members of a military unit (a *shehui juntuan*) working together against the common enemy. Class differentiation was thus absolutely necessary since different individuals were endowed with different abilities. Yet this should not cause any problem as long as all individuals realized that, whatever their station, their task was to work for the good of society.[16]

Class, in other words, provided a quasi-rational way to analyze how society could best function in the modern era. Society was no longer simply an amorphous collectivity. Instead society could now be seen as a structured and ordered totality, which could be literally dissected and broken down into its constituent classes, that is, into different segments. And such divisions would not necessarily generate conflict. Indeed, different versions of such ideas could be found among fin de siècle European theorists. Emile Durkheim (1858–1917), for instance, argued that the increasing division of labor, so characteristic of modern society, could actually result in "organic solidarity" among its constituents.[17] For society—and by extension the "nation"—to be strong, its members, as Liang pointed out, must be organized into different classes, working together to ensure the health of the organic whole.

It is not surprising that many Chinese elites of the early Republic, concerned with the fate of the country, were attracted to the discourse of class as a way to analyze society. Guomindang luminaries such as Hu Hanmin and Lin Yungai, for example, began to publish studies on class, exploring its implications for morality or conflict.[18] To them, for China to be modern, society had to be vitalized. By providing a specific and concrete paradigm for the mapping of society, the discourse of class purportedly enabled the different social segments and their interests to be methodically identified and mobilized. Furthermore, if the Guomindang was to establish a government befitting a modern nation, and if the legitimacy of modern government was grounded at least in part on its claim to represent the people, it would also be useful for the people to be represented as an organism—society—comprised of neatly categorized classes or segments, whose interests the government could then claim to know. Indeed, in the rapidly changing physical and social landscape of urban China, as in the case of Canton, the discourse of class seemed to offer the governmental authority a guide to map its complex contours. That was why, despite their reservations about the notion of "class conflict" popularized by the more orthodox interpreters of Marxism in

China, many members of the Guomindang continued to employ the language of class in articulating their worldview.

POLITICAL LANDSCAPE

At first glance, the history of Canton during the decade after the collapse of the Qing is one of almost unmitigated disaster. Despite the fact that Guangdong was one of seven home provinces which escaped direct occupation by the Beiyang forces in 1913, the debacle of the so-called Second Revolution nonetheless brought the Yunnanese militarist Long Jiguang back to the province.[19] Long became noted primarily for his brutal repression, as he faithfully executed Yuan's policy of wiping out the remnants of the opposition. At the same time, Yuan's administration intervened to try to rescue the province from complete financial chaos and to regain some control over the provincial revenues. Still, despite his allegiance to Yuan, Long basically ruled Guangdong as his personal domain, if by default rather than by design. As Peking's presence in the south remained circumscribed, Long was able to take the initiative in such matters as retaining funds bound for the central administration in order to enlarge his own army, or mortgaging the potential income from local taxation to secure foreign loans.[20] Indeed, particularly toward the end of his tenure, Long was to give Canton a taste of things to come. His demand, for example, for "mobilization payment" for his troops prior to their departure at the end of 1916 was to become a familiar form of extortion by militarists in subsequent years.[21]

Long was driven out of Canton in late 1916 by the old Guangxi clique,[22] headed by the ex-bandit Lu Rongting, whose henchmen Chen Bingkun and Mo Rongxin successively held the post of military governor of Guangdong from 1917 to 1920. If Long was only a prototype, the Guangxi militarists represented everything usually associated with the phenomenon of so-called warlordism. Not only were they no longer subject to the control of the central authorities, they existed seemingly for no other purpose than to perpetuate their own power. For a brief period, they tried to bolster their legitimacy by giving refuge to Sun Yat-sen while the latter organized his protect-the-constitution (*hufa*) movement against the Peking regime.[23] Sun returned to Canton in July 1917, but left less than a year later after discovering that the militarists had little but their own interests in mind. Meanwhile, an array of taxation was imposed to sustain the bloated armies and their many skirmishes with rival forces. Local assets were mortgaged for still more foreign loans to continue the cycle of violence. According to Liao Zhongkai (who took over the administration of the treasury following the ousting of the Guangxi militarists), during its years in Guangdong the Guangxi clique accumulated about C$10 million worth of debts (both internal and external), most of which were short-term loans for military purposes.[24]

The Guangxi period ended when units under the command of Chen Jiongming succeeded in capturing the province toward the end of 1920. Regarded by the British military attaché as "one of the two most able soldiers" in China in the early 1920s (the other being Wu Peifu), Chen is an enigmatic figure in modern Chinese history.[25] Reliable information on his life is scanty, in part because his rebellion against Sun Yat-sen in mid-1922 led to his permanent characterization as a pariah in the orthodox annals.[26] Trained with a classical education before graduating from the new Guangdong Academy of Law and Government in 1908, Chen was a vocal member of the Provincial Assembly during the late Qing. As a supporter of the republican cause in 1911, he organized the revolt against the ancien régime in his native Huizhou in eastern Guangdong, paving the way to a military career. After the fall of the Qing, Chen rose to become the commander of the military forces of the province under the new republican government. His brief tenure ended, however, with the failure of the Second Revolution and the arrival of Long Jiguang.

Despite his allegiance to the republican cause, Chen was never a member of Sun Yat-sen's inner circle. Still, upon Chen's defeat of the Guangxi militarists, Sun was invited back to Canton in late 1920. Chen was named governor, responsible for the daily operation of the administration. For the next two years, Chen tried, albeit with only limited success, to organize elections for self-government at the county (xian) level as well as for the new municipal government of Canton.[27] But he is more often remembered for transforming Canton into a center of "progressive" activities in the early 1920s.[28] Chen's most dazzling initiative was perhaps his decision to bring the prominent radical intellectual Chen Duxiu, who went on to become the first general secretary of the Chinese Communist Party, from Peking to Canton to head the project for educational reform. While Chen's attitudes toward workers can be described, in Winston Hsieh's words, as "austerely paternal-istic,"[29] under his administration labor organizations in Canton were first publicly recognized by the government as both a key element of modern so-ciety and a potential constituency of support.

Unlike Sun, however, Chen was an advocate of federalism (*liansheng zizhi*) for China, and he was decidedly unsympathetic toward the idea of embarking on a military campaign against the north shortly after the recap-ture of Canton.[30] Whether Chen's position stemmed from tactical maneu-vering or political conviction, the result was an open break with Sun that led to the latter's dramatic escape to the gunboat *Yongfeng* in June 1922. Sun re-mained on the vessel for almost two months before leaving for Shanghai.[31] Six months later, however, Canton again changed hands. This time it was taken by what became known in the local parlance as the "guest armies" (*kejun*): a combined force of splinter units from both Yunnan and Guangxi. Their commanders' nominal allegiance to Sun allowed the irrepressible vet-eran to make yet another comeback. With the assistance of the Soviets and the Chinese Communists, both of whom had only recently appeared on the political stage, Sun's reorganized Guomindang was able to turn Canton into a base for its project in the mid-1920s.

REORDERING CANTON

Given the incessant political strife in Canton during the first decade of the Republic, it would appear difficult enough for the city to have weathered the turbulence and emerge unscathed. Yet the metropolis somehow even man-aged to thrive during this period. The decade witnessed some of the most significant changes to the city since the Ming-Qing transition in the seven-teenth century, laying the essential groundwork for what was to become the city of Guangzhou that we know today.

Even before the founding of the Republic, the initial impetus to modern-ize the infrastructure of Canton was provided by the New Policy in the last years of the Qing. The insolvency of the government then, however, meant that it had to turn to nonofficial sources for financial support to take even tentative steps toward the renovation of the metropolis. The waterworks project, for example, was created in 1905 by the then governor-general of

Guangdong and Guangxi, Cen Chunxuan, with an initial capitalization of 1,200,000 taels to be shared evenly between the government and private sources. Much of the nongovernment funding initially came from Shanghai.[32] As the cost of construction increased, however, another 300,000 taels were raised from the private sector. In 1915, the dire financial condition of the republican government led to the sale of the official share of the waterworks to investors, most of whom were from the local merchant community. A completely private enterprise, named the "Canton Waterworks Company," then came into existence.[33]

In much the same vein, the late Qing authority succeeded in putting together a sum of C$1.5 million in 1909 to purchase the first electric lighting plant in Canton from the British, who had installed it in 1901. Two-thirds of the amount was raised from private investors, in part through the issuing of shares with an initial value of C$10 each. As in the case of the waterworks, the initial capitalization was found to be inadequate, and was raised to C$3 million in 1919. At the same time, all the government shares were sold, again mostly to merchant holders.[34] One should not, however, read too much into the sale of these enterprises, still less conclude that it was a testament to the strength of society. The merchant investors did not exactly wrest control of the enterprises from the government. The utility companies were handed over to the nongovernment sector simply because the political-cum-military authorities in Canton then were unable and, more significantly, unwilling to handle the task of operating them.

Another initial force which drove the renovation of the city was the émigré community. Many of its members were supporters of the anti-Qing movement. With the establishment of the republic, they were eager to invest in the city they had left decades earlier. One of the first conspicuous symbols of their investment was the department store.[35] In 1912, the Sincere (Xianshi) Company, which had begun its operation in Hong Kong at the turn of the century after being founded by a group of émigré investors from Australia, opened its first store in China on the midwestern section of the Bund—commonly known as Changdi—in Canton. It was ten years earlier that the then governor-general Cen authorized the addition of another 12,000 feet to the Bund, which had hitherto stretched a mere 120 feet along the river, thus providing a new thoroughfare for a city best known for its web of crisscrossing lanes of no more than twelve feet in width.[36] Now on the new section stood the five-story Sincere building. Towering by the standards of the time, the new store featured, in addition to an impressive array of merchandise, an open-air amusement park on its top floor which carried regular perfor- mances of opera, acrobatics, and movies.[37] It proved to be a prime attraction. The company, moreover, had constructed another equally imposing build- ing next to the store to run as a hotel. Indeed, the midwestern section of the Bund along the Pearl River was to become almost a replica of the famous Nanjing Road of Shanghai.[38] With its new department stores, cinemas, and other avenues of entertainment, the area was transformed into an urban magnet for the rich, the curious, and the unsavory.

Sincere's system of management was borrowed directly from its Western (and Japanese) counterpart.[39] It was characterized by the institution of a clear bureaucratic hierarchy and division of labor coupled with a strong dose of paternalism designed to engender unswerving loyalty to the company.[40] Moreover, unlike the small retailers who were dependent on the old import- export firms for their orders, the sheer volume commanded by the depart- ment store meant it could purchase in bulk directly from manufacturers abroad, or at least negotiate directly with their representatives in China.[41] The Sincere Company, in fact, went further. Emulating the strategy of the pioneering stores of the West, it established a number of facilities for man- ufacturing "in-house" products, including soft drinks, biscuits, and footwear, as well as glassware (for bottling) and wooden containers (for pack- aging).[42] The department store, then, not only took the world of retailing to a new frontier, but also contributed to the modest beginnings of the indus- trialization of Canton.

As a symbol of modernity, the organization of the department store stood in stark contrast to the commercial quarter of Qing Canton. The latter was protean, unruly, and chaotic; while the former, with its world of goods, was nonetheless enclosed, rational, and ordered. Sincere, however, did not bask in the glamour of being the sole department store of Canton for long. Its success soon attracted a neighbor further west on the Bund: the Daxin Department Store, another émigré concern which housed itself within a seven-story building with its own rooftop entertainment park.[43] Both stores became instant landmarks of the metropolis, meccas to the local population with their often bewildering range of practical as well as exotic items. The Daxin store was located on the section of the Bund where the western end

The Daxin Department Store with its rooftop
entertainment garden was a distinctive feature
on the Bund and a symbol of modern Canton.

of Changdi adjoined the southern tip of Xiguan. The area was referred to by
the local inhabitants as Xihaokou, and it was reputedly the liveliest part of
town.[44]

However, despite the impact of the department stores, it was only with
the complete transformation of Canton's spatial structure that its economic
and social geography was truly recast. A new municipal council (*shizheng
gongsuo*), which was to give the city its own governmental authority and to
free it from the dual jurisdiction of Panyu and Nanhai counties, was established in 1918. The council was the precursor to the full-fledged municipal
government founded just over two years later. In what amounts to a local
version of Haussmannization, it was decided that the old sixteen-gate city
walls would be demolished. The contract for the demolition work was con-

Yonghan Road, one of the newly paved and widened thoroughfares of Canton in the mid-1920s, viewed from where the old city wall used to stand.

cluded between the new municipal council and the Canton Tramways Syndicate.[45] The latter was a private company which put up the financing for the project. The walls, which averaged 25 feet in height and between 15 and 25 feet in width,[46] subsequently took three years to tear down. At the end, the space formerly occupied by the walls was turned into over 67,000 feet of wide if not exactly well-paved streets. The syndicate had begun to operate about twenty gasoline buses as early as 1921, covering a stretch of about 17 kilometers which linked Xiguan in the west to Dongshan in the east through what was the old walled city.[47] Together with construction in other parts of the city, there were by 1922 about 137,000 feet of new roads in Canton.[48] The inner and outer sections of the metropolis were thus physically integrated, and hitherto virtually inaccessible areas were now open for commercial and industrial activities. They were also brought under the jurisdiction of the new municipal authority.

The material impact of the transformation of the city's physical structure can hardly be overestimated. One of the immediate results was the emergence of a new center of commerce at the heart of the Old City, around what used to be the official quarter at the junction of the northern section of

Yonghan Road (now Beijing Road) and Huiai Road (now Zhongshan Road), in a section popularly known as Shuangmendi. Two of the earliest tenants of the new district were, as could be expected, branch stores of Sincere and Daxin. Opened in the early 1920s, they were reportedly even more glamorous than their main outlets on the Bund. The Sincere branch, Huiai shangdian, was touted as one of the largest enterprises in south China, while the Daxin branch was housed in a recently constructed five-story building nearby.[49] There were also the new general stores—miniature department stores—dealing in an assortment of products, many of which were foreign-style items (yanghuo). Defying the codes of the old commercial establishment where every trade was supposedly restricted to its own quarter, these new medium-size retailers stocked a range of goods under one roof, in turn reflecting the larger market created by a more integrated city. Mimicking the practice of department stores, their merchandise was clearly categorized, labeled, and priced, with emphasis on efficient service.[50]

Also ubiquitous at Shuangmendi were bookstores, many of which were branches of chains, catering to a growing audience whose interests ranged from Western political philosophy to the latest romance novels.[51] Such developments were further spurred by the availability of novel modes of transportation—buses and particularly rickshaws—on the newly paved roads. In fact, the Shuangmendi section quickly became the nodal point of a new transport system, from which bus and rickshaw routes were to spread throughout the city.[52] As the most popular mode of transportation, the operations of the rickshaws, ranging from their fares and designated stops to the cleanliness of the vehicles and the manners of the pullers, were all subjected to the regulation of the municipal government.[53]

A modern city, moreover, was not just a center of consumption. It was also a place of industrial production. The new city center was to be flanked by the outlying areas, particularly those to the east and across the river, which served as the sites for the growing number of industrial enterprises. With the development of communications, as a municipal government report later put it, the country would then be able to supply the city directly with its produce; while the city would then sell its industrial products directly to the country.[54] The aim was to get rid of the mediation of greedy and unprincipled merchants (jianshangtangu). Indeed, whenever it was possible, the report stated, major public-interest enterprises should be operated by the municipal authority. Hence the waterworks, for instance, was incorporated into the structure of government.[55]

Like most modern governmental authorities, the new municipal government, following its inauguration in 1921, took as its first order of business the claiming and consolidation of all the territories supposedly under its jurisdiction. A surveying commission was thus constituted to map and to demarcate the boundaries of the new entity: the municipality of Canton.[56] It was stipulated that "areas already deemed to be part of the Canton municipality cannot secede [*tuoli*] to form their own autonomous entity."[57] The administrative authority was to be centralized in the hands of the mayor and a commission.[58] The latter, headed by the mayor, consisted of six bureaus with responsibilities ranging from public utilities to education.[59] Interestingly enough, all six bureau heads were students returned from the United States, Japan, and Europe, as were reportedly over 80 percent of the section chiefs (*kezhang*) and their immediate subordinates.[60] To underscore the need of the new administration to manage with "unified authority," all the various *yamen* of previous administrations were earmarked for demolition. A new building to house all the different bureaus of the administration and to be known as the Municipal Administration Offices (*shizheng heshu*) was to be created as the literal and metaphorical nerve center (*zhongshu*) of the government. The progress and complexity of society, according to the authority, meant that such a building was necessary to save time and labor for the purpose of governance.[61] Just as the social realm was increasingly viewed as an interconnected and organic whole, then, governmental power was also articulated and coordinated in new ways. Indeed, such administrative centralization, in the view of one contemporary commentator, constituted an "unprecedented new system" (*potianhuang zhi xinzhidu*) of government.[62]

For the purpose of policing, for example, the municipality was divided into twelve wards. The police force consisted of about 4,500 members. Since the population of the municipality, as a new government survey discovered in 1923, was 801,646,[63] that would translate into a ratio of about 1 policeman for every 180 residents, which was higher than, say, the ratio in mid-nineteenth-century London (1 to 350).[64] In addition to the standard duties of maintaining order, the police were entrusted with the tasks of guarding the inhabitants' morality and closing down unlicensed enterprises.[65] The policeman was to become, to use the apt words of Robert Storch, a "domestic missionary."[66] Moreover, as befitting a modernist administration, a special bureau had been established for the maintenance of health standards (an undertaking which hitherto tended to fall under the purview of the police). The bureau of health divided the city, for regulatory purposes, into six districts. New rules and codes were enacted to regulate the use of public space, as an elaborate hierarchy of functionaries was organized to inspect and license public establishments.[67]

Even more revealing was the jurisdiction of the education bureau. The development of a more integrated city, while allowing the government to institute specific forms of management, also led to an often unchecked growth of unregulated entertainment. The educational mission of the bureau was thus broadly defined: In addition to being the regulator of the institutions of schooling, the bureau was also the overseer of the general conduct and welfare of society. It thus had the authority to shut down theaters, cinemas, and various venues of public entertainment. It also took on the responsibility to operate municipal charities and to supervise nonofficial philanthropic organizations.[68] Furthermore, the creation of new public space provided the opportunity for the construction of new facilities to "educate-and-reform" (*ganhua*) the residents. The government was to build a public theater for the purpose of "social education" (*shehui jiaoyu*) and of raising "consciousness."[69] Outside the schools, public lecture series were organized to "enlighten" the city's inhabitants. Topics included, for example, "Science and superstition" and "Principles of science." The bureau apparently also tried to organize courses on child-rearing, family education, and hygiene for women, but was forced to abandon those plans for want of funds.[70]

This headlong attempt to bring Canton into the modern world did not, however, go unchallenged. Many small merchants saw the process of reconstruction as posing a threat to their livelihood. Students of economic change have long suggested that the advent of the department stores usually led to tension with the small retailers. The former are said to enjoy the advantage of the economies of scale: reduction of overhead, large inventory, velocity of trade, and so forth, all of which signal the despair if not the demise of the traditional shopkeepers. Some have also maintained that it was the fear induced by the age of the department store that drove the political activism of threatened shopkeepers in nineteenth-century Europe. Still, the impact of the *grands magasins* on small business was by no means uniform. Some small retailers were victimized by the intrusion of the large stores while others thrived alongside them. Moreover, the conversion of economic discontent into political organization was often a complex and mediated process.[71] We will return to the predicament of the ubiquitous shopkeepers in Canton in the next chapter. Suffice it to say here that to many self-proclaimed apostles of modernity, resistance from the merchant community was regarded simply as evidence of the latter's backwardness.

Instead, the attention of the governing elites was seized by what they saw as the positive results of the transformation of the city, such as the roads and the transportation system, the new commercial district, and the enhanced opportunity to educate and direct their constituents. Above all, they were pleased to witness the expansion of industry and the metamorphosis of the suburb of Honam into an industrial enclave. The increasing visibility of two classes of people—industrialists and workers—particularly captured their imagination.[72] Whether one found in these two groups confirmation of the wisdom of organic solidarity or the seeds of class conflict, all could agree that they were the essential segments of a modern social body. Industrialists and workers, in other words, were the harbingers of modernity, the vital fabric with which a brand new society-and-nation was to be woven together.

THE PROMISE OF INDUSTRY

According to a survey taken in 1933, Canton had the third largest number of non–foreign owned factories among Chinese cities.[73] Yet the metropolis entered the twentieth century with little more than a handful of manufacturing industries. With a few notable and usually government-sponsored exceptions such as the arsenal (*jiqiju*) founded by Governor-General Rui-lin in 1873 (and subsequently expanded by his successors Zhang Zhidong and Cen Chunxuan), most industrial concerns were of the backyard variety. They employed at most a dozen or so workers each, usually operating in the rear of a shop, with the front serving as a retail outlet. There was, in short, not always a clear distinction between commercial and industrial establishments. Only in the last decade of the Qing, and in particular following the founding of the Republic, did modern industrial enterprises become a discernible part of the local economy. Even then, industries in Canton were heavily tilted toward small-scale organizations. For example, while Canton claimed a total of almost 30 percent more factories than Wuhan, those enterprises together commanded only about 65 percent of Wuhan's assets in terms of capitalization and number of workers. Indeed, the capitalization of the Canton concerns was even less than that of those at Qingdao, despite the fact that Qingdao had only about a tenth as many factories as Canton.[74] In a separate survey on manufactories in eight Canton industries in the same year, only 31 out of a total of 205 sampled employed more than a hundred hands.[75] Their modest scale meant that industrial enterprises in Canton were particularly vulnerable to changes in the market or government policies, and they often started up and folded with alarming rapidity. Stability was decidedly not a feature of the industrial landscape of Canton during the early Republic.

A prominent example of the new manufacturing industries in the early Republic was the production of rubber goods. Unlike most other ventures, the latex industry was first started in Canton rather than in the industrial capital of Shanghai, reflecting Canton's close commercial ties with southeast Asia where the raw materials were produced. An archetypal light industry with modest need for capital investment, rubber goods quickly came to symbolize Canton's quest for industrialization. The first enterprise, the Guangdong xiongdi gongsi xiangjiaochang, otherwise known as "The First in China," was established in the industrial enclave of Honam in 1919.[76] The founders were a member of the gentry, Deng Fengchi, and his dentist friend Chen Yubo, with capital raised from their relatives in southeast Asia and Canada.

Inspired by the then familiar call to promote industries in China, Chen apparently parlayed a knowledge of latex acquired through his dental practice into successful production of rubber soles for shoes. The cost advantage of rubber quickly rendered it a popular replacement for leather, and by the early 1920s there were over twenty factories engaged in its production in Canton.[77] The number of workers at "The First in China" increased from about two dozen to over a hundred.[78] The boom, however, did not last long. The fierce competition led to general cost-cutting in production and deterioration in quality. By 1923, the heavy taxation imposed by the government,

Small-scale manufactories typical of republican Canton located along the city's congested riverfront.

in addition to the rising cost of raw materials, had resulted in a severe depression of the industry. By then, only five enterprises remained.[79]

Yet, even in 1923, one of the five, the Feng Qiang Rubber Factory, had already begun to explore other business options. Feng Qiang was named after its founder who, like his partners, was an émigré from the Straits Settlement.[80] Feng realized that the future of latex products lay in expansion into other areas of the market. Sales of rubber shoes (rather than simply soles), for instance, had hitherto been dominated by imports from southeast Asia. What was lacking in Canton, however, was the technical expertise for production of more sophisticated goods. Eventually, after Feng made a personal trip to Japan, the company was able, with the assistance of Japanese technicians, to produce rubber footwear for the first time at its Hong Kong branch factory around 1927.[81] Production began in Canton the following year. As the market responded favorably, the number of latex enterprises shot back up to 28, capturing the market from imported goods in the process. The production figure for rubber shoes just before the onset of the depression in the early 1930s was estimated to be over 800,000 pairs from local manufacturers.[82] The most dominant was undoubtedly Feng Qiang, its premier position illustrated by the fact that "fengqiang shoes" (*fengqiangxie*) was widely accepted as being synonymous with footwear products from Canton.[83]

The search for technological transfer from abroad was by no means restricted to the latex industry. In an era of increasingly strident nationalistic rhetoric, many of the budding industrialists of the early Republic often faced the dilemma of having to choose between their objective of promoting "native" manufacturing and their reliance on foreign expertise and machinery for economic viability. Another example is the manufacture of matches. Match production, which required even less capital investment than the latex industry, was one of the oldest major industries of Canton.[84] But it was in the town of Foshan, about 25 kilometers west of Canton, that the first match manufactory, Qiao Ming, appeared in 1879. Its founder, Wei Shengxuan, had been a longtime resident of Japan.[85] Qiao Ming was soon followed by several similar concerns in Canton, again funded mostly with émigré capital.

The golden age of match manufacturing, however, did not arrive until the first decade of the Republic, toward the end of which 30 factories were to be found in Canton alone.[86] A significant percentage, perhaps as high as 85 percent, of the investment continued to come from émigré communities, particularly those in Japan and the United States.[87] Moreover, members of this flourishing industry, save a couple of notable exceptions, were dependent on Japanese raw materials, machinery, and technicians for their daily operation.[88] The most conspicuous exception was the almost fully mechanized plant installed by the Xing Ya Company, a creation of émigré investors from the United States in 1921. The company's capitalization was estimated to be around HK$400,000, making it the best-endowed match manufacturer of the region. As might be expected, all of its machines were imports from the United States. Its owners, however, soon found out that despite their expensive and sophisticated equipment, the "American-style" matches—long and cylindrical, with only 50 to 60 in a large box (in contrast to the "Japanese-style" square sticks with about 100 to a smaller container)—were not competitive locally.[89] Adding to their woes were the renewal of Japanese efforts to penetrate the local market, defective machinery, and the unfavorable taxation policies of the government. The company never recorded a profit and went out of business after three consecutive years of losses.

An even more instructive example of the predicament of the new industries of the early Republic is the case of the Dongshan Match Factory. Dongshan's credentials as an example of indigenous entrepreneurship were impeccable. Unlike most other match producers in Canton, it was the creation of two local academics (both returned students), Luo Jieruo and Chen Dachu, with the collaboration of a laboratory technician, Li Yaofeng. Luo's father was a typical merchant entrepreneur of the older generation, who specialized in the production of straw mats for export from workshops in both the surrounding counties and Canton, and was also involved in the native banking business. It was the Luo family's financial support which underwrote the venture. Like many of their contemporaries, the Dongshan founders saw their task as laying the material foundation for a modern society-and-nation. It was their avowed intention that the enterprise, which was named after the newly developed eastern suburb of Canton in which they set up their plant at the end of 1919, was to use only Chinese machines, materials, and technicians.

In an attempt to take advantage of a burgeoning local machine-tool industry, the partners contracted two manufacturers in the Honam area to produce the necessary machinery. Unfortunately, the Chinese machines not only required more manpower to operate and were cumbersome to use, but managed only about 50 percent (instead of the projected 95 percent) of the productivity of their Japanese counterparts. The materials used for the matchsticks were also substandard. Although Dongshan's product, riding on the tide of the campaign of the 1910s to use native goods, did sell well in the market for a brief period, they eventually stockpiled even when priced below cost. As Li Yaofeng recalled wryly in his reminiscences, even his own family members balked at using Dongshan's matches.[90]

After a year of losses, the young owners were forced to bow to the imperative of survival and turned to Japanese machines. Indicative of the predicament of many of the fledgling industrialists—and the hazards of developing self-reliant indigenous industries in early republican China—was the fact that Dongshan was also compelled to import matchsticks from Japan. Not that suitable sticks were unavailable within the country: They were produced in Shanghai and had been successfully utilized by manufacturers there. Those sticks, however, were not cost-effective for the entrepreneurs in Canton, as lower productivity, to say nothing of unreliable transportation, meant that the Shanghai shipments were priced 10 percent more than Japanese imports. Although Dongshan never did employ Japanese technicians, its founders nonetheless felt that their original vision had been compromised. Such sense of disillusionment was probably made even more acute by the fiery rhetoric of the Guomindang and the Communists in the 1920s, which drew a sharp imaginary line between "national bourgeoisie" and "imperialist lackeys." By 1924, Luo had departed for Peking to resume his academic career, while Chen was on his way to Germany. Li alone remained to see the company through the hard times.[91]

The story of latex and match production is in many ways representative of the problems faced by the new class of industrialists. The absence of a domestic capital market meant that funds for the enterprises, as in the case of the department stores, often came from the émigré communities. The foreign banks were reluctant to lend directly to indigenous entrepreneurs, while the Chinese-owned modern banks in Canton generally preferred to earn their profits by engaging in long-distance transmittal and exchange of funds rather than by financing infant industries. The local merchants and their native banks, to be sure, were sometimes involved in providing backing for ventures in the new manufacturing sector, usually through personal connections as demonstrated by the Luo family and the Dongshan company. As a whole, however, their role seems to have been limited by both their mode of operation and modest assets.[92] In many cases investment in the new industries was the result of a few partners pooling their resources, with perhaps additional input from relatives and friends. Out of seventeen latex manufactories surveyed in the mid-1930s, for example, there were fourteen partnerships in contrast to only one joint stock company and two single ownerships.[93] The depth of resources in the new industries was decidedly limited.

In addition to the problem of financing, competition in early republican Canton was also ruinously intense. Take the example of mechanized rice husking (*nianmi*). Following the influx of superior-quality, mostly machine-husked rice from southeast Asia toward the end of the nineteenth century, the first mechanized plant for husking appeared in Canton in 1906. By 1921, the number of husking factories, the majority of which were located in

Honam, had reached a total of 32.[94] But even as these enterprises flourished, many merchants from the surrounding rice-producing counties had already begun to establish their own mechanized workshops to do the husking. The result was a precipitous fall in the business of the plants at the metropolis. Over half of them went out of business within a decade. Not until the mid-1930s, when an import tax imposed by the government led to an almost 75 percent reduction in the volume of foreign rice available, did the industry regain a degree of vitality.[95]

To the governing elites, the promise of industry was considerable. Not only would industries be instrumental in the modernization of the country, they would also provide renewed impetus for national construction. The industrialists, for example, stood to benefit most from an integrated national market. In a series of articles published in 1919, the Guomindang stalwart Liao Zhongkai lamented that the Chinese government had never carried out a comprehensive survey of its territories, and nobody knew the exact size of the country. For China to progress, Liao believed, it had to seek detailed knowledge about its rightful territories (*lingtu*). That could not be done, however, without better communication systems. That was why Liao, like Sun Yat-sen, believed that railroad development was essential for constructing the nation (*zuzhi guojia de yaosu*).[96]

The vision of a physically integrated nation was undoubtedly attractive to the industrialists. The products of the new industries were clearly aimed at a different kind of market than that of the manufacturing enterprises operated by members of the established merchant community of Canton. The latter, as symbolized by the silk industry, were part of a triangular network of commercial-banking-export activities which was a legacy of the nineteenth century. Production was determined by the demands of the foreign market, with Western traders as its representatives. Taking advantage of locally produced raw materials, such export-oriented manufacturing work was often carried out in the surrounding counties, or distributed to urban artisanal workshops.

By contrast, the new industries, while obviously not closed to the possibilities of overseas expansion, directed their products first of all to the domestic market. The sale of rubber goods in China, for instance, was dominated by products from Shanghai and Canton, with the latter almost monopolizing the market in Guangdong, Guangxi, and the southwestern provinces.[97] There were often wholesale representatives of the larger latex companies of Canton in other major cities. Similarly, matches produced in Canton were a major force south of the Yangzi, including Jiangxi, Fujian, and Yunnan.[98] Even more important, these products were marketed not as luxury items but as daily necessities to the consumers. The logic of the marketplace, in other words, did point to this class of industrialists as a feasible building block for a new polity.

Yet, the world of industries in the early Republic was unstable and fragile. The government, its proclaimed commitment to industry notwithstanding, was frequently forced by its own dire financial needs to squeeze the fledgling entrepreneurs. As mentioned earlier, most of the new industrialists in Canton were returned students or émigrés, and they often lacked the kind of organizational network which had served the merchant establishment so well since the late Qing. Only toward the mid-1920s, for instance, did several founders of major match manufactories begin to schedule regular, albeit still unofficial, meetings to discuss issues common to the industry, such as the problems of "overcompetition" and pricing strategy.[99] Even their enterprises were found mostly in the newly carved outlying areas of the city, as if to symbolize their limited impact on the core of the metropolis.

On the whole, the existence of many of the new industries in Canton was too precarious, and their interests too splintered, for the owners to assert themselves effectively. The harsh business imperatives of many industrialists, moreover, often conflicted with the muscular nationalistic rhetoric of a self-reliant community of producers. Industrialists, however, were not the only class brought by the proliferation of these enterprises which accompanied the spatial transformation of Canton. To many political and intellectual elites bent on reconstructing (*gaizao*) China in the image of a modern nation, there was another class which figured prominently in the discourse of society: the workers.

REORGANIZING WORKERS

A leftist intellectual from central China, Gao Yuhan, upon visiting Canton in 1921, was impressed by the labor force's standard of living in comparison to that in Shanghai.[100] It was, to be sure, a somewhat fleeting observation, and its accuracy is hard to verify with the available data. But there was undoubtedly a widespread consensus by the early 1920s that Canton had become a stronghold of progressive thought and, depending on one's ideological leanings, democratic or subversive political practices. More significant, the city had acquired a reputation as the hotbed for labor organizations, which prompted Gao to speak enthusiastically of turning south China into a "red" zone (*chihua*)[101] The city was singled out in a Western report on the relationship between "dangerous doctrines" and labor unrest in the major urban centers of China. "Except perhaps at Canton," the report states, "the movement [of ideas such as Bolshevism] exists at the present stage almost entirely among the educated classes."[102]

Neither the concept of labor nor labor organization were, of course, new to China. The closest Chinese term for labor, *gong*, denoting the physical work necessary for the production of the arts or material goods, can easily be found in classical texts. Like the merchants, those who engaged in *gong* for a living in imperial China had also long learned to organize themselves. And such organizations—which often carried the label *bang* or "gang"—were formed on the basis of native place, trade, or segregated sphere of operation.[103] Indeed, these labor gangs, whose functions ranged from the provision of mutual aid to securing access to work, were an integral part of the daily existence of most workers. At times of turmoil, they also often provided the organizational basis of the workers' collective action. If labor organizations were not a new phenomenon, why then did the workers, particularly those in early republican Canton, become the focus of so much attention?

There was, to be sure, the founding of new industries in early-twentieth-century Canton. Yet, as will be shown later, its immediate impact on either the relations of production or labor organizations was rather circumscribed. In her research on Shanghai, Elizabeth Perry, a sympathetic student of the labor movement, also finds that even during what she calls the "heyday of radicalism" in the 1920s, "the working class remained embedded in preexisting forms of solidarity despite its growing cosmopolitanism."[104] Nor was the since canonized May Fourth incident of 1919 a catalytic event in the laboring world of Canton. The local rally in support of the May Fourth demonstration in Peking, which took place on May 11, was dominated by students.[105] It was again the students, protesting the sale of Japanese goods, who occupied the department store Sincere for an evening following another rally on May 30.[106] But the students' efforts to organize workers to carry out sustained collective action produced little result. Unlike in Shanghai, the workers of Canton staged no symbolic political strike in solidarity with the students.[107]

Moreover, whatever stirring of labor there was in Canton, it did not occur where one might expect, in the relatively large-scale factories of the modern sector. Rather it stemmed from the likes of handicraft workers, service employees, and that historically most volatile segment of the laboring population, transport workers. This was partly due to the structure of the labor market. In addition to his favorable assessment of local conditions, the visitor Gao Yuhan also pointed out in passing the use of female labor in Canton.[108] Indeed, the modern industrial sector of the metropolis, particularly the plants with a sizable workforce such as those in the match and to a lesser extent the latex industries, was sustained primarily by female and child labor, as the following account describes in some detail:

> Of the typical match factory, the Wen Ming Match Factory, on the Northwest outskirts of Canton city, may be taken as a good example. About two hundred workers are employed, mainly small children of both sexes and a fair number of women, together with a couple of dozen men to do the heavy work and attend to machinery, etc. . . . Only the men are regular employees, paid by the month (averaging $15 a month), the children and women engaged in packing, labeling, box-making, drying, and employed on the various pieces of machinery, etc.: are all paid daily by piece work. . . . The hours of work amount to twelve hours a day, seven days a week. . . . The machinery used is both Japanese and Chinese (the latter made in Canton, Honam suburb), and consists of a gas-engine (Chinese) to run the belts driving the other machinery, and other small light pieces of machinery for various different operations. Most of the work however is still done by hand.[109]

Li Yaofeng, one of the founders of the Dongshan Match Factory, once suggested that he joined the Merchant Corps in the 1920s in part because riffraff and off-duty soldiers often gathered around the factory site to offer their unwanted attention to his three hundred–odd female staff.[110] A survey carried out in the mid-1930s revealed that of the 3,514 workers in eleven match manufactories (an average of 319 workers per factory), about 76 percent (2,680) were women, with the remainder comprised of 10 percent children (the figure 345 was probably low due to underreporting) and 14 percent men (488).[111] Women accounted for about the same proportion of the workforce in the latex industry. Of the 3,128 hands in seventeen plants (an average of 184 per plant), 77 percent (2,400) were women in contrast to 23 percent (726) men.[112]

The concentration of female workers and tough conditions notwithstanding, the larger enterprises in Canton were far from being the center of labor agitation. There were occasional outbursts of activity, such as the unionization of the hundred-odd women operators of the Canton Telephone Company in 1924.[113] On the whole, however, the predominantly female workforce of the modern sector remained relatively quiet during the turmoil in the early Republic. The reasons were manifold. The female industrial workforce, for example, often lacked the established network of organizations into which their male counterparts in the handicraft or transport sectors could tap. More importantly, official labor organizers, including the Communists of the mid-1920s, had largely stayed away from this segment of the workforce, as indicated clearly in their own reports.[114] It seems that the mostly male leadership was either unable or unwilling to overcome their preconceived notions about the passivity of women workers and their prejudice against the "weaker sex."[115] Thus in spite of the official promotion of a women's movement, intervention by women as a group in the political process in Canton in the 1920s was confined largely to the symbolic realm, as in the case of the annual celebration of Women's Day.[116]

The emergence of a labor movement in Canton in the early 1920s, then, seems to stem less from the founding of new industries than from the efforts of the governing elites in (re)organizing the workers and generating a new discourse of labor. Instead of simply representing a specific form of occupation, *gong* came increasingly to signify, following most nineteenth-century Western social theories, a specific social stratum or segment—or class—which was central to the systematic formation of a modern social body. Seen in this light, the myriad preexisting labor gangs were a mixed blessing to the elites. To be sure, the fragmentation of the workers into various gangs constituted on the basis of native place or sphere of operation did not necessarily hamper labor militancy. It has even been argued that regional or other parochial affiliations actually served to foster labor activism.[117] Still, activism clearly did not necessarily translate into class unity.[118]

On the other hand, the labor gangs did provide a readily available group of organizations, divided as they might be, for those who tried to mold the workers into a cohesive constituency for their project. Thus with the return of Chen Jiongming and the founding of the new municipal administration under Sun Fo in Canton in 1921, more than a hundred labor organizations were encouraged to modernize and to register themselves with the government. A plethora of groups, usually consisting of teachers, students, clerks, or functionaries, was established with the aim of fostering new and modern representative organs for the workers, rejecting old institutions such as the guild (which often included both employers and employees of a given trade) or the gang in the process. Yet, as the government was soon to find out, although many of the old institutions renamed themselves "unions" (*gonghui*) or "labor associations" (*gongshe*), the structure of their organizations often remained largely unchanged.[119]

Indeed, the line between the old and the new labor organizations was not always easy to define. Take the powerful machinists as an example. An elite stratum of workers with a history of participation in the organization of their trade that dated back to the late Qing, the machinists in 1921 established their own union, the Guangdong Machinists Union (*Guangdong jiqi gongren weichihui*), in distinction from the employer's organ, the Federation of Machine-Tool Trades (*Jiqi shangwu lianyi gonghui*).[120] The leader of the new union, Huang Huanting, was an ex-machinist turned labor organizer. He was, however, at the same time also the owner of a machine-tool shop in the Honam area. Huang was moreover a seasoned politician, who had purchased a rank in the imperial army, joined Sun Yat-sen's Revolutionary Alliance in the last years of the dynasty, and been active in both the Merchant Self-Government Association and the guild of the machine-tool trade during the late Qing and the early Republic.[121] Huang's background was hardly atypical of those who ran the new labor organizations. As we will see, Communist activists were at pains to point out that even by the mid-1920s, most of the so-called modern unions were dominated by people like Huang or leaders of the labor gangs.[122]

The fact is that the labor movement of Canton in the early 1920s consisted of little more than a tapestry of multifarious organizations. There was, for example, the Mutual Aid Association (*Huzhu zongshe*), founded in 1920, which comprised perhaps 30 to 40 labor organizations under the direction of that maverick Marxist follower of Sun Yat-sen, Xie Yingbo. The objective of the association was allegedly to secure future control of the government by workers, although it actually operated, in the words of a contemporary report, more in the fashion of a "faithful agent of the Kuomintang [Guomindang]."[123] It refused, for instance, to support organizations which would not follow the official policy of the Guomindang.[124] Other involved groups included the declining yet still active clusters of anarchists. Although the anarchists did not directly command any labor organizations, they had long sought to spread their message among the workers. Some of them, for example, were at work within those associations affiliated with the Guangdong Workers' Federation (*Guangdong zonggonghui*), founded in 1921, a motley collection assembled initially by organizers from the émigré communities.[125] All of these groups tried to claim the allegiance of the various labor organizations, which reputedly commanded a combined following of over 200,000 members by 1922.[126]

While the elites were eager to recruit bona fide workers into the leadership ranks of the labor movement, the task was not easy. A glimpse of the difficulties involved can be found in the experience of the Socialist Youth Corps (SY), which was described, with some justification, as "by far the most important Communist Association in Canton [in 1922]".[127] Among all the labor organizers, the SY perhaps made the most conscious attempt to bridge the gap between the elites and the toilers, and to connect with the grassroots of the laboring world. Still, the result of its effort was disappointing. The monthly reports on recruitment compiled by the Canton SY show that while the corps absorbed 58 new members in 1922, 47 of them were students in contrast to only 11 workers. Considering the predominantly female workforce of the new manufacturing enterprises, even more telling is the column on woman recruits, which remained consistently blank throughout the year.[128]

Despite Canton's reputation, therefore, there is scant evidence to suggest the successful politicization of labor there at the beginning of the 1920s. To be sure, the workers, many of whom belonged to the handicraft and service sectors (including pottery workers, teahouse waiters, and printers), were adept at taking advantage of a new milieu favorable to labor activism. The number of labor conflicts, for example, soared in 1921, prompting comments of a "melancholy tale" or "epidemic" of strikes from westerners.[129] But the strikes were often spontaneous in nature and had something of a "wildcat" quality, as was the case when the workmen at the Waterworks Company put down their tools after a colleague was dismissed.[130] The majority were economic strikes: The objective of the workers was usually either a wage increase or improvement in their working and living conditions.[131] Violence, moreover, seems to have been a regular part of the collective actions of workers, an unfortunate feature that drew comments even from such a sympathetic observer as Gao Yuhan.[132] The analysis from the Communist labor organizer and historian Deng Zhongxia, who described the strikes in Guangdong during the early 1920s as "backward" (*luohou*),[133] typified the views of the political and intellectual elites.

In the annals of Chinese history, the Hongkong Seamen's Strike of 1922 has often been represented as a watershed in the narrative of the labor movement. Not only was it one of the first large-scale organized labor strikes in the early Republic, it also marked, as some might argue, a new phase in the awakening (*juewu*) of the workers. By striking against the shipping companies, most of which were foreign-owned, the seamen were said to have engaged in an act of anti-imperialist struggle, and "anti-imperialism" was to become central to the Guomindang-led project of constructing society-and-nation in the mid-1920s and beyond.[134] Yet, initially, the seamen, like most workers of the period, sought little more than economic betterment for themselves.[135] Nor was the Leninist message of anti-imperialism an integral part of the Guomindang repertoire in 1922. Indeed, after Sun Yat-sen's return to Canton in late 1920, he continued to talk about nationalism simply in terms of the equality of nations and races.[136] Even in the aftermath of the strike, the Guomindang leader, perhaps in an attempt to allay the fear of many westerners, stated that he was sympathetic toward the workers only "as far as their strike was economic," but that he "absolutely repudiate[d]" the use of the dispute "to damage British interests."[137]

What ultimately lent a political dimension to the strike was not so much its initial objectives as the effects of the bungling of the British administration. The colonial government's unnecessarily intransigent stance succeeded only in coalescing support against the British. In particular, the callous shooting of sympathy strikers in Hong Kong on March 3, almost two months after the walkout by the seamen, caused an outburst of unprecedented anti-British feeling in the Canton area[138] and created an impact that lasted far beyond the strike itself. It was, in other words, through the unexpected twists and turns of the strike that the Guomindang leadership first learned how different classes could apparently come together *in practice*, and how the working class could play an instrumental role in the process.[139] The turn to the discourse of anti-imperialism to undergird the project of national reconstruction was thus more a result than a progenitor of the Seamen's Strike. This result was, of course, reinforced by the Sun-Joffe Agreement reached between the Guomindang and the Soviet Union in early 1923.

The plight of Chinese seamen has often been noted, and there is no doubt that they were one of the most economically exploited groups of workers.[140] Even the British consul-general in Canton, in the aftermath of the strike in which the workers won a substantial proportion of their wage demands, conceded that "the settlement is not an unfair one."[141] The initial strategy of the shipowners and the Hong Kong government, however, was to break the strike, which started with a walkout on January 12. A curfew was quickly imposed. Although an offer of a modest wage increase was extended by the employers on January 17, the gesture was clearly a ruse as the offer was withdrawn within 24 hours, before any serious negotiations could have taken place. Concessions made by the workers in late January were also summarily rejected by the shipowners.[142]

Meanwhile, the strikers began to retreat to Canton where the leaders of the strike had established their headquarters away from the tentacles of British authority. Assistance was offered by local labor organizations. Although the Canton government was not officially a party to the dispute, its provision of wherewithal, in the form of supposed loans, was crucial for the sustenance of the strike. Support for the workers, of course, was not without political rewards. By mid-February, there were probably about 6,000 striking workers in Canton alone.[143] They were issued identity cards with a portrait of Sun Yat-sen on one side.[144] The British even accused the Guomindang of demanding 50 percent of the increased wage from the workers as a contribution to its campaign against political and military rivals to the north.[145]

The hard line of the employers, however, backfired. The dockers and the stevedores, whose original reaction to the call for solidarity from the seamen was at best lukewarm, decided to go on sympathy strike on January 27. This immediately sent alarm throughout the colony as the strike was now capable of paralyzing Hong Kong. The colonial administration reacted on February 1 by declaring the recently founded Seamen's Union an illegal organization. As attitudes hardened, coercive and violent tactics were deployed by both sides. The seamen seem to have been particularly successful in their intimidation of "scabs," most of whom, like some of the strikers themselves, were hired from the Shanghai and Ningbo areas.[146] The result was a stalemate. By then the dispute had begun to take on the tone of a broader struggle against the British authorities. For example, the leaders of the seamen in Canton proclaimed on February 20 that the strike was a "bloodless revolution," and that the issues at stake were nothing less than "human value" and "national prestige."[147]

Nevertheless, the turning point of the strike did not come until early March. Toward the end of February, the workers began to threaten a general strike which would further cripple the colony. As more strikers began to leave for Canton, the governor of Hong Kong, Reginald Stubbs, panicked. In response, he issued a controversial order forbidding anybody to leave Hong Kong without a permit. The problem of legality aside, such a decree was bound to be tested under the circumstances. On the morning of March 3, hundreds of workers were marching to Canton when they were spotted in the outskirts of Hong Kong by a small patrol unit of policemen and soldiers. As the workers ignored the order to return, they were fired upon. There were at least three deaths and eight injuries.[148] Public outcry followed, and the British consul-general in Canton distanced himself from such wanton disregard for human life.[149] Realizing that they had lost substantial moral ground, the shipowners were forced to return to the table and reached a settlement on March 4 which was largely in favor of the workers.[150] Two days later the Order in Council outlawing the Seamen's Union was rescinded, and those being held in custody in connection with the strike were released. The government was "to consider favorably" the provision of compensation to those injured or to the families of those killed. A sum of HK$1,000 each was reportedly paid.[151]

In view of the subsequent Canton-Hongkong Strike of 1925–26, Governor Stubbs for once seemed rather prescient in his report on the Seamen's Strike. "The Kwok Man Tong [Guomindang] has undoubtedly gained 'face' as a result [of the strike]," he wrote. "It has shown that it can paralyse the trade of HK, and it must be expected that it will again employ similar tactics whenever it desires to gain some object." The British authority therefore "must assume that next time a general strike will be declared without warning."[152] If Stubbs's remarks were informed by his unabated hostility toward the Guomindang, there is little doubt that the latter had emerged from the episode a more potent force. In fact, the Guomindang gained more than merely "face" from the experience. It had learned a valuable lesson in the working of society.

Members of the Guomindang initially turned to the discourse of class as a guide to understanding the putative structure of modern society. While they recognized class interests as a legitimate way of analyzing the social body, in their quest for a cohesive society-and-nation they were understandably wary of any notion of class conflict. The Canton government under Chen Jiongming in the early 1920s, despite its embrace of labor as a constituency, actually spent much of its effort trying, through the use of posters and educational campaigns, to dissuade workers from striking.[153] To Chen, labor organizations were to be encouraged for the enlightenment of the workers. In an interview with worker representatives, Chen reportedly stated that labor organizations then were still too immature (*youzhi*), and that workers should keep their distance from political turmoil. He justified his stance with utopian rhetoric, saying that while the goal of political movements was to ameliorate the prevailing system, the labor movement should aim instead at the wholesale abolition of every kind of system.[154]

Still, if Chen's language was eclectic, his reservations about the politicization of workers were undoubtedly shared by the majority within the Guomindang leadership then. In a speech at the inauguration of the new Guangdong branch of the Guomindang in 1921, for example, Sun Yat-sen himself made it quite clear that his own understanding of social justice entailed a kind of "state capitalism" (*zichan guoyouzhi*) in which the country was to industrialize through mechanization without "class conflict."[155] The role of the Guomindang was to ensure the harmony of different "class interests." This is what the historian Arif Dirlik refers to as the Guomindang's engagement in "class politics without class struggle" and in fashioning a "corporatist" solution.[156]

It is within this context that the Seamen's Strike is particularly significant. It demonstrated to the Guomindang how labor could be fully appropriated for its political project. The working class did not only symbolize a modern society: Through the clash with the British it had also become a sign of the nation. The potential tension between the different segments or classes of society, even in a place with such a complex social formation as Canton, was seemingly suppressed in a moment of common struggle against foreign exploitation. To the Guomindang, the politics of class, with the working class situated at the forefront, could now be articulated with the erasure of any trace of endogenous conflict. Indeed, in a speech to the newly founded Council of Workers' Deputies on Labor Day (May 1) of 1924, Sun Yat-sen went so far as to say that "not only are Chinese workers not oppressed by indigenous capitalists, they actually think of various ways to oppress them." He then posed the rhetorical question: "If the position of the workers is already superior to that of the indigenous capitalists, why can all economic oppression not be got rid of?" The problem, Sun declared triumphantly, was that most oppression came from foreign capitalists. As a result, if the workers wanted to improve their own position, they must first of all shoulder the burden of raising the position of the nation.[157]

As the most organized of the modernist elites in the early 1920s, members of the Guomindang were armed with the conviction that their mission was to construct a new society-and-nation. They set out to transform Canton into a modern city and to establish the conditions conducive to the institution of a new form of government as well as a modern social formation, signified in particular by the industrialists and workers. Their project was to ground their party's claim to power on its representation of a cohesive body social. If the industrialists turned out to be too marginal a force, the workers seemed to be in a position to play a leading role. Bolstered by the success of the Seamen's Strike and by the apparent possibility of the formation of a disciplined and cohesive *shehui juntuan* consisting of the various social segments under the rubric of anti-imperialism, members of the Guomindang were able to elide the potentially disruptive thrust of the discourse of class in their articulation of a unitary nation. As it turned out, however, the Guomindang in Canton encountered the stiffest resistance not, as might be expected under the circumstances, from the foreign powers, but from part of the very society it sought to represent.

CHAPTER THREE

The Contested Nation

> Alas! What has happened to the zealousness of the people
> of Guangdong in the struggle against imperialism! Not
> only do you not dare to resist, you have to succumb to
> imperialism, even elevating its lackeys to become your
> leaders and attacking organizations that fight against im-
> perialism. . . . You beg foreign consuls to threaten this
> government with something akin to an ultimatum, what
> a crime that is! To beg the foreign governor of a colony to
> interfere in the affairs of this government, what a disgrace
> that is! Such behavior is not unusual when perpetrated by
> the lackeys of imperialism. What is surprising, however, is
> that it is supported by ordinary merchants. Even more sur-
> prising is the fact that the ordinary people show absolutely
> no reaction or fury toward such behavior and carry on as
> if nothing has happened. . . . Oh, people of Guangdong!
> Don't insult your ancestors! Oh, people of Guangdong!
> Don't forget the origins of the struggle against imperialism!
>
> — *Guangzhou minguo ribao*, 1 9 2 4 / 1 0 / 2 7

At dawn on October 15, 1924, the police forces of Canton under the command of Commissioner Wu Tiecheng, together with army units loyal to Sun
Yat-sen and cadets from the Whampoa (Huangpu) Military Academy,
blasted their way into the city's Xiguan district and routed the quasi-insur-

rection staged by the local Merchant Corps.[1] The event, which became known as the Merchant Corps incident, represents the final explosion of a bitter yearlong tussle between the Guomindang-led government and the merchant community of Canton. It was also a turning point in the Guomindang's project to reconstruct society-and-nation.

At the time of the rebellion, Sun was actually about to abandon Canton and head north. He was reportedly frustrated by the apparent indifference, if not outright hostility, of many of the local inhabitants toward his government. Thus following the outbreak of conflict in the lower Yangzi area in early September of 1924, a precursor to the second full-scale Fengtian-Zhili war, Sun issued a proclamation stating his intention to lead his followers to head north to join the Fengtian side, leaving the people of Guangdong province to their own self-government.[2] Despite obviously insufficient funds, arms, and logistical support, he ordered his troops immediately to Shaoguan in northern Guangdong in an almost comic attempt to join the northern war. By all accounts, it was only at the insistence of his key followers that Sun decided to confront the insurrection which had by then broken out against the Guomindang government back in Canton.[3] Crushing the Merchant Corps would enable the Guomindang to hold on to Canton for another two critical years during which it not only consolidated its grip on the rest of the province of Guangdong, but managed to establish, with Soviet aid, an army which was key to its successful military campaign to the north in 1926–28.

Initial opinions, however, weighed heavily against the Guomindang immediately following the suppression of the Merchant Corps. To most westerners, the episode presented further evidence, in light of the agreement reached between Sun Yat-sen and the Soviet representative Adolf Joffe in early 1923, of the Bolshevization of the Canton government. The English press in Hong Kong in particular was virulent in its condemnation, reporting unsubstantiated rumors that women and children were being bayoneted by government soldiers under instructions from Sun "in order to save ammunition."[4] More important, perhaps, was the shock and outrage aroused in the émigré communities which had been a major source of financial support for the Guomindang's project. Many of their members came from the Canton area, were engaged in mercantile activities, and felt a certain affinity for their brethren back home.[5] Destruction was undoubtedly extensive.

In the wake of the Merchant Corps incident of 1924, destruction is evident in one of the narrow main streets characteristic of the old commercial quarter of Xiguan.

Although the notoriously narrow lanes of Xiguan rendered the site ideal for barricading, the wooden gates erected by the Merchant Corps provided but little resistance to the artillery fire of the government forces. As fires caused by the shelling swept through the area, the burning continued into the following day. Almost a third of Xiguan lay in ruins as a result, and an estimated 750 to 1,000 houses burned or were looted by marauding troops.[6] Casualties numbered at the minimum in the hundreds, although most civilians had by then fled the Xiguan district. By the government's own admission, close to a hundred soldiers were shot on the day for breaching discipline and committing crimes.[7]

Seen through the lens of the Guomindang, however, the Merchant Corps insurrection was more than simply an antigovernment rebellion. It was an overt threat to the vision of a cohesive society-and-nation which lay at the very heart of the Guomindang's project. The Seamen's Strike might have been an encouraging moment for the advent of society. But the Merchant Corps incident revealed, in an equally dramatic manner, that the social was an infinite and unpredictable play of differences rather than an easily manageable organic and finite whole.[8] Still, if an invigorated and disciplined body social indeed constituted the foundation of a modern nation, then this play of differences had to be somehow domesticated and controlled. Coercion in the form of crushing the insurrection, while essential, was clearly inadequate. The analysis, representation, and memory of the incident also had to conform to the official discourse of the making of a cohesive polity.

As the Guomindang regained control of the city, the initial tale of carnage faded into the background. It was replaced by an officially sanctioned narrative. To place itself as the architect of a new political order—the nation— the Guomindang explained the body social's convulsion as the work of exogenous forces: A conspiratorial plot had been masterminded by the imperialists, primarily the British. Wu Tiecheng, for example, described the British as the "director" (*daoyan*) of the incident in his memoir.[9] The British themselves, of course, did not barricade Xiguan—their work was purportedly carried out for them by the compradors and the grande bourgeoisie of Canton. These agents of foreign companies, who relied on imperialist profit to gain wealth for themselves, Sun Yat-sen said, were a carbuncle on the nation.[10] In a still authoritative account of the Nationalist Revolution by a leading Guomindang historian, first published in 1966, the comment that "the British authority covertly supported the Merchant Corps rebellion" is deemed so self-evident that it needs little elaboration or supporting evidence.[11]

Interwoven with this narrative was the notion that the merchant class was split between big and petty merchants. For example, a booklet which appeared following a skirmish between the corps and pro-government militiamen and cadets, just days before the events of October 15, insisted that small merchants and shopkeepers were on the side of the government.[12] As will be shown, it was an assertion which flew in the face of evidence and was contradicted by other government statements. But in the aftermath of the Merchant Corps incident the Guomindang did begin in earnest their attempt to organize and to reinscribe the "middling and small merchants" as a discrete constituency of support.[13] Meanwhile, an undifferentiated working class was privileged in the narrative. It had become the standard bearer of the masses (*qunzhong*), an alliance of different classes which supposedly formed the bedrock of a reconstituted society. Much ink was spilled on what turned out to be a rather exaggerated role of the worker militias (*gongtuan-jun*) in the storming of Xiguan.[14] Yet this narrative, or a significant part of it, has often been reproduced even outside the realm of official history. One Western historian, for instance, describes the incident as displaying "all the violence of class warfare,"[15] while another notes enthusiastically that "for the first time the Chinese proletariat had an armed force of its own."[16]

Finally, in its proclamation after the incident, the Guomindang urged the people of Canton to remember their dual "qualification" (*zige*), as both citizens of the nation and residents of the municipality. To fulfill the duties of citizenship, according to the announcement, meant to try one's best to carry out, or at the very least to understand and feel empathy for (*liaojie*), the doctrines and platform of the Guomindang.[17] Membership in the nation, in other words, was now explicitly identified with the specific ideas and practices of a political apparatus, in this case the Guomindang. And if society was the nation's foundation, and if the Merchant Corps incident revealed all too clearly the former's ills, it was then the duty of the Guomindang to intervene and to ensure the health of this organic body. Whatever the necessary means, then, the boundaries of society—and thus the nation—must now be rigorously policed to suppress any further disruption. Yet, the complexities of the social invariably mean that its constituents will exceed or subvert any attempts to delimit or discipline their unpredictable play. As a result, the Guomindang, as would soon become evident, had in effect set itself an impossible task.[18]

MERCHANTS AND THE MODERNIST PROJECT

Cheng Tiangu, a Guomindang official who also operated several factories in Canton, professed in his memoir an intense antagonism toward the local merchant community. His short-lived (three-month) tenure as officeholder of a merchant association in the mid-1920s convinced him that "it is not easy for old and new forces to co-exist."[19] Cheng, who was born in nearby Xiangshan county in 1889, left for Singapore at the age of thirteen to seek a better living as an apprentice mechanic. He subsequently graduated from the University of California, where he earned a master's degree in political economy. By his own admission he was completely out of touch with the conditions at home during his years abroad.[20] If Cheng was unusually frank, his attitudes were by no means atypical of the members of the modernist elite. And they were certainly an integral part of the Guomindang's image of itself as a force of progress dedicated to the eradication of the backward traditionalism of the old.

To the Guomindang leaders, the merchants in Canton then occupied a rather ambiguous position in their vision of society-and-nation. Not only did the merchant notables dominate most of the civic organizations which once claimed to be representatives of society, they also commanded financial resources without which any plan of national construction was doomed. At the same time, it seemed self-evident to the governing elites that the merchants, who prospered in a socioeconomic system that smacked of a bygone era, belonged to the traditional segments of the population. In the modern world, industries and science were the keys to the future, and the old-style merchants were often regarded as recalcitrants who resisted, no doubt fruitlessly, their own relegation to the margin of a new society.

This articulation of a simple dichotomy between new and old forces, with its implication of an inevitable clash, was useful for positioning the Guomindang as the engine for change. But it could hardly survive critical scrutiny. First of all, the merchant leaders of post-Qing Canton consisted of mostly the nouveau riche of the city, who were themselves responsible for the displacement of the old guard of the mercantile community. Most of them gained prominence after making their fortunes in the newly booming sectors of the economy, such as sericulture, the export of silk products, or the native banks. Nor did the personal backgrounds of these merchant notables reveal hardened traditionalists. For example, Cen Bozhu, who in 1912 became the founding leader of the Merchant Corps, eschewed classical education as a youth in the 1870s. Instead he spent four years in Canada with his father before returning to China at the age of 21 to try his hand in the mining industry. Lack of success then drove him to a brief stint in South Africa. His breakthrough as an entrepreneur finally came when he took advantage of the growing silk trade by establishing a chain of over ten silk filatures in his nearby native county of Shunde in the late nineteenth century.[21] Cen was active in the merchant organizations which sprang up in the late Qing, and was one of the chief patrons of the Guangren Charitable Hall. Together with another silk merchant, Li Liangfu, and others, Cen was also responsible for founding the Guangdong Merchant Association for the Maintenance of Public Order in 1912.

Cen's successor and the "arch villain" of the Merchant Corps incident, Chen Lianbo (1884–1945), belonged to the next generation and was the scion of another prominent silk family. He was a graduate of Queen's College, one of the most prestigious schools in Hong Kong. As a young man he started working for the British Hongkong and Shanghai Bank in Canton and was given the financial portfolio of the Merchant Association for the Maintenance of Public Order after the fall of the Qing in 1912. He was also the chair of the Canton General Chamber of Commerce in 1920–22.[22] His deputy at the Corps, Jian Jinglun, also known as Jian Qinshi, was a nephew of the founder of the "patriotic" Nanyang Tobacco Company, Jian Zhaonan.[23] The elder Jian, a native of Nanhai county who had spent much of his life abroad, built a factory in Hong Kong in 1905 and initially confined his cigarette marketing to the British colony and southeast Asia. Jian Jinglun (1888–1950) himself grew up in French Indochina. When his uncle decided to enter the China market with full force in 1915, the younger Jian was made the official representative of Nanyang in the company's first Chinese office in Canton.

Under his direction, Nanyang was deliberately visible in generously supporting local philanthropy. Jian was also careful in cultivating a network of influential associates, including Chen Lianbo.[24] His assumption of a leadership role in the corps seems a clear indication that the effort was well spent. The backgrounds of the rank and file of the corps were equally diverse. Among them, for instance, were the two young industrialists, the chemist Li Yaofeng and the geologist Luo Jieruo, of the Dongshan Match Factory. They apparently joined the corps in 1923 to provide security for their fledgling business in face of the constant breakdown of order within the city.[25] All told, the merchant notables and their organizations in early republican Canton could hardly be described as representatives of the old.

In fact, the merchants of Canton had not always been at odds with Sun Yat-sen and his entourage. After their initial vacillations, most of the merchants welcomed the founding of the Republic, a feat which they attributed in no small measure to Sun. Many viewed the beginning of a new regime as a time of opportunity. In the spring of 1912, in a welcoming party thrown in honor of Sun in Canton, organized by a committee headed by none other than Chen Lianbo,[26] the merchant notables referred to the establishment of the Republic as marking "the leveling of the mighty and the humble as well as the end of [the ritual of] subservience [*pingguijian zhijie, feibaigui zhili*]."[27] The leaders of the Merchant Association for the Maintenance of Public Order described Sun's greatest achievement as "returning the republic to our citizens, and returning Guangdong to the people of the province."[28] As Li Liangfu and his associates put it, "everyone must accept the responsibility of being a citizen of the Republic."[29] It is perhaps important to emphasize that to the merchant notables, the rhetorical flourishes on Guangdong did not signal that the province was turning its back on the nation, but rather indicated that the health of the province was tied to the strength of the new republican regime.[30] The merchants, in other words, did not challenge the conception of a cohesive "society-and-nation." No irony was intended when they ended their address by hailing "long live the Republic of China" followed by "long live Guangdong."[31]

In 1912, leaders of the then newly established Merchant Corps actually voiced their hope that the corpsmen "would some day become an awe-inspiring crack regiment, so that they could, at the very least, protect their own families, and at their best be able to fortify the republic."[32] Indeed, the very presence of the Merchant Corps was a sign of a new era for the merchants, for the Qing government in its twilight years had repeatedly spurned their requests to organize their own militia. And with just over five hundred members initially, the Merchant Corps was reportedly well disciplined and well trained. The corps's insignia proudly displayed both its own emblem and the new national flag, with the words "The First Year of the Republic of China" engraved above.[33] Most of the founding corpsmen were either actual owners of the numerous enterprises in Canton or members of the owners' immediate families or senior staff. Hu Hanmin, Sun's lieutenant who headed the provincial government in 1912, was said to have been so impressed by the first parade of the Corps that he decided to encourage the creation of similar forces throughout the province, in part as a way to reduce the administration's overextended military budget.[34]

The alienation of the merchant community was thus not the result of a conflict of old and new forces. Rather it stemmed initially from the general disenchantment with the failed promise of the new regime in the years following the fall of the Qing. To most of the country, the experience of the early republican administration would have been farcical had it not had such disastrous consequences. Referring to the National Assembly in Peking in 1913, Liang Qichao wrote that "in less than three months all that the nation expected from it has evaporated . . . if by chance a meeting is held, there is an uproar like quarrelling village wives or uncouth screaming school-boys. Having wasted half a day in such bedlam, they disperse like birds and beasts."[35] In Canton, popular apathy and indeed hostility, which developed as a result of the political and economic mismanagement by the local administration headed by Hu Hanmin, helped to doom Sun and his followers' challenge to Yuan Shikai in the so-called Second Revolution of 1913. Sun Yat-sen, who had once commanded considerable respect especially in the south, sank to the nadir of his political fortune and prestige. When the death of Yuan Shikai plunged the country into a political crisis in 1916–17,[36] Sun attempted to spearhead a much heralded, if completely ineffective, protect-the-constitution movement. It was then that a series of rather acerbic articles appeared in the influential promerchant newspaper of Canton, the *Guangdong Seventy-two Guilds News*. They allow us a glimpse of the sentiment of the merchant community.

Like most of their compatriots, the merchants' initial enthusiasm for the Republic had by 1917 turned into profound skepticism akin to cynicism. One commentator described how in recent years the monarchical regime was overthrown ostensibly to make way for the republic for the people, and how the republic for the people (*minguo*) existed only in name while it was a republic for officials (*guanguo*) in practice. The republican polity, to be sure, now had the institution of assembly, but that only provided autocratic officials with an extra channel to shirk (*weixie*) their responsibilities, as they resorted to condemning each other in the public forum.[37] Another article offered a thinly veiled rebuke to Sun, who urged support for "true republicans" like himself struggling against the "pseudorepublicans" of the north. The author lamented that while most political leaders claimed to be in favor of the republican form of government, they never actually delineated their positions so that the people could judge for themselves. "Our country's republican form of government," the observer wrote, "is truly without any standard at all [*manwu biaozhun*]. Just like the objective of revolution, the way different groups of people use it to rally support for themselves is tantamount to simply using 'revolution' to attack each other."[38] In another apparent slight to Sun and his associates, one contributor registered his estrangement not because, as he said, he did not care about the nation, but because powerful people merely used Guangdong to further their own ambition rather than to help the country. For both the people of Guangdong *and* for the nation, he felt obliged to speak out.[39] To understand the meaning of the words "people's republic" (*gonghe minguo*), according to a contemporary, one had to engage in a kind of doublespeak. Every word denoted its exact opposite meaning, and nothing was what it was supposed to be.[40] There were, in other words, no longer any principles, just forms.

There were, to be sure, occasional pieces written in support of the political order. One commentator, for instance, urged "Guangdong patriots" to refrain from betraying what they themselves had painstakingly created in the past.[41] Yet the exhortative and defensive tone of the writing indicated that the author was quite aware that he was swimming against the tide. On the whole, what the articles suggest is how quickly the goodwill generated at the founding of the new regime in 1912 dissipated in the political chaos of early republican China. Despite his often lofty rhetoric, Sun Yat-sen's increasing tendency to hastily form expedient alliances with various militarists clearly

did not help convince his audience that he was different from the other contenders for power.

The distance between Sun and the merchant community of Canton can
perhaps be gauged in a speech the former delivered at a meeting to enlist
support from the local notables in 1918. The seasoned orator was at his best,
projecting an image of a strong and prosperous China where the government
would be instrumental in creating large-scale commercial enterprises and
factories.[42] Such a vision, alluring as it might be, must have struck those in
attendance as grandiose or unrealistic within the context of the time. The
polity then, after all, was seemingly falling apart. This kind of rhetoric certainly helped to account for the increasingly frequent use of the pejorative
label "Sun the Windbag" (*Sun Dapao*). To the merchants, skepticism or even
cynicism in response to the turmoil of the early Republic was not unreasonable. To Sun and many other members of the political and intellectual elite,
however, the merchants' attitudes bordered on the abrogation of their duty
as constituents of the new society-and-nation.

In an attempt to circumvent what they considered to be the pernicious
influence of the merchant leaders in Canton, Sun and his entourage established an organization called the Guangdong Association of Chambers of
Commerce (*Guangdong shanghui lianhehui*) in March 1922. The new organization was supposed to bring together all the representative institutions of
the merchants from the towns across the province, with the aim, as one
report puts it, "of creating a body of opinion favourable to himself [Sun]
among the trading classes, on whom up to the present he had made little
impression."[43] Adhering closely to the government line and dominated by
political operatives, it was a prototype of the kind of officially sponsored
"mass organizations"—founded to represent the different classes or segments
of the people—which were to appear in scores in the mid-1920s. The
Canton Chamber, the leading merchant association and home to the merchant notables since the fall of the Qing, was barely a part of the proceed-
ings at the founding ceremony of Sun's organization. Rather conspicuous, in
contrast, were Sun's followers who had been active among labor circles, perhaps a curious sight at the launching of a putative merchant group.[44]

As was the case later with many other "mass organizations," this attempt
to create and command a constituency by the government resulted more in
political theater than in substantive support. Despite an initial flurry of

activity, the association quickly lost its momentum after Sun was briefly forced out of Canton by Chen Jiongming in the latter part of 1922. Thereafter the association seems to have existed only as a marginal force, as the Canton Chamber remained the dominant voice of the merchant community. Little wonder that the Guomindang and the merchants were suspicious of each other. When Sun once again set foot in Canton in February 1923, he was undoubtedly a battered political figure. Even though his prospects then looked somewhat better with the promise of Soviet aid, he seemed a long way from his subsequent enshrinement as the venerable "father of the nation" (*guofu*).

FISCAL MANAGEMENT AND GOVERNANCE

For a regime whose self-imposed mandate was to construct society-and-nation, the Guomindang faced a formidable task when it returned to Canton in early 1923. The ousting of Chen Jiongming meant that Sun Yat-sen and his associates were then almost completely dependent on the good will of the so-called guest armies, mostly splinter units from the Yunnan and Guangxi forces, for their hold on the city. As reward for their role in the defeat of Chen, the leaders of these units intended to squeeze as much out of the metropolis as possible for their own benefit. The Guomindang, moreover, continued to face military threats from the remnants of Chen's forces which had withdrawn to the eastern part of the province. With Soviet material aid still yet to come, 1923–24 was thus a difficult year for the Guomindang. For Sun and his followers, the first priority was, simply put, to survive.

For any political apparatus with a pretension to govern, however, even mere survival requires access to revenues. And revenue collection proved to be an intractable problem to the Guomindang. While historians have often swept the blame for the financial chaos in Canton then at the feet of the guest armies,[45] it was really the cumulative result of years of political instability, local warfare, and fiscal mismanagement dating back to the late Qing. The Canton government's ambitious plan to remodel the city in the early 1920s undoubtedly added to the financial turmoil.[46] The plundering by the guest armies was thus simply the last straw. For instance, the official paper notes of the Republic, issued by the Provincial Bank and often printed as the need for cash arose, had long ceased to command confidence and were traded on the market for less than 20 percent of their face value.[47] Even the "twenty cents" (*shuanghao* or *xiaoyang*) silver coin, which had been the most popular medium of transaction in Canton, had lost much of its stature due to substandard minting, if not downright counterfeiting, by the successive regimes. The decade following the founding of the Republic saw an almost fivefold increase in the number of *shuanghao* of varying quality in circulation.[48] Hence the head of the treasury of the Guomindang administration found that the mercantile world was dominated by the Hong Kong dollar.[49] One account estimated that almost two-thirds of the notes issued by the Hongkong and Shanghai Bank, amounting to around HK$30 million in the 1920s, were circulated within China, mostly, though not exclusively, in the south.[50] Despite the government's intent to expand its disciplinary power, even basic fiscal matters were rapidly slipping from its regulatory control.

Under the circumstances, the response of the Guomindang government was predictable. Even at the risk of further straining an already fragile relationship, it asked the merchants to come up with the financial backing to allow the government to redeem the almost worthless official paper notes.[51] Denying the legitimacy of the central government in Peking, Sun's administration also seized control of the local salt tax revenues. It was, however, rebuffed by the Western powers when it tried to lay claim to the proceeds of the Guangdong Maritime Customs in late 1923.[52] While the Guomindang did stage a demonstration against the powers in December, there was not the popular support to turn it into a sustained effort. The merchant organizations were accordingly condemned for their reticence on the issue.[53]

Beyond that, the government launched its famous campaign to "unify financial administration" (*caizheng tongyi*). What the campaign did in practice was both to levy a litany of consumer taxes and to try to bring the various autonomous revenue-collecting agencies of the guest armies under the jurisdiction of the Guomindang administration.[54] Most of the taxes were regressive in nature. It would not be much of an exaggeration to say that everything, from foodstuffs to brothels, was taxed.[55] Rates seem to have been randomly fixed according to the whim of the government. There were, in addition, other forms of extraction. Landlords as well as their tenants, for instance, were periodically required to "donate" or "lend" the government one or two months' worth of rent.[56] Worse still, taxes for the various trades were farmed out to different individuals, usually local notables with connections to the government, who in turn would squeeze their constituents for a profit.[57] Tax farmers could, to be sure, deliver their funds months in advance to bolster, if only temporarily, the balance sheet of the regime, but ultimately the burden fell squarely on the people in general.[58] It was a sad comment on this group of modernist elites who were bent on remaking the world, that they were forced to rely on such a mechanism of revenue collection for their own sustenance: a mechanism which had, of course, plagued generations before the twentieth century.

But if the taxation was extortionate and demoralizing, its impact paled into insignificance compared to the government measure euphemistically entitled "guaranteeing people's properties" (*minchan baozheng*). The measure originated in a scheme to expropriate temples and religious estates as government properties.[59] Spurred by their hostility toward what they considered to be backward practices as well as by financial need, the Guomindang confiscated religious properties, often in conjunction with campaigns against superstition.[60] Many of the religious institutions in Canton were owned or sponsored by clans, lineages, or other civic groups such as merchant associations. As one government proclamation somewhat cavalierly stated: "Since these religious estates were usually collectively rather than individually held, their seizure should not really be considered oppressive [*shangbu weinüe*]."[61] Properties seized were offered for sale in the market. In fact, expropriating or destroying these institutions helped the Guomindang achieve multiple objectives. It not only enabled the government to bring in revenues, it also made it possible for the regime to redirect social life away from those institutional anchors toward the new officially sponsored mass organizations. The price was the resentment and disorientation generated by the scheme among the local inhabitants. Not surprisingly, one of the first signs of open confrontation between the Merchant Corps and the government sprang from incidents where corpsmen were acting as guards for temple properties.[62]

The government's demand for revenues, however, could not be met simply by the conversion of religious properties into public funds. As religious landholdings began to be exhausted, the government took the desperate step of extending its assault to all landed properties within the city. Not only were small owners now also at risk, but the measure had such a destabilizing effect that it almost completely crippled the economy. For instance, banks, fearing arbitrary expropriation, would no longer accept immovable assets, the most common form of collateral, as guarantees for loans.[63] The Guomindang's position was that all landed properties belonged to the government unless the owner could discharge his onus of proof by presenting documents of legal entitlement. Such requirements, which became increasingly stringent as the regime's financial needs mounted, created tremendous turmoil. For example, many of the properties in Canton had undergone substantial modifications during the years of rapid change since the founding of the Republic, with the result that the descriptions on the title deeds were often no longer technically accurate, a predicament that the government did not hesitate to exploit. The uncertainty of whether a piece of property came under the purview of provincial or municipal authorities also added to the confusion.[64] To maximize income, moreover, the Guomindang administration encouraged informants to uncover government properties.[65] Since the purpose of the seizure was to put the assets up for resale to fill the government coffers, reports of illegally held "government properties" began to pour in, often from people who were just interested in purchasing a particular piece of real estate.[66] It hardly needs pointing out that the socioeconomic life of the city was hence severely disrupted, if not indeed paralyzed, by a pervasive sense of insecurity among many of its residents.

It was against such background that the Guomindang administration unveiled its measure to "guarantee people's properties" in December 1923. The measure led to the establishment of a Bureau of Guarantee of People's Properties early the following year.[67] The idea was that owners could present documents proving their entitlement for adjudication by officials, who, if satisfied, would issue a certificate that safeguarded the property from any possible further infringement, in return for a fee set in theory at 3 percent of the value of the property. The fact that this amounted to government blackmail was by then beside the point; what should be noted is that the opportunities for corruption and abuse in the implementation of such a policy were literally endless. Bribery became almost institutionalized.[68] To cite another example of how far the government was prepared to go in fulfilling its rapacious demands: As the market for the certificates of guarantee began to be saturated in mid-1924, the administration reverted to its old practice of squeezing the tenants, as it announced yet another plan to issue certificates, this time to renters within the city in return for a month's worth of rent. The certificates, according to the government, could then be used in lieu of cash as rent for landlords. The latter, needless to say, were less than disposed to accept the government paper as sufficient payment. Despite considerable coercion, the scheme was short-lived because tenants simply refused to oblige.[69]

The oppressive measures of the Guomindang were a reflection of its weakness in 1923–24. It is perhaps a testament to the desperation of the Guomindang that, despite the tension with the foreign powers, as late as May 1923 Sun Yat-sen still sought the assistance of "British experts" from Hong Kong in reorganizing his administration.[70] Subsequent confrontations regarding the customs proceeds as well as access to the concession area of Shameen, however, further strained the relationship between the two sides.[71] At the same time, with the lesson of the Seamen's Strike, and with the establishment of an alliance with the Communists and the increasing influence of Comintern representatives (particularly following the arrival of Michael Borodin in October 1923) in Canton, the Guomindang also began to rearticulate its project more vocally under the banner of an anti-imperialist struggle. In the proclamation of its First Party Congress held in Canton in January 1924, for example, the Guomindang claimed that both industries and labor had suffered under the bondage of imperialism, and that the impact had been felt in all classes—merchants, workers, tillers, and intellectuals.[72] All these classes, the proclamation continued, should then come together as one organic entity to fight against foreign oppression. By mid-1924, however, it seemed that the Guomindang-led government had made little headway in bringing the different segments of society together under its direction. In fact, it had achieved exactly the reverse: the alienation of most of the residents of Canton.

FOR THE SAKE OF MODERNIZATION

It was a controversy over the related issues of shop ownership and the construction of new roads in early 1924 that paved the way for the subsequent armed confrontation between the government and the Merchant Corps in October. To suggest, as Yokoyama Hiroaki does, that the conflict reflected the Guomindang's attempt to carry out progressive reform of the "feudal" commercial order is surely to accept uncritically the official narrative of the government.[73] The origin of the controversy lay in a specific custom which had been part of local commercial practices since late imperial times. Not unlike the so-called one-field-two-lords system (*yitian liangzhu*) in parts of rural China, ownership of shops in Canton had often been divided between the "shop front" (*pumian*) and the "shop bottom" (*pudi*). In this case, however, the "shop bottom" right, which included claims to the name of the shop, guild membership, the goods, other fixtures, accounts, and all structural changes and decorations of the shop, was owned by the tenant.[74] The arrangement was intended, of course, to protect the investments of the tenant merchants. The landlords had no right to interfere in any transaction of the shop bottom right. The tenant could, for instance, transfer his right and receive a compensatory fee (*dingshoufei*) from the new tenant. Alternatively, he could simply choose to be a secondary landlord, leasing the shop while keeping his shop bottom right. He might even engage in what in local parlance was known as *maitai*: leasing to a third party with the restrictions that both the name and the nature of the shop must not be changed, and that no further subletting was permissible.[75] To the tenant merchants, most significant of all was the security afforded by the shop bottom right that enabled them to use their rented properties as collateral to raise capital.[76]

Although the stated objective of the Canton government since the early 1920s had been the modernization of the city, the Guomindang initially had little problem with this structure of dual ownership or the shop bottom right. In fact, it saw the custom as another opportunity to collect revenue. Tenants were asked to register their ownership of the shop bottom. They would then be issued a certification in return for a fee.[77] The purpose was, at least in theory, to protect the right of the tenant in the hazardous world of property transactions. The government even proclaimed that once the shop bottom was properly registered, the right would then be "protected by law" and that it would be held "in perpetuity" by the tenant.[78] Yet the promise proved to be rather short-lived. What caused the Guomindang administration to renege on its word was, simply put, an attempt to elicit more funding from the merchants. Officially the revenues were to be used for the continual effort to modernize the city: specifically, for the construction of new roads.

Road construction had always been a contentious issue with many merchants. Not all merchants, to be sure, were always against the paving of new roads. After all, the Canton Tramways Syndicate, which assumed the initial contract for demolishing the city walls and thus making the road construction plan possible, was in part financed by merchant investors.[79] Still, it is not difficult to see why the plan resulted in constant friction with members of the merchant community. First of all, the restructuring of the road network caused prolonged disruptions to the normal flow of trade and not infrequently forced the actual relocation of the shops. Merchants, understandably, were often reluctant to leave a familiar locale with an established clientele, to say nothing of the possible offense to their geomantic sensitivities caused by extensive physical destruction around them. That was why many merchants resisted the early attempts to demolish the city walls shortly after the founding of the Republic, and there was considerable opposition when the government decided to force the issue in the early 1920s.[80] But once the road construction plan was implemented, even more controversial was the way that its cost was to be accounted for, and the uncertainty over how it was to be apportioned.

Merchants whose properties needed to be destroyed or modified to make way for the road work were supposed to receive financial compensation. The government, however, had put forward the disputed claim that since the very same merchants were going to benefit from the access provided by the new roads, they should therefore contribute to the cost. As might be expected, by the administration's calculations, most of those affected ended up owing the government money for pulling down their properties. While new roads did improve transportation and enlarge the catchment areas for many shops, though, they also led to new competition for the merchants. Adding to the confusion was the separate ownership of shop front and shop bottom in many enterprises, and thus the question of who should be responsible for the contribution. Under Chen Jiongming, for instance, it was vaguely stipulated that if the landlord did not pay his allotted sum by the deadline, tenants who had shop bottom right would then be held accountable.[81]

As the Guomindang-led government resumed the demand for contributions in 1923, the merchants were so clearly reluctant to come forward with the funding for road construction that the administration was compelled to appeal to the chamber of commerce to act as an intermediary for collection.[82] Moreover, although the administration promulgated that the "construction fee" should be evenly split between landlord and tenant,[83] the dual ownership of the shops became a common excuse for the merchants to avoid their obligations. Landlords, for example, declined to contribute for lack of full ownership due to shop bottom rights which, they said, prevented them from enjoying the supposed fruits of the new construction. Tenants, on the other hand, claimed exemption because they, after all, did not own the properties.[84] To make matters worse, at a time when there was already strong resentment against the myriad taxes imposed by the government, even the Guomindang conceded that the people were suspicious of its intentions for the collected funds.[85] Still, determined to finish what it had started, the government chose this rather inopportune moment to strike at the rights which many local merchants held to be sacrosanct.

At the end of March 1924, the government announced its plan to "unify the ownership of shops" (*tongyi puyequan*) as a measure to rationalize the commercial structure of the city.[86] Shop front and shop bottom rights were to be unified under a single ownership. Depending on whether structural improvements had been made, either the landlord or the tenant would have the preferential right to buy out the other party's share of the property at predetermined prices. More importantly, if the parties failed to comply with the promulgation, the government would force the sale of the property to a third party by putting it up for auction. In either case, 20 percent of the proceeds would go to the road construction fund.[87] The order created tremendous commotion within the merchant community, and almost immediately galvanized many of its rank-and-file members: the middling and small merchants who constituted the core—perhaps about 85 percent—of the mercantile world of Canton. These were the merchants whose enterprises were capitalized at around C$5,000 or less, and whose livelihood depended on their ability to hold on to their rights.[88] As the bulk of the merchant class, they also constituted a significant segment of society, which the Guomindang claimed to represent.

Although the government insisted that its policy affected only around seven hundred shops located along the new roads, the implication for the others was clear.[89] For the tenant merchants with shop bottom rights, who were mostly concentrated in these small establishments, the decree meant that they had to either come up with a substantial amount of money to purchase the properties themselves, or risk being forced out by their landlords or new owners exercising their right of full ownership. Further problems arose following the stipulation that landlords were only required to compensate tenants for their shop bottom right according to the value registered with the government by the latter. Since merchants almost always underreported their net worth to the authorities for fear, with good reason, of further extractions, many would suffer large financial losses even if they were not subsequently evicted.[90] Furthermore, the loss of security would undoubtedly have adverse effects on their access to capital and loans.

Resistance to this government initiative prompted the establishment of a new, initially ad hoc merchant organization, known as the Canton Municipal Association for the Maintenance of Shop Bottom Right (*Guangzhoushi pudi weichihui*). This turned out to be the first step toward the creation of an independent and permanent merchant association for the middling and small merchants. In its first proclamation, the association bluntly condemned the government for betraying its words, saying that "even such an autocratic regime as the Qing dared not openly strip [*boduo*] the merchant community of shop bottom rights that went back hundreds of years."[91] This proclamation was quickly followed by another appeal from the Canton General Chamber of Commerce, arguing that the war-torn, depressed economy of the metropolis meant that few merchants then were in a position to purchase the properties.[92] The statements by the merchants were backed by threats of commercial strikes which would paralyze the city. After a war of rhetoric, and faced with open defiance from a large segment of the population, the administration finally backed down and rescinded the decree in late May on the grounds that "most people regarded the measure as having a detrimental effect on commerce and property rights."[93]

Despite the rescission, it was clear that the episode had seriously compromised the standing of the Guomindang in its own backyard. The drive for industrialization notwithstanding, Canton remained a commercially oriented city, in which the merchants were a major force. For a government whose claim to authority and legitimacy rested in significant part on its identification with society, such an overt act of disobedience on the part of the latter could not but present a grave challenge. Indeed, shortly afterward, editorials appeared in both the *Guangdong Seventy-two Guilds News* and the semiofficial *Canton Republican Daily* which questioned, for different reasons to be sure, the ability of the administration to govern under such circumstances.[94] In late May leaders of the merchant establishment held a meeting which resulted in an explicit petition for the resignation of Sun Yat-sen.[95] At the same time, the Merchant Corps under the direction of Chen Lianbo announced that it sought the formation of a centralized command for all the local corps around the Canton area.[96]

In July the Association for the Maintenance of Shop Bottom Right was reincarnated as the Canton Municipal Association for the Maintenance of Commerce (*Guangzhoushi shangye weichihui*). More than a hundred representatives of stores and shops met and resolved that not only was organization necessary, but a permanent municipal chamber should be established in order to "supplement the strength of the general chamber."[97] Membership of the new organization was based on the shop (*puwei*) rather than on the individual merchant. Each street was required to elect one particular shop to keep accounts for the contributions of its members. Fees were extremely modest in contrast to the General Chamber. Rather than the C$1,000 reportedly required to join the latter, each shop was asked to pay C$1 for enrollment in the new association, plus a 50 cents annual fee and voluntary contributions for the monthly operational expenses of the organization.[98] According to a pro-Guomindang source, over five thousand shops joined within the first two weeks of the recruitment drive.[99] For a government with a self-proclaimed mission to bring together different classes for a cohesive society, it was surely ironic to witness the enthusiastic backing given by the "middling and small merchants," a group which the Guomindang sought as part of its foundation of support, to an association with a clear agenda to challenge its policies. Thus by the summer of 1924 Sun Yat-sen was forced to reconsider the viability of Canton as a base for his government.

THE MERCHANT CORPS INCIDENT

The founding of the Merchant Corps in early republican Canton initially served not only as a sign of the empowerment of the merchants, but also a practical purpose. With the constant breakdown of the political order, the corpsmen offered in Canton, as their counterparts did in other urban centers in China, a modicum of protection for the merchants in an often chaotic and militarized milieu. As relationships with the mercantile community became strained, however, the governing elites no longer necessarily viewed the Merchant Corps in a benign light. When Chen Lianbo announced the imminent creation of a centralized command (*lianfang zongbu*) for all the corps around the Canton area in late May 1924, the government was wary of the specter of a united force of potentially hostile corpsmen spread through the Pearl River delta area.[100] Moreover, many of the corps by then were made up of hired toughs rather than bona fide merchants or their senior employees, as was originally the case.[101] It was within such a context that a dispute arose regarding a shipment of arms. For some time the government, as another means to raise revenue, had been selling arms to the merchants.[102] In late July 1924, Chen Lianbo applied for and got a permit to import a shipment of arms.[103] But when the consignment carried by the Norwegian freighter SS *Hav* from Europe arrived at Canton only days after the application was made, the suspicion of the Guomindang-led government was aroused. Delivery to the merchants was denied by Sun, and the shipment was held up at the port of Whampoa. The government alleged that the corpsmen were the intended recipients for less than half of the weapons, with the remainder being destined for various militarists, some of whom were hostile or even at war with the regime.[104] The accusation of collusion between Chen Lianbo and antigovernment forces was never proved, although, given the petition for Sun's resignation earlier on, the suspicion was not without foundation.[105]

To many members of the merchant community, though, the seizure was simply another example of the arbitrary actions of a predatory government. Their resentment grew particularly when the administration indicated that part of the consignment could be reclaimed for a fee of C$60 per rifle, lending fuel to the suggestion that the whole affair was nothing but one more excuse to squeeze the merchants.[106] Meanwhile, when the Merchant Corps, after an initial delay, announced its plan to open the headquarters for the central command on August 13, the government tried unsuccessfully to stop the operation by claiming procedural irregularities.[107] The opening ceremony took place with much fanfare in a show of defiance and support, and the Merchant Corps threatened to paralyze Canton with a general commercial strike.[108]

There were many attempts at mediation. The major points of contention remained the amount of "donation" or "purchasing fee" demanded by the government and the question of the latter's control over the corps. There was certainly no lack of willing mediators. Some were members of the guest armies, more interested perhaps in lining their own pockets than in solving intricate problems.[109] Others were leaders of civic organizations such as the Nine Charitable Halls and the General Chamber of Commerce. Most were less than effective. It was particularly difficult for the leaders of the civic organizations to intervene, as they had close personal, if not institutional, ties to the Merchant Corps. The then president of the General Chamber, Chen Lianzhong, for example, was the treasurer of the corps and the younger brother of Chen Lianbo.[110] The elder Chen himself, as mentioned, headed the General Chamber from 1920–22. Chen Lianbo had also been closely associated with philanthropic organizations, in particular the Aiyu, the most prominent of the charitable halls.[111] While it is true that there were diverse opinions within these organizations, their leaders were hardly in a good position to resolve a conflict of which they were very much a part.

More interesting was the intervention of the Municipal Association for the Maintenance of Commerce. Their already severe losses in recent months had made the middling and small merchants cautious of leaping into another commercial strike. It was the Municipal Association which took the initiative in bringing together the leading civic organizations of the city for a meeting at the General Chamber, during which one of its leaders suggested that the Nine Charitable Halls, the General Chamber of Commerce, the Guangdong Association of Chambers of Commerce, and the Municipal Association for the Maintenance of Commerce should together guarantee the legal use of the firearms if they were returned.[112] According to the letter of invitation sent by the Municipal Association to the General Chamber in August, the former was approached by both the government and the corps and took on the task of mediation for the sake of "local peace and order."[113] At the same time, an "emergency flier," distributed under the slightly different name of the Guangdong Association for the Maintenance of Trade (*Guangdong weichi yingyehui*), stated that "our organization considers commercial strikes to be a negative response. Just like committing suicide, unless there is absolutely no alternative, it should not be carried out." The merchants should wait before striking, according to the flyer, to see whether the government first fulfilled its word and abolished all the taxes and demands for "donations."[114] The middling and small merchants were in a rather delicate position. While they undoubtedly wanted to keep the pressure on the government, they were also concerned that the confrontation should not go so far as to bring destruction literally to their own doorsteps.

Indeed, it is precisely because of such nuances and ambiguities that it is impossible, despite the official position of the governing elites, to reduce the plurality of the social to neatly categorized, often opposing, groups, segments, or classes. Not only was the position of many middling and small merchants ambiguous, the so-called grande bourgeoisie was hardly a monolithic group. For example, a careful reading of the press reports reveals that the differences in support afforded the commercial strike, called by the corps for the last week of August when the weapons were still not returned to them, lay not so much between big and small merchants. Rather, it was shaped by the city's geography and the trades' varying ties to the Merchant Corps.[115] The strongholds of the strike were located along several streets in lower Xiguan, where the staunchest support was found among native bankers, the long-distance *sanjiangbang* merchants, and import-export traders. Activities in areas around Datong Street, Shisanhang, and the stretch of the Bund at the southern tip of Xiguan (where many of the stores specializing in long-distance trade [*banzhuang*] were concentrated) came to a grinding halt. This section of the city was essentially dominated by the trades which had been best represented in the merchant establishment.

By contrast, the resolve of the merchants in the new downtown commercial district was considerably weaker, as they appeared to be rather more ready to be "persuaded" by the police to open their doors. The government was particularly concerned that the two major department stores, Sincere and Daxin, be kept open as a symbol of normal business activities. At one stage armed guards were assigned to "protect" them.[116] These enterprises in the new commercial districts had less robust ties to the Merchant Corps than did their counterparts in Xiguan. Both Ma Yingbiao and Cai Chang, the owners of Sincere and Daxin respectively, reportedly had reservations about the promise of still more disruption rather than solutions.[117] Meanwhile, other parts of the city, such as the suburb of Honam across the Pearl River, were effectively beyond the reach of the Merchant Corps. Part of the reason was that Honam, where many of the new industries were located, was the domain of Li Fulin, a longtime local militarist who had worked closely with

the Guomindang.[118] That partly explained why even those enterprise owners in Honam, who had joined together to form a unit that served nominally
as part of the corps, were for all practical purposes segregated from the main
body of the force during the dispute.[119]

Even though support for the corps from the merchants themselves was in
many cases less than vigorous, Sun Yat-sen was nonetheless frustrated with
the increasingly hostile environment of Canton and with the open defiance
of his government's authority. Still, few expected that Sun, who had once
chided the governor of Hong Kong (during the confrontation over the customs revenue in late 1923) for threatening "to bombard an unfortified and
defenseless city like Canton,"[120] would himself resort to such a step. As the
commercial strike got underway, however, Xiguan was threatened with
naval bombardment by the Guomindang-led government. The foreign powers, already suspicious of Soviet influence on the Canton regime, became
alarmed. They particularly feared that the foreign enclave of Shameen island,
located directly across Xiguan on the river, would be endangered if Xiguan
came under fire from the government gunboats as Sun intended. It was thus
not without a touch of irony that the acting British consul-general in
Canton, Bertram Giles, issued a warning on August 29 that British naval
forces would intervene if the Canton government proceeded to commit the
"barbarity of firing on a defenseless city."[121] Sun Yat-sen was reportedly in-
censed, and the government promptly used the warning as "evidence" for its
claim that foreign powers were actually the force behind the strike.[122]

Thus when the Jiangsu-Zhejiang war broke out on September 3, leading
to a full-scale second Fengtian-Zhili war shortly thereafter, Sun seized the
occasion as a great opportunity to head north to join what many then considered to be a decisive struggle between the major military contenders for
control of the country. His enthusiasm for a northern venture, however, was
apparently not shared by many of his associates. Despite their differences,
most of Sun's lieutenants agreed on the perils of leaving Canton and of rush-
ing north to join the battle with a small and ill-equipped force. Undaunted,
Sun left Canton for Shaoguan in northern Guangdong with some of his rag-
tag units on September 12, after leaving a vaguely worded proclamation
promising the people of Guangdong their own "self-government." In doing
so, he left the status of Canton uncertain. He also asked for the distribution
of the confiscated weapons to his units, lending fuel to the accusation that

Government troops reclaim part of the city following the suppression of the Merchant Corps.

he had coveted the arms of the corpsmen for his own purposes all along.[123] Meanwhile, those who opposed the government must have been emboldened by Sun's departure, believing that the end of the Guomindang regime in Canton might be in sight.

It was in such a state of confusion that negotiations dragged on between the government and the corps. Tensions mounted as the merchants began to talk of another round of strikes in early October. An arrangement was finally made in which the government was supposed to deliver over five thousand pieces of weaponry to the corps in return for a loan of C$200,000 (to be repaid from the "rent donation" fund) and presumably pledges of loyalty.[124] The delivery was scheduled to be made on October 10, the designated day of the celebration of the founding of the Republic. Early that afternoon, as corpsmen unloaded and transported the weapons along the river south of Xiguan, they encountered a progovernment procession of cadets, students, and workers celebrating the republican day. Fire was exchanged and a stampede followed, which led to at least several dead and dozens injured.[125] As the government condemned the corps for causing the incident, the latter escalated its defiance by closing the street gates and barricading its members within stretches of Xiguan, perhaps calculating that the Guomindang was no longer committed to staying in Canton. The corps also claimed that only half of the firearms and one-tenth of the ammunition had been returned and called for further action.[126] Meanwhile, Sun Yat-sen, faced with uncertain prospects in the north and urged by some of his closest advisers, decided, at least halfheartedly, to try to reassert the Guomindang's authority in Canton.[127] Some three thousand men finally returned from Shaoguan. If those units were not quite ready to do battle with the Zhili army, they were more than enough to handle the Merchant Corps. The scene was set for the carnage in Xiguan on October 15. Sun himself finally returned to the metropolis on October 30.

In his study, Martin Wilbur finds that the British manager of the Hongkong and Shanghai Bank in Hong Kong helped to finance the arms shipment for the merchants, and that the commissioner of customs in Canton was also implicated, although the British government itself was unaware of their involvement until late 1924.[128] To the Guomindang-led government, however, such muddled details of the British role in the episode were less relevant than the specter of an imperialist plot. There were, in fact, obvious differences even between the various British representatives in the Canton area. For example, A. G. Stephen, the said manager of the Hongkong and Shanghai Bank, actually approached Consul-General James Jamieson in Canton as early as October 1923. In his letter, Stephen wrote that he believed "the Hongkong Government would preserve a benevolent blindness to any measures likely to secure peace and good order in Canton city."[129] His request for assistance from Jamieson for arming the merchants, however, was flatly turned down.[130]

On the other hand, the governor of Hong Kong, Reginald Stubbs, a figure whose erratic judgments had earlier prompted a call from the Foreign Office for his removal, once said that he doubted if Sun Yat-sen "has a single positive good quality."[131] He had previously advocated an advance of HK$2 million to Chen Jiongming in support of the latter's fight against Sun. That suggestion was also resisted, successfully as it turned out, by Jamieson on the grounds of the British policy of neutrality. Stubbs then dismissed Jamieson's complaint as "academic."[132] In his report in late 1924, Stubbs confirmed that he indeed had a meeting with Stephen, who had conveniently passed away in the meantime. Stubbs claimed that in their discussion he simply informed Stephen that he "was certain His Majesty's Government would not listen to the suggestion" about British intervention in Canton, and that he "could not, of course, do anything without their permission." The governor then said, somewhat disingenuously, that he was "at a loss" as to why "anybody who knew me as intimately as Mr. Stephen did could have formed this opinion" regarding the intention of the Hong Kong Government.[133]

DISCIPLINE AND NATIONAL COMMUNITY

"To every social class, the meaning of nationalism," according to the proclamation of the First Guomindang Congress in 1924, "is none other than to get rid of the encroachment of imperialism." Furthermore, "the people's rights [*minquan*] of the Republic can only be enjoyed by its citizens, and these rights must not be bestowed lightly upon those who oppose the Republic, lest they use such rights to destroy the Republic. To elaborate, all those individuals and organizations which genuinely oppose imperialism can enjoy every liberty and right; all those who betray the nation and its people [*maiguo wangmin*] in order to be loyal to imperialism and warlords, be they organizations or individuals, will not be entitled to such liberty and rights."[134] Similarly, Sun Yat-sen delivered, on the eve of his departure for Shaoguan in early September, one of the most vitriolic attacks on the foreign powers of his career, accusing the imperialists of consistently sponsoring the forces of "counterrevolution."[135]

Such proclamations were based on the premise that the realm of the social—the modern foundation of governmental legitimacy—could be dissected rationally. Boundaries could be drawn clearly between, say, those who were for and against the imperialists. Yet, instead of compliantly subjecting itself to the disciplinary regime of such a well-ordered society, the social was actually characterized by the endless play of differences of its constituents. It was thus consistently resistant to any mechanism of systematic ordering. As a result, the quest for boundaries was perforce an unceasing endeavor and would always necessitate the use of governmental intervention in deciding who should belong. The notion that the social body was reducible to a taxonomy of different classes or segments, the exact configuration of which could be easily rearranged if necessary, was hence key to the modernist project of constructing a cohesive polity.

Seen in such light, it is clear why the Merchant Corps incident was reduced by the Guomindang-led government to a simple Manichaean conflict between the petty merchants and the working class on the one side, and the grande bourgeoisie and compradors on the other. The latter, as represented by Chen Lianbo and his supporters, were deprived of their own agency and vilified as mere accessories (*fushuwu*) of the imperialists and their allies, such as the warlords.[136] Indeed, simplicity was what the Guomindang was seeking: a simplicity of discipline which would clearly demarcate the boundaries of the national community. As a Guomindang proclamation issued shortly after the incident clarified: Between those who have submitted themselves to the imperialists and warlords, and those who seek their overthrow (*dadao*), there is absolutely no middle ground (*juewu zhongli de yudi*).[137] To sustain the vision of a cohesive society-and-nation, anti-imperialism was invoked as the boundary marker. Those excluded were delegitimized as constituents of the social body and were therefore to be banished from the national community. Violence was justified as a means to maintain the integrity of the polity.

Emblematic of those who opposed imperialism was the working class, which had now been elevated to center of the political stage. As the Guomindang official Liao Zhongkai declared during the dispute with the Merchant Corps: "Let them [the merchants] go on strike," he thundered, for it was the hope of the generalissimo (Sun Yat-sen) that workers "could engage in business and direct management themselves . . . as a way to test their knowledge, skill, and power."[138] A symbol of this new focus on the working class was the much-heralded formation of the Worker Militia.

Although there had been calls for the formation of the militia in early 1924, it was not until mid-August that concrete steps were taken.[139] The date was surely not coincidental. The second clause of the charter of the militia stated that its objective was "to assist the revolutionary government in suppressing counterrevolutionary activities."[140] Its six hundred—odd members, however, turned out to be less than impressive bearers of the struggle. Despite the publicity, the government had neither the resources nor the arms to provide for even such a small symbolic unit. The militiamen were thrown into a crash two-week course of basic education and training before being sent off to Shaoguan, completely unarmed, to "concentrate on propaganda work" as part of Sun Yat-sen's plan to move north in early September.[141] The role of the militia in the storming of the "counterrevolutionary" stronghold of Xiguan was undoubtedly token at best. According to the Russian military adviser A. I. Cherepanov, out of a government force of over 4,000 which took part in the conflict, "mass support" amounted to 320 militiamen (plus an unspecified peasant unit), who were armed and trained for three days for the occasion.[142] Little notice has been taken of the fact that the militia disappeared just as abruptly as it arrived. A fortnight after the routing of the Merchant Corps and the aborted northern campaign, the government declared that the worker militia had fulfilled its term of service. The force was disbanded for "further political training" following a brief ceremony.[143]

In an article published in 1919, the Guomindang luminary and theorist Hu Hanmin maintained that "[if a person] does not recognize the demands of society, or does not follow the customs of society, he or she definitely cannot co-exist with that society [*juebuneng yu na shehui xiangrong*]."[144] To Hu, it was natural, indeed necessary, for a society, for its own survival, to reject those who did not follow its rules, a view which resonated with the earlier writings of Liang Qichao.[145] As a modernist regime, however, the Guomindang-led government was not interested only in the elimination and destruction of its opponents. As Hu's fellow Guomindang theorist Dai Jitao once emphasized, the genius of a leader was to expose the defects in the constitution of society (*shehui zuzhi de quexian*) and then to reconstruct it.[146] Thus, for example, the intervention in the merchant establishment of Canton did not end with the suppression of the Merchant Corps, even as it no longer necessarily took the form of an armed conflict.

The subjection of the merchant class to the new disciplinary regime began with a reconstruction of its organizational structure. The Nine Charitable Halls, a symbol and bastion of the merchant establishment of Canton since the turn of the century, were formally put under the control of the municipal authority in October 1925. In the government pronouncement, most of the administrators of the charitable halls were described as people with "old ideas," who were "opposed to modern social policies in which self-governing civic organizations [*zizhi tuanti*] exist in order to com-

Residents make their way through the rubble as sections of Canton lie in ruins in late 1924.

plement the government." Their incorporation into the municipal administration was thus touted as a passage of progress (*jinhua*).[147] The roles of the General Chamber of Commerce and the Municipal Chamber (*Guangzhoushi shanghui*) were also greatly reduced. This happened despite the fact that the latter was the successor to the Municipal Association for the Maintenance of Commerce, and could thus reasonably claim to be the representative of the so-called petty merchants, whom the Guomindang had designated as core supporters of its government. In their place a new government-sponsored Merchant Association (*shangmin xiehui*) was founded in early 1925 to represent and mobilize the merchant class.

One should be careful, however, in assessing the role of the Merchant Association. As in the case of the numerous other mass organizations which were established to mobilize the various social segments or classes in this period, it is not always easy to generalize the extent of its impact. These mass organizations were not grassroots institutions. Indeed, they could at times be reduced to simply churning out official propaganda. Yet, it would be erroneous to assume that just because they were sponsored or sanctioned by the government, these organizations always acted in accord with official policies.

The Guomindang might have envisaged them to be a straightforward medium through which its government could orchestrate social support. But it was not infrequent that their constituents actually took advantage of the presence of these organizations to negotiate positions favorable to themselves vis-à-vis the authorities. With the working class at center stage, for example, there were then in existence myriad officially endorsed worker organizations. Nevertheless, the government was soon to learn that, despite its efforts, the establishment of these worker organizations did not always generate the anticipated results.

CHAPTER FOUR

Privileging Labor

> Whatever kind of "ism" it is, it has always been trans-
> formed into a deceitful trick once it reaches the hands
> of the Chinese. Today is the famous Labor Day. This day
> of course holds great meaning for Western societies. It
> symbolizes the class struggle of the propertyless class, that
> is, the laboring class, against the class which exploited
> them. . . . Some years ago I gave a lecture somewhere
> [in China] and was received by a group of peasant associa-
> tions, merchant associations, and worker associations.
> Dozens of their representatives were there, none looked
> like a peasant, merchant, or worker. They all rather
> appeared to be members of the elite. . . . It is mournful
> that within the country the untold multitude of the
> productive class, going about their business, are not
> even aware of the representations which are being made
> in their name by those people.
>
> — LIANG QICHAO, 1925[1]

On May 1, 1926, the main streets of Canton were, as on many other occasions in recent months, adorned with a sea of red flags and banners proclaiming social solidarity or the need to be vigilant against the imperialists.
Thousands of workers from the area were directed into the center of the city
in preparation for a demonstration to celebrate May Day (International

Labor Day). The ritual had been carefully organized and promoted by the Guomindang and its Communist allies, both as a symbolic display of the vigor of the masses—with the working class in the lead—and as a show of support for the government. By 1926, such demonstrations, which often commenced in the newly constructed parks of the city, followed by processions routed along the new thoroughfares with participants distributing leaflets and chanting slogans, had become standard fare in the public arena. Thus what occupied the attention of the government on that particular May Day was, perhaps, not so much the celebration but the escalating brawls between rival factions within the Union of Rickshaw Pullers. The fighting eventually left four dead and scores injured before the day was over.[2]

The incident was both embarrassing and frustrating for the Guomindang and the Communists. The latter, in particular, had actively taken upon themselves the task of organizing the workers. And the rickshaw pullers' organization was reputedly one which had come under their control. For the political elites in Canton, a unified working class had become, in the aftermath of the Merchant Corps incident, the symbol of a new realignment within society, signifying the surge of mass support for their cause. Supposedly no effort was spared to awaken the class consciousness of the workers. The political discourse was saturated with reference to the sanctity of the working class. "Words," as Lynn Hunt wrote in reference to the French Revolution, "did not just reflect social and political reality; they were instruments for transforming reality."[3]

But even before the problem of friction within the working class itself is addressed, it is important to note that there were many within the Guomindang leadership who, although they believed that the strength of a society depended on the mobilization of its different segments or classes, continued to be concerned about the potentially disruptive effects of the notion of class conflict. The Guomindang theoretician Dai Jitao, for instance, wrote in 1925 that the political project should be based on an alliance of various classes. The way that classes opposed each other, in Dai's words, was an "ailment of society" (*shehui de bingtai*). In an interesting twist, Dai argued that in order to avoid conflict, the ruling class must be awakened to act on behalf of the ruled. Ultimately, the objective was to enable members of the ruling class to shed their class nature (*paoqile ta de jiejixing*).[4] But for the moment, despite his reservations, Dai accepted class as the defining feature of contemporary society.

Similarly, in his last series of lectures on the Three People's Principles delivered in Canton in early 1924, Sun Yat-sen, as expected, emphasized that "nationalism" meant the joining together of all Chinese people in a single organization (*guozu tuanti*). However, in contrast to the prevailing opinions of most political and intellectual elites, he also suggested that lineages (*zongzu*) could serve as the building blocks for such an organization.[5] Sun, to be sure, was probably pandering to his lineage-conscious audience in Canton, and his rhetoric in this case was never translated into concrete policies. Yet it was also clear that Sun, like many of his associates, was not entirely comfortable with an image of a world shaped by the potential confrontation between different classes. To Sun, the question of equity concerned not just the workers. Even in the highly industrialized countries, he maintained, there were conflicts between all those who were useful and capable on the one side, and the capitalist class on the other. Reiterating one of his favorite themes, Sun suggested that was why "public authorities" (*gongjia*) were needed to ensure equitable adjustments among the people.[6]

In Sun's view, Marx might have correctly identified certain ills of society, but he failed to discover the "law of societal progress" (*shehui jinhua de dinglü*). Its primary impetus, according to Sun, was provided not by class warfare, but by the human struggle for survival. Chiding gently what he called the "fashionable intellectuals" who claimed otherwise, Sun pronounced that his focus on solving the problem of people's livelihood was thus "very much in line with the logic of societal progress."[7] Class conflict and the sufferings of the workers occurred, Sun reasoned, only because the issue of people's livelihood had not been properly addressed. His own Principle of People's Livelihood, Sun declared, was hence conceived in the same spirit as communism and socialism.[8] Indeed, all three shared the modernist view of the centrality of the social realm, and of the reordering of social relations as the linchpin of change. The difference was that the proponents of People's Livelihood, while recognizing class differences and social inequities, relied on public authorities rather than class struggle to achieve progress.

While Sun and his lieutenants sought to domesticate the disrupting effects of the politics of class, their strategies had, however, run up against the practical needs of their political project. To put it bluntly, if the Guomindang-led government was to retain a semblance of social support, it had, by late 1924, little choice but to privilege the working class. The Comintern advisers had, to be sure, pushed for a more prolabor policy. But in the aftermath of the bloody fiasco in Xiguan, the labor movement had really become the only readily organized constituency for the regime.[9] The memory of the Seamen's Strike of 1922 was certainly still fresh in the minds of the governing elites. An anti-imperialist struggle led by the working class might just be the recipe to reinvigorate a passive, if not outright hostile, local society.

To most members of the Guomindang leadership, then, the privileging of the workers was meant, first and foremost, to rally support from society. It was to get the workers, as a cohesive force, to take the lead in marching behind the banner of the government. Such a stance was quite different, of course, from that of the Communists (and some more radical members of the Guomindang), who subscribed to the Marxian notion of the inevitability of class conflict. To the Communists, the privileging of the working class was historically determined. The self-perceived role of the Communists was to lead the workers toward their destiny as the dominant class. Communist activists were hence particularly eager to restructure the labor organizations, and to insert themselves into leadership positions within the movement. They also then had to confront the very real problem of how to get through to the grass roots of an often insular laboring world.

What these official labor organizers, Communist or otherwise, purported to do was to turn the workers into a cohesive segment of society endowed with class consciousness. Through a thorough restructuring of their organizations, the workers were supposed to learn to transcend what many elites had long condemned as their parochialism, and to base their solidarity on class affinity rather than, say, local or regional ties. The impressive statistics furnished by the numerous new unions of the mid-1920s often led historians to sing the praises of the success of the movement. A survey carried out by the Municipal Government of Canton in 1926, for example, listed 180 more or less modern unions that claimed 298,632 members out of an estimated total work force of fewer than 500,000, a large percentage by any standard.[10] Thus one labor historian wrote that, in 1925–27, "the mainstream of the politicized labor movement in the [Canton] delta first turned radically to the left as vanguard of the revolutionary united front against domestic

With Guomindang party and national flags hoisted in the background, delegates to the Council of Workers' Deputies in Canton assemble for a photograph, ca. 1924.

warlords and foreign imperialists."[11] The working class, in other words, had by then become the standard bearer of the project to reconstruct society-and-nation.

This chapter will look at several key constituents of the labor movement in Canton. It will begin with an examination of the rickshaw pullers' union and the May Day Riot, followed by an analysis of the protests of the oil-processing workers and the Machinists' Union, and, finally, by an appraisal of the railroad workers. It will end with a critical scrutiny of an overall assessment of the movement provided by its most active organizers: the local Communist cadres. Most of the workers discussed here were products of the transformation of the city in the late Qing and the early Republic. They were, in other words, part of the drive to modernize Canton as envisaged by the elites. Moreover, the leaders of the rickshaw pullers, oil-processing workers, and railroad crews were all represented in the seventeen-member Executive Committee of the Council of Workers' Deputies (*Gongren daibiao xiehui*), an officially sponsored umbrella organization established on May Day of 1924 in an effort to unite most of the unions in Canton.[12] By encouraging, organizing, and endorsing the new unions, the governing elites sought to revitalize society by rallying its different segments behind the struggle of the working class. Yet, as they soon found out, the process of forging the heterogeneous laboring population into a disciplined and cohesive force—the vanguard of the *shehui juntuan*—was not nearly as straightforward as they had thought.

THE RICKSHAW PULLERS
AND THE MAY DAY RIOT

The Union of Rickshaw Pullers (URP) was the first successful union reorganization carried out by Chen Yannian (1898–1927), son of Chen Duxiu, the radical intellectual and the first general secretary of the Chinese Communist Party (CCP). The younger Chen succeeded the subsequently famous Zhou Enlai in heading the Guangdong branch of the CCP, as Zhou became increasingly involved in the various military expeditions launched by the Guomindang-led government after 1925.[13] Officially founded (or, more accurately, reorganized) in August 1925, the URP claimed an estimated membership of 7,000, of whom some 1,400 were considered literate.[14] It did not, however, appear to include the unemployed within the occupation.[15] Still, it represented precisely the kind of effort advocated by the elites: getting the people to unite to form new kinds of collectivities as the basis of a vital society.

At first glance, the May Day Riot of 1926 seemed, at least from a modernist perspective, like an atavistic feud. The battle line was drawn primarily between two different "ethnic" groups of pullers: one from the Canton area and the other from the Chaoan region of eastern Guangdong. "It is well known," as stated in a recent work on territorial bonds, "that for those in southern China who claim to be Han Chinese the home county and village are major markers of identity."[16] Yet, while organizations based on alleged common ethnicity, usually traced to some common place of origin, had been widespread since the late imperial period, the criteria for the boundaries between these groups were actually neither always clear nor consistent. Depending on the time and place, commonalities could be established on the basis of county of origin, provincial identity, dialectal grouping, other perceived cultural traits, or a selective combination of the above. The two groups of pullers involved here, for instance, were from the same province but spoke different dialects, and, depending on one's perspective, might or might not belong to the same cultural grouping.[17] Indeed, the concept of ethnicity, to borrow the words of a cultural critic, "changes as it repeats, but it also repeats as it changes."[18] To maintain that the bloody brawl on that May Day was simply an old-fashioned conflict between rival ethnic groups is thus to slide dangerously close to the ahistorical view that ethnic differences are immutable.

There are a multiplicity of mechanisms, contingent upon the context, through which ethnic boundaries can be drawn and imposed. Ethnic differences, in China as elsewhere, have always been the product of a perpetual process of re-creation throughout history. In fact, the ethnic demarcations within the laboring world of Canton were in many ways a by-product of the drive to modernize the city. As Quan Hansheng once observed, while the intrusion of "Western capitalism" had undermined much of the old guild system of China, the labor gang, or *kulibang*, with its exclusionary spirit, remained defiantly in place.[19] Indeed, the labor gang seemed to have enjoyed a period of growth rather than decline in early republican Canton, as the city went through a rapid process of change. In trying to forge a working class out of the laboring world of Canton, then, the political elites were not only engaged in obliterating vestiges of the past (as they thought), they were actually combating and suppressing alternative modes of organization for the workers of the present.

The recasting of the physical and commercial geography of Canton in the early 1920s had made the rickshaw the dominant mode of transportation within the city. Although the old city walls had been almost completely demolished by 1922, and the once legendary narrow lanes had been replaced by boulevards in parts of the city, the new roads were often too poorly paved for travel by motor vehicle to be comfortable and safe. The omnibuses that came into service in 1921 were, in the words of a contemporary, "very clumsy large bod[ies] on small chassis."[20] Accidents were frequent, and the transport company and the municipal government maintained an ongoing dispute over the problem of laying proper tramrails. Meanwhile, the two to three hundred automobiles which appeared in Canton were conspicuous within a sea of rickshaws, the number of which swelled to around four thousand at the

A ubiquitous sight in early republican Canton: rickshaws and their pullers awaiting customers.

end of 1923. The rickshaws had quickly established themselves, as one report puts it, as the "favorite among the people of Canton."[21]

The rickshaw pullers, many of whom were recent rural migrants from other parts of the province, were part of the expansion of Canton in the early twentieth century. The metropolis's inhabitants increased from perhaps around 600,000 at the beginning of the period to reportedly 801,646 in 1923 and 1,122,583 in 1932, reflecting in part a gradual stream of migrants, many of whom were young male itinerants, into the city to seek work.[22] Most of the pullers, for instance, were not even from the areas immediately surrounding Canton.[23] Of the 5,253 pullers found in 1933, almost 60 percent (3,110) were from three relatively distant counties—Huiyang, Chaoan, and Qingyuan. The group also consisted mostly of men 40 or younger (4,270). Although about half of them were married, the majority came to the city on their own.[24] Such trends were also reflected in the larger laboring population. According to a survey of worker families in Canton in 1933, for instance, only 257 of the 1,425 respondents (18 percent) were natives of the municipality, while of the remaining 1,168 (82 percent), many had family members residing in their homes outside Canton.[25] To the elites determined to organize labor into a cohesive force, the modernization of the city appeared to have produced the ideal conditions for their project: an assembly of displaced and, as a whole, relatively young workers, such as the rickshaw pullers, simply waiting to be awakened.

Indeed, the backbreaking work of the rickshaw pullers, to say nothing of their centrality and visibility in the modern urban life of early-twentieth-century China, had clearly captured the imagination of the elites.[26] It was surely no accident that Chen Yannian chose to organize the pullers first. As an official report on the conditions of Canton later put it, even among the toiling masses life was the hardest for the rickshaw pullers.[27] But to organize them, one first had to contend with the intricate matrix of work relations which mediated the lives of the rickshaw pullers in Canton.

Work organization in the rickshaw trade was a variant system of contract labor. Historians are by now familiar with the system of contract labor (*baogong*) in China, but its salient features in relation to the labor gang bear brief reiteration. A gang was usually headed by a labor contractor (*gongtou*), who was responsible for recruitment and negotiation for work. Employers dealt with the contractor, who in turn guaranteed the conduct of his men. As a rule, the contractor retained a percentage of the men's wages as his compensation, the exact amount being contingent on the type of work, market conditions, and so forth. In addition, he usually deducted another sum to support a kind of rudimentary insurance and emergency fund for the workers. The contractor tended to cull his labor from a familiar locality, often the area from which he came.[28] Thus once a contractor established himself in Canton, a flow of workers from his home region usually followed. Patronage was then reinforced by putative native-place ties (*tongxiang*), and it was such contracting systems which formed the nuclei of the labor gangs.

In the rickshaw trade, the system meant that the pullers in Canton generally did not own the vehicles nor rent them directly from the companies, the largest of which claimed over a thousand rickshaws, but leased them from a contractor. Most companies charged a daily deposit of C$5 plus a rental fee of about C$1 for each rickshaw. The amount was paid by the contractor, who assumed full responsibility for the vehicles. A puller had to pay the contractor a commission for his service, in addition to the cost of leasing the rickshaw. Rickshaw pullers in Canton were divided into two shifts, from 6 A.M. to 2 P.M., and then from 2 P.M. till midnight. For each shift, a contractor usually charged a local puller 60 cents. Those from the outlying counties of Chaoan and Huiyang, who were obviously even more dependent on the contractors, were saddled with an extra 10 cent surcharge.[29] For all the pullers, however, the availability of work was contingent upon their access to the contractors, who in turn competed fiercely with each other for a greater share of the market. Each contractor, then, constantly tried to consolidate and expand his own band of followers.

The dominance of the contractors over the pullers extended well beyond the arena of work. More often than not, the former controlled not only the working but also the living and social space of the latter. Most of the pullers lived in dormitories (*guankou*). These were usually small houses with as many beds as space would allow, and were provided by the contractors for a monthly fee of about C$1.[30] A government report of 1933 found, for example, that almost half of the pullers (2,391) were crammed into the many dormitories located in the section of town along the eastern Bund, commonly known as *Dongdi*.[31] To some extent, such isolation in their own living quarters or ghettos, as it were, contributed to the development of an "imagined community" of pullers. Large congregations of pullers were, for instance, a regular feature of the eating houses in the *Dongdi* section, not to mention the various gambling establishments and brothels. Rickshaw pullers were inscribed in the popular imagination as an often rowdy and obstreperous group, an image reinforced by the frequent arguments between pullers and riders over disputed fares in the streets of Canton.[32] But the pullers' sense of community, if it indeed existed, was extremely fragile, as it was constantly under challenge from the imperative of access to contractors and competition for work. There was certainly no illusion among the elites but that the parameters of the pullers' existence were set largely by the contractors. As the local branch of the CCP reported in unequivocal if despondent terms, "to be realistic, this union [the URP] has no alternative but to cooperate with the contractors, for only then can it retain its influence."[33]

If there is one word which captures the world of the labor gang, it is perhaps "violence." For transport workers in particular, and not only in Canton, rival claims to turf—areas which a given gang was allowed to monopolize—were almost invariably settled by force.[34] It was a world with its own code of conduct and was often brutish, as illustrated by the numerous press reports and government proclamations devoted to the subject in Canton. In this context, the outbreak of violence between the two rival group of pullers within the URP on that May Day of 1926 was merely symptomatic of the problems of imposing a union onto the prevailing structure of work organization. As a modern union, the URP was obliged to observe Labor Day. There was, however, considerable resistance from the ranks, as the loss of a day's income threatened the livelihood of many. At the same time, the union lacked any authority to enforce discipline independent of the contractors. Indeed, the new union was itself little more than a loose coalition of contractors, each of whom actually depended on that very divisiveness among the ranks for his livelihood.

An emergency meeting was held on April 30, 1926, in which a resolution was passed to allow work to be resumed by 7 P.M. on May Day. By about six o'clock the following evening, however, three pullers, one from the Canton region and the other two from the Chaoan area, were found working and were confronted by a group of Chaoan pullers. Serious injuries were inflicted upon the Cantonese, while the attackers left their *tongxiang* relatively unscathed. The result was street warfare. Much was made of the reports that the fighting, which quickly spread from the Bund to the heart of the city, was conducted largely along ethnic lines. The whole transportation system was paralyzed. In addition to the four deaths and other injuries already mentioned, over a hundred rickshaws were destroyed. The commotion subsided only when police fired repeated warning shots and confiscated weapons.[35]

The fighting, however, dragged on for another three days. A violent protest was staged by over a thousand pullers at the union headquarters. Two union officials, both of whom were from the Huiyang region and were probably contractors, were assaulted and severely wounded. The building itself was vandalized. The Council of Workers' Deputies could do little more than issue an obligatory statement condemning the incompetence of union officials as well as the lack of education, to say nothing of consciousness, on the part of the workers.[36]

It was easy to view the May Day Riot of 1926 as simply a trivial incident in the grand narrative of the labor movement, but the larger issues of which it was a mere symptom could not be quite so summarily dismissed. To accuse the workers of backward parochialism and lack of enlightenment, as members of the elite were wont to do, was to remain willfully blind to the fact that the very nature of the rickshaw pullers' work organization militated against worker unity. Yet, convinced of the viability of a cohesive and disciplined society in the modern era, the governing elites were bent on constructing an organic entity whose health was contingent upon the coming together of its constituents. The working class, real or imagined, had become an emblem of the enterprise.

To be sure, some might discount the rickshaw pullers as simply a marginal element. They were recent rural migrants. Their work was unskilled and often transient, and they lacked an institutional base. Such inherent instability undoubtedly contributed to their volatility, resistance to discipline, and apparent propensity for reckless violence. Yet, as the political elites were repeatedly reminded, the problems they encountered with the URP were by no means confined to the unskilled or the illiterate, but were rather endemic within the laboring world.

THE OIL-PROCESSING WORKERS AND THE MACHINISTS

According to a municipal survey carried out in 1926, the Union of Oil-Processing Workers (UOPW) was founded in 1921. The UOPW represents a good case study of labor organization in early republican Canton. It was, first of all, part of the artisanal industry, characterized by small-scale production and semiskilled labor, which was typical of the metropolis in this period. In 1933, for example, out of the 205 factories surveyed in Canton, a total of 119 still consisted of only 10 to 50 workers.[37] At the same time, like many other industries, the craft tradition of oil processing was under threat as enthusiastic entrepreneurs, many from the émigré communities, began to introduce mechanization to improve productivity. Moreover, the UOPW was reputedly one of the best organized and disciplined modern unions. In a generally critical review of the labor movement in Canton, the Russian adviser General V. K. Blyukher (pseudonym "Galen") singled out the UOPW by name as the one in which the Communists, who spent the most effort organizing the workers, were effective. Indeed, according to Blyukher, the UOPW had by far the largest number of Communist organizers (sixteen) among its members.[38] The UOPW, in short, was in the forefront of the labor movement.

"Oil processing" here refers to processing edible oils, the most common of which, known as *shengyou*, was made from groundnuts. *Shengyou*, however, had uses other than human consumption. Prior to the widespread distribution of kerosene and cigarettes after the turn of the century, *shengyou* was also used for lighting purposes and for percolating local tobacco. The initial method of oil processing was a purely manual operation. The nuts were first ground into powder. The powder was then steamed and compressed into cylindrical form for the first round of pressing for oil. A secondary grinding then took place, producing a bran-like residual substance that was fried and molded into a patty, followed by two more rounds of extraction. An average processing yard thus had maybe three or four wooden presses (*muzha*) and no more than twenty workers. Such simple infrastructure requirements allowed the establishment of a large number of small enterprises: there were over 70 in Canton as of the last decades of the Qing.[39] There was, however, as in many other industries, a rush to experiment with mechanization during the heady days of the early Republic. The first phase of the process, which brought in machinery to grind the nuts while leaving the actual pressing to manual labor, was generally a success. Problems arose when several companies attempted to introduce full-scale mechanization of production in the early 1920s.[40] Tension mounted not only between owners and employees, but also between traditional craftsmen and another group of workers ready to exploit the opportunities afforded by the advent of machinery.

Like rickshaw pulling, oil pressing required such sheer physical strength that the industry was almost completely free of women and children.[41] During the height of the industry in the mid-1920s, there were reportedly 13,500 workers (including those in the surrounding counties) employed in oil processing, making them easily one of the largest groups within the laboring population.[42] Unlike the solitary pullers, however, oil-processing workers did operate in a factory-like environment. Work was usually organized in teams of six or eight, which included a couple of apprentices. Each team worked basically as an autonomous unit, organizing its work around the *muzha*. It had its own leader, who acted as a kind of foreman, enforcing discipline and monitoring productivity.[43] The autonomy of the team could be seen in the decision of the workers to demand, during a strike in 1923, a raise and compensation calculated on the basis of each *muzha*.[44] Thus even though some of the newer enterprises claimed over a hundred hands, the workers were not necessarily integrated at the workplace.

Moreover, the kind of recruitment pattern which characterized the rickshaw trade also operated in the oil-processing industry, with workers from the same locality forming a work unit together, creating ethnic divisions in the process. The two major groups, which undoubtedly encompassed further subdivisions, were the so-called *xijiangpai* (those who came from counties along the West River, such as Sihui, Guangning, and Gaoyao) and *dongjiangpai* (those from counties along the East River, such as Dongguan, Heyuan, and Huiyang).[45] Not only were most workers in the oil-processing industry recent migrants from the surrounding counties, they also often returned to agricultural work during the low season of the oil-processing trade. With the ties to their agrarian homes still relatively intact, it is little wonder that workers were strongly influenced by what Elizabeth Perry calls "the politics of place," as embodied by organizations based on *tongxiang* allegiance.[46]

According to Hou Guiping, an oil-processing worker who was recruited into the Communist Party after leading the strike of 1923, the early history of the UOPW was not unlike that of most other unions in Canton. Organization was weak. Its first leader, Zeng Xisheng, was allegedly in the business mostly for the money, although he was briefly a Communist.[47] Hou's own background was probably representative of the majority of oil-processing workers. Born into a peasant family in Huaxian (about 40 kilometers north of Canton) and having barely any formal education, Hou did not move to the metropolis until 1920. While in Canton, Hou came into contact with young Communists like Liu Ersong and Ruan Xiaoxian, who were attracted to the UOPW by the sheer size of its actual and potential membership.[48] Although the strike of 1923 was purely economic in nature and ended only after the union had made substantial concessions, the workers nonetheless held out for several months, despite occasional internal friction, and managed to force the owners to raise wages and provide compensation for work lost.[49]

The crucial factors for the success, however, had relatively little to do with union leadership. Apart from the support of the government, it was actually the decentralized team structure which enabled flexibility and effective coordination for the strike (provided, as in this case, that most of the team leaders shared the same agenda). Just as important was the oil-processing workers' continued close ties to the land which allowed many of them to return to tilling the soil and so weather the hard times.[50] For those labor organizers striving to "enlighten" the workers and to drag them into modern times, it was surely ironic that such "backward" features within the movement made the "progressive" collective action possible. To be sure, the fragile solidarity did not last long. Many subsequent brawls, with clubs and even revolvers, took place between UOPW members themselves.[51]

In the 1920s, though, the oil-processing workers faced a threat even more ominous than either internecine warfare or employers' sanctions: the introduction of mechanized production. The machine-tool industry in Canton had a history which stretched back to the nineteenth century, stimulated particularly by the then booming silk industry in the surrounding counties and to a lesser extent by the development of the shipping trade. Starting with repair work, the industry, dominated initially by small workshops with no more than a handful of workers each, soon grew to construct basic machine-tools. Entrepreneurs would try to imitate or modify expensive foreign models.[52] The founding of the Xietonghe Machine-tool Factory in 1912, for example, with only three machinists and five apprentices, symbolized an increasingly ambitious approach. Its legendary rice mill, the *mimoerhao*, quickly established the reputation of the factory. By the middle years of the decade, it had over 60 workers and was manufacturing, among other products, diesel engines.[53] Xietonghe, to be sure, was the largest and the most successful of the machine-tool enterprises. Nonetheless, in the 1920s a number of them were confident enough to produce more sophisticated models that needed a higher degree of precision, including ones which could replace the manual *muzha* in oil processing.

The skill level required to work in the machine-tool trade meant that the machinists constituted a distinct stratum of workers in late Qing Canton. This stratum had grown considerably with the introduction of the railroads and the expansion of the arsenal.[54] The contrast between the machinists and the oil-processing workers was stark. Take, for instance, the difference in literacy rates. While 90 percent of the machinists were considered literate, only ten percent of the oil-processing workers qualified.[55] The machinists were also among the best paid in Canton: Their monthly income ranged from C$30 to C$75 (UOPW members by contrast earned between C$10 and C$20).[56] It is perhaps to be expected, therefore, that the Machinists' Union (MU), which after several earlier incarnations came into formal existence in

1921, was one of the most powerful labor organizations.[57] It claimed a sizable membership of around 12,000 in the mid-1920s.[58] As one contemporary observer noted, the machinists were clearly a "labor aristocracy" of Canton.[59] The machinists' unique position also explained why supporters of Sun Yat-sen had long cultivated ties to them. The machinists, indeed, played an important role in the Guomindang's success in ousting the old Guangxi clique from Canton in 1920.[60]

When a number of oil-processing concerns in Canton, encouraged by their own success in instituting machine-grinding as well as by the growth of the local machine-tool industry, began to introduce wholesale mechanization in the 1920s, many oil-processing workers were confronted with the specter of displacement.[61] The conflict between the machinists and the oil-processing workers, however, was not simply a matter of the latter's resistance to the "inhuman" machines, characteristic of displaced craftsmen everywhere. It was also entangled with the politics of labor organization then within Canton. Given the importance of the machinists, it was logical that the corps of modern labor organizers, most of whom were Communists, initially tried to gain a foothold within their organization. Indeed, the machinists were one of the few groups of workers in Canton who might pass for proletarian in the strict sense of the term. They were urban: The often harsh apprenticeship of four years ensured that the qualified machinist was unlikely to be a recent immigrant to the city.[62] Their skill had also endowed them with a degree of autonomy not commonly found among other workers. Furthermore, their involvement with the Guomindang in the early Republic meant that collective political actions were not alien to them. In their internal report, the Communists characterized their relationship with the machinists in the period between 1921 and 1924 as "co-operation."[63] As was the case with most other labor organizations, however, the work of the Communists then was largely confined to the leadership of the MU, with little contact with the rank-and-file members.[64] Another Communist report in 1923 lists the MU and the UOPW in the same category as unions which were "relatively organized."[65]

Overt tension, however, began to emerge between the machinists and Communist labor organizers by mid-1924. Confident of its own strength, the MU chose to remain independent of the new officially sponsored umbrella labor organization, the Council of Workers' Deputies. The Communists, meanwhile, were increasingly frustrated by their inability to reorder and discipline effectively the factious laboring world of Canton. They had decided that one reason for the lack of class consciousness among the workers was that unions were often organized along discrete craft lines, of which the Machinists' Union was the obvious example. The Communists suggested, somewhat dogmatically, that industrial unions represented a more progressive form of organization. This, of course, set them on a direct collision course with the powerful machinists by late 1924.[66] The machinists were regarded by the labor organizers, not without justification, as a privileged group which, upon taking advantage of its historical connection to the Guomindang, was bent on protecting its own special position. The MU, in other words, had become an obstacle in the effort to forge the working class. It was within such a context that the conflict between the oil-processing workers and the machinists unfolded.

The conflict erupted in early 1925 when the owners of an oil-processing factory named Changtaihou decided to install locally manufactured machines to replace manual presses. As expected, the move encountered strong opposition from the oil-processing workers. As the self-proclaimed champions of the working class, the new corps of labor organizers was saddled with a dilemma. They were, after all, the apostles of modernity, and mechanization of the industries was surely the future of the nation. At the same time, they were also supposed to fight against the displacement of workers, particularly since they had painstakingly cultivated support within the UOPW and were loath to see its demise. The fact was that if the oil-processing factories were mechanized, many of their workers would then be open to recruitment by the Machinists' Union, in effect sounding the death knell of the UOPW. Given the growing hostility between the Communist labor organizers and the machinists, that would hardly aid the former's quest to restructure the labor movement under its leadership. The labor organizers could presumably have assumed the role of mediator and tried to facilitate some settlement between the two unions in the name of class unity. Instead, they took the conflict as an opportunity to split up the MU.

The labor organizers chose to fan the Luddite sentiment of the oil-processing workers.[67] In late March, gangs of oil-processing workers charged into Changtaihou, denouncing the evil "man-eating" machines, and promptly destroyed them after clashing with members of the Machinists'

Union. There were scores of injuries, with the machinists claiming two or three of their fellows missing. The result was a drawn out standoff between the two unions which was never genuinely resolved.[68] The Public Security Bureau's attempt at mediation seems to have bogged down on who should qualify as a machinist, and on whether machinists working in the oil-processing industry should also belong to the UOPW.[69] There were still calls for a settlement even in the midst of the fervor of the Canton-Hongkong Strike later in the year.[70]

The results of the incident, however, were not exactly what the labor organizers anticipated. If the Changtaihou attack was aimed at weakening the Machinists' Union, it hopelessly backfired. In an internal report compiled shortly afterward, the Communists described their strategy during the episode as their "biggest error" which constituted a "great blow" to their leadership of the labor movement.[71] The cadres also conceded, in a later report, that the conflict played into the hands of the machinists, and actually served to strengthen the organization of the MU.[72] This was partly because, despite a growing interest in machine-tools in Canton in the 1920s, the conversion to mechanized production, often constrained by the want of capital and the instability of the market, was proceeding at only a gradual and piecemeal pace. Mechanization was not, in other words, necessarily perceived by most workers in the small-scale artisanal industries as a general and immediate threat. The call for industrial unions also meant little to most workers. On the other hand, the machinists had long played a vital role in certain key sectors of the local economy, such as silk or shipping. Many of those who worked in those industries believed that their own well-being was linked to the fate of the MU.

In addition, backed by the Communist labor organizers, the aggressive and destructive behavior of the oil-processing workers made the UOPW appear unreasonable. Meanwhile, the machinists accused the UOPW and its supporters of being the cause of internal strife among workers.[73] It was their claim that the UOPW was depriving them of their means of livelihood and starving them to death that aroused empathy in the laboring world.[74] The MU even appropriated the rhetoric of the labor organizers as its members marched defiantly in the streets, proclaiming that only mechanized production could rescue the nation from its woes, and touting slogans such as "Down with imperialist society" and "Machines are omnipotent" (*jiqi wan-*

neng).[75] Indeed, the extent of support for the machinists was such that the UOPW was eventually forced to make concessions in late 1925 in order to prevent the MU from "further using the slogan [the Changtaihou incident] to rally the masses."[76] There was even a slight hint from the local cadres that the Communist Party dogma regarding the preference for industrial unions might need to be reassessed.[77] And if the labor organizers hoped that the conciliatory approach might divide the machinists or encourage the emergence of an alternative leadership for the MU, they were also to be disappointed.[78]

In the annals of history, the Machinists' Union has often been described as anti-Communist. The MU was supposedly a clear example of a "yellow" (reactionary) union in contrast to the "red" (revolutionary) unions, the latter being those which supposedly followed the leadership of Communist labor organizers.[79] Such convenient political labels, needless to say, obscure the complex conditions at work in Canton of the 1920s. In fact, almost every labor organization in Canton, including the machinists and the oil-processing workers, became more "militant" in this period. Taking advantage of the prolabor government policies and their privileged position in the discourse of society, workers were more than ever able to organize, strike, and fight collectively—whether as a gang or as a union—to secure their livelihoods. The problem for the political elites was that the militant collective actions of the labor organizations did not transform the workers into a cohesive and disciplined force, that is, a working class. In fact, the opposite seems to have been true. The more the workers organized, the more factious they became. As the labor historian Elizabeth Perry emphasizes, "intraclass divisions did not immobilize the workers," but even she concedes that "labor militancy . . . is not tantamount to class consciousness."[80] To the governing elites searching for a new form of collectivity in Canton in the 1920s, the sight of the workers, mobilized yet tearing at each other, could be of scant comfort indeed.

THE RAILROAD WORKERS

Railroad workers hold a venerable position in the history of twentieth-century China. The railroad was a potent symbol of modernization which had long captured the imaginations of the likes of Sun Yat-sen and his associates.

The railroad workers, who manned those modern arteries of transportation on which the strategic movement of both troops and goods increasingly relied, were thus often considered to be in the vanguard of the labor movement. The Communist activist and historian Deng Zhongxia, in his widely read essay on Chinese labor in this period, credited the strike on the Jinghan (Peking-Hankou) railroad in early 1922 as the turning point at which the focus of the labor struggle shifted from economic amelioration to political emancipation.[81] In Canton of the 1920s, there were over three thousand workers, perhaps close to three quarters of whom were considered literate, who operated the three railroad lines which converged in their hub at the metropolis.[82] The intervention of the railroad workers in June 1925 was often cited as critical to the success of the Guomindang-led government in suppressing the rebellions of the militarists Yang Ximin and Liu Zhenhuan, the leaders of the so-called guest armies.[83] It was also among the railroad workers that the Communist labor organizers in Canton carried out one of their attempts to institute their cherished industrial union at the expense of craft-based organizations.

The first railroad line to reach the city of Canton was the Canton-Sanshui railroad, a 48.92-kilometer stretch to the west of the metropolis constructed in 1901–1904 by the American China Development Company.[84] As the Americans were granted the right to the Canton-Hankou railroad in 1898, the Canton-Sanshui section was initially conceived as a branch to the soon-to-be-built main line. The construction of the Canton-Hankou line, however, proved to be a drawn out process. The Qing government's concession to the powers regarding control of the railroads quickly became the focus of protests against foreign domination after the turn of the century. The right to the Canton-Hankou railroad was redeemed in 1905 largely by a loan secured, ironically, from the colonial government of Hong Kong arranged by the Qing official Zhang Zhidong.[85] The management of the redeemed railroad, however, ran into a succession of problems, and the whole length of the line did not become fully operational until 1936. In the mid-1920s, the southern section of the line starting from Canton still went only as far as Shaoguan in northern Guangdong, a 224-kilometer stretch which was completed in 1915. Meanwhile, the Canton-Kowloon (Hong Kong) railroad (182 kilometers), financed by the British, came into service in 1911 after four years of work.[86]

Despite their checkered history, the impact of the three railroads was quickly felt. The Canton-Sanshui line was important in facilitating the important trading route along the West River, connecting the towns of Sanshui and Foshan (where the West River runs its course) to Canton. The Canton-Kowloon line, on the other hand, enabled Canton to gain better access to the superior port facilities of Hong Kong, which had become the major distribution center of south China. The Canton-Shaoguan section not only linked up with the North River trade but also became a crucial launching pad, as demonstrated repeatedly by Sun Yat-sen and his followers, for military campaigns northward to the heart of the country.[87]

According to the Canton municipal survey of 1926, the monthly income of railroad workers ranged from about C$20 to C$70, which was similar to that of the machinists.[88] Unlike for the machinists, however, the income differentials between the railroad workers represented not only the gradations of skill and experience but clear divisions of labor within the industry. A wide range of occupations came under the rubric of railroad work. An investigation of 21 major railroad lines in the country in 1931, for example, found that the workers could be broadly divided into 27.21 percent skilled, 50.92 percent semiskilled, and 21.87 percent unskilled.[89] They also tended to cover a wide spectrum in terms of age. Thus out of a total of 582 workers at the Canton-Sanshui railroad in 1929, there were 185 between the ages of 20 and 29, 210 between 30 and 39, and 119 between 40 and 49.[90]

But even such categorizations masked the sharp demarcations between the various types of work: carpentry shop, machine-tool shop, and engineering (track) work, in addition to services on the train and at the station. Thus the head of a train crew, for example, for the Canton-Sanshui railroad in 1926 not only earned more per month (C$52) than, say, a foreman of the engineering team (C$31.50), but actually shared little daily work experience with the foreman. The same, of course, could be said for the station heads (C$60) and the cooks on the trains (C$9).[91] Different groups of railroad workers were initially organized, if at all, around their separate workplaces, as each group established its own "clubs" (*julebu*) for recreational and liaison purposes. At the same time, those who worked for the machine-tool shop (or on the locomotive) tended to follow the lead of the Machinists' Union. Nor should the profound variations in the culture of work between the different groups be overlooked. While the track workers, for instance, had to labor in rather harsh and often hazardous conditions, the train crews hardly considered themselves as part of the laboring world. As some exasperated labor organizers put it, "With regard to the train crews, most have petit-bourgeois characteristics and habits. Moreover, it is easy for train crews to seek private gain and smuggle, and as a result of such contamination, these workers do not even know what class is."[92]

To those determined to forge a working class, the challenge was to overcome such inherent divisiveness. Using the same strategy they employed in other industries, the organizers first attempted to arrange the workers into core groups of ten (*shirentuan*) as the basic unit of association. They quickly learned, however, that such an arbitrary scheme was far from effective, as it was divorced from the actual work organization of the railroad industry. Starting with the Canton-Shaoguan line, then, the labor organizers turned to the work unit as the basis of their organizational activities. Track workers would be recruited as a team, locomotive operators would group themselves according to shifts, station crews would join as a cohort from each station, and so forth.[93] Such an approach, while undoubtedly expedient, did little to surmount the want of unity among the railroad workers.

To be sure, each of the three lines based in Canton had reputedly established its own railroad-wide union by the spring of 1925. Still, the old workers' clubs, now rechristened "branch associations" (*fenhui*), often insisted on their own integrity within the main union and remained wary of surrendering their prerogatives to others with whom they did not necessarily identify. Such tendencies were reinforced by the structure of work relations within the industry. Typically defined by the contract labor system, leadership positions in the work units were usually occupied by the contractors or foremen, even though labor organizers subsequently had some success in placing ordinary workers in union roles.[94] As resistance against a genuine integration of authority and organization within a single railroad-wide union continued, the labor organizers could in reality only manage to put together a coalition of different groups of workers, which often existed in uneasy tension with one another. As late as the fall of 1925, the Communist cadres reported that the Canton-Shaoguan union, the best organized of the three, still suffered from the fact that "different occupations [within the line] are still segregated from each other," and that many of them continued to have their own branch associations.[95] Although conditions of the union at the Canton-Shaoguan

line were upgraded to "unified" by the labor organizers in the summer of
1926, evidence of unity consisted of little more than the establishment of several railroad-wide organs for education and entertainment. Meanwhile, relations between the different groups at the Canton-Sanshui union could be
described only as "alliance," with its Canton-Kowloon counterpart lagging
still further behind.[96]

The fact that many activities were carried out in the name of the unions
in this period often obscured both the internal complexities and the weaknesses of their organization. Take the four-month-long "strike" which paralyzed the Canton-Sanshui railroad, for example. The conflict occurred in the
summer of 1925 in the midst of the Canton-Hongkong Strike, and led to the
offer of resignation by the head of the Peasant and Labor Bureau in
September.[97] At first glance, the episode appears to be a typical example of
struggle against management. Led by the machinists, a group of workers including carpenters and printers went on strike demanding the dismissal of
the new director of the railroad, Chen Yaozu. They accused Chen of attempting to instill discord among workers, to employ machinists from elsewhere, and to use armed inspectors to suppress the labor movement.[98]
Meanwhile, Chen fired the man in charge of the machinist section, a union
official named Liu Gongsu, accusing Liu of irresponsibility regarding the actions of his subordinates.[99]

The stage thus seems to have been set for a classic confrontation between
the two sides. Such a description, however, is highly misleading. It conceals
the crucial cause of the strife, a problem which the Communists had clearly
diagnosed in one of their internal reports. "Despite the founding of the railroad union," the report states, "owing to the fact that most of the officials
were our comrades operating without worker participation, and that they
had different views among themselves, the four-month-long conflict ensued."[100] These "comrades," it hardly needs stating, were often none other
than the leaders of the individual sections, the contractors and the foremen,
who were prone to see power in the new unions as a means of ensuring their
own control over the workers. To put it bluntly, the strike was not so much
a struggle of the workers against oppressive management, but a result of the
bickering and jockeying which grew out of the labor politics of Canton.

The leadership of the machinists was close to the former director of the
railroad and had resisted the appointment of Chen Yaozu from the begin-

ning. Quite a few other labor leaders, however, viewed the change at the top as an opportunity to enhance their own positions. Thus at the time when the machinists and their associates were declaring a strike, the engineering and track workers and the train crews, together with a minority of carpenters and printers, issued a statement proclaiming that they had nothing to do with the current strife with the management. Instead, the latter group concentrated on discrediting Liu Gongsu, the machinist leader, claiming that he abused his union office for private gain.[101] Demonstrations were staged demanding Liu's punishment.[102] Meanwhile, one of the leaders of the train crews, identified as Huang Hansheng, was attacked by the machinists as a key figure who had been colluding with the new director.[103]

For the machinists and their supporters, the defense of Liu Gongsu against the oppression of the new railroad administration and its collaborators had become the rallying cry. Much of the agitation was carried out under the banner of legitimate union activities. But workers were mobilized not so much to further the cause of the labor movement than as loyal troops assembling behind their individual commanders. The attempt by the government at arbitration could only result in the conclusion that both sides' arguments were vitriolic but short on evidence. In fact, animosity between different groups of workers within the Canton-Sanshui line became so intense that the government had difficulty even locating a willing candidate for the directorship, once it had decided to replace Chen Yaozu as a compromise gesture.[104] The machinists only resumed work after the railroad management, with the help of the army, agreed to fire all the scabs hired during the strike.[105] According to the Communist labor organizers, following the strike the whole railroad union was dismantled. In its place a new union was set up, allegedly with bona fide workers as its officials. Nonetheless, the cadres would still only conclude somewhat cryptically that "the state of [the new union's] organization was not very good, but it was a lot better than before."[106]

In the aftermath of the strike, there was of course no shortage of finger-pointing, with each group blaming the other for sowing the seeds of disunity. The fact was that the reasons for the discord among the railroad workers were not that different from those in other sectors of the laboring world. To many workers and particularly their leaders, the official call for unionization was more a license to assert their sectorial rights than a quest to find common cause with their fellow proletarians. Organization did not lead to discipline, but rather to more conflict and strife between workers. To the members of the elite who set out to create a strong and cohesive social constituency—the working class—upon which their political project could be constructed, such results must have been disheartening. Indeed, they were to lead to a searching reevaluation of the labor movement by the Communist organizers themselves.

WHITHER LABOR MOVEMENT

Toward the end of a detailed internal report on the labor movement filed in mid-1926, the Communist organizers observed that, although the process of unionization in Canton appeared to have then enjoyed extraordinary growth, the conditions were in reality fraught with danger.[107] In their view, there were challenges from four principal areas. First, there was the problem of fragmentation of unions. To cite but one example from the report, the mere five hundred sanitation workers were somehow divided into two unions. The result, according to the cadres, was almost daily armed conflicts between unions, not for claiming the ideological high ground, but for the mundane purpose of grabbing members, financial contributions, and government benefits. Second, to many, the establishment of unions had become just another way to get rich in what must have seemed to be a topsy-turvy world of the mid-1920s. Tactics which several years earlier would have brought prompt and severe suppression from the authorities were now openly tolerated, if not encouraged, by the government. Extracting contributions from their employers, which in Canton often meant entrepreneurs with only limited resources at their command, had, for example, become a favorite practice. Worse still, according to the report, the "propaganda team" of each union was usually not involved in propaganda work at all. Rather, they typically went around the city, armed with wooden clubs, coercing unsuspecting workers to join their unions in order to collect membership fees and garner other government subsidies that came with large recruitment.[108]

Third, the unions faced competition from employer-sponsored labor organizations. Surprisingly, the report devotes relatively little space to this issue. Perhaps the problem was so self-evident that the cadres deemed it in need of little elaboration. The same, however, could not be said of their fourth point, in which the cadres assailed what they called the "excessive economic demands" of the workers, which ranged from insistence on a universal eight-hour day or refusal to work after dark to outright blackmail of employers. In the opinions of the labor organizers, the nature of work organization in most local industries meant that a universal eight-hour day was "obviously unacceptable." Despite the spread of mechanical clocks, the concept of precise timekeeping as a cornerstone of discipline was still rather novel in local practices. Also, emboldened by the tolerance of the government, workers often pressed for unrealistic wage increases which could run as high as 100 percent. Most alarming of all, the cadres reported, was that even after some enterprises were forced to shut down, they continued to be harassed by unions levying their mixture of threats and demands. The result, as the report bluntly puts it, was that "not only small-scale entrepreneurs felt extremely uneasy, but the public at large was disgusted [*taoyan*] with the workers."[109] Astonishingly, the Communist organizers conceded that while the proposal to restrict the labor movement might have stemmed from the "right wing" of the Guomindang, it could also in fact represent the "public opinion" (*gongzhong yulun*) of Guangdong.[110]

In their conclusion, the Communist labor organizers warned that the Council of Workers' Deputies (CWD), the umbrella labor organization, was a purely political creation. "Any union wishing to establish itself can only do so after inspection [by the council]; they have no choice but to join the CWD. The CWD is thus not the product of our work [in the labor movement]. Instead its existence is dependent on our authority in the government," the cadres wrote, "if the right wing of the Guomindang should hold sway . . . we will lose immediately our authority to lead the CWD."[111] Many of the unions would simply dissolve, the authors suggested (prophetically, as it turned out) if there was a change in the direction of the government. The apparent success in unionization, in short, was due less to a genuine reordering of the laboring world than to the organizers' ability to set the political agenda. Too many battles had been fought in the offices instead of on the shop floor. Since the movement lacked firm organizational foundations, the cadres remarked wistfully, from then on more work must be done among the grass roots of the working population.[112]

Even if one considers the report as in part a self-serving exercise of the local Communist cadres to cover up their incompetence or mistakes in organizing the workers, it is nonetheless clear that, contrary to the initial belief of the elites, the creation of representative collectivities such as unions did not in itself entail unity, much less the successful forging of a class. For the workers, this period of official support of their activities had undoubtedly brought concrete benefits. A partial survey of conflicts between employers and workers in Canton between 1923 and 1933, for instance, reveals that after two years of limited activity, there was a sharp rise in disputes between 1925–27, during the height of the prolabor policies. A precipitous fall in the number of cases then followed, indicating that the fortune of labor was indeed closely tied to the political ebb and flow of the time.[113] It is also surely not mere coincidence that while the wage index lagged consistently behind the wholesale price index in Canton during the so-called golden age of Chinese industries in the post–World War I years, it suddenly surged ahead, again, from about 1925 to 1927. Such gains, however, did not turn the workers into a disciplined segment which might constitute the basis of a cohesive society. Instead, as the elites learned, the establishment of the veneer of a formal organizational structure meant little in terms of the daily management and control of the unions and their constituents.

When Liang Qichao wrote the article "Propertyless Class and Unemployed Class" (*Wuchan jieji yu wuye jieji*) in 1925, he was expressing a sentiment that was increasingly pervasive in China at the time. Liang mocked the curious phenomenon in which a rash of official representative associations, the so-called mass organizations, had been established in the name of workers, merchants, peasants, and so on, even though they were often little more than the invention of the political elites. He even repeated a widely circulated (and probably apocryphal) story of a bespectacled, westernized young intellectual in Shanghai, who cursed, kicked, and beat a rickshaw puller with his cane in full public view for not getting him to a labor solidarity meeting on time.[114]

The reason for the phenomenon described by Liang, odd as it might seem, was not difficult to fathom. As the governing elites saw it, the mobilization of the different segments or classes of people, as represented by their respective organs, was key to their enterprise. These organizations were to be the foundation of a disciplined society-and-nation. If many of these officially endorsed associations failed to generate the kind of mass support anticipated, the problem, according to the elites, lay not with their own vision of the working of society but with the people themselves. The latter were often

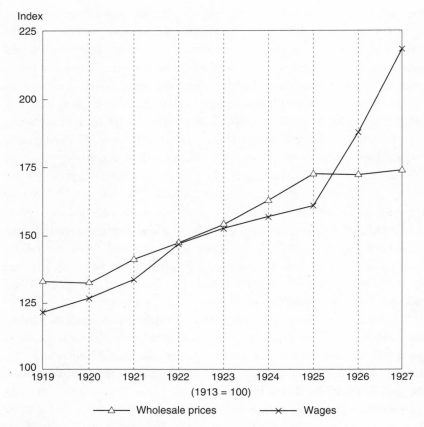

Wholesale Price and Wage Indexes for Canton, 1919–1927

said to be narrow in their outlook, hampered by their petty concerns and parochial ties. Those who, wittingly or otherwise, challenged or resisted the elites' attempts to reconfigure the social realm were invariably castigated as backward or worse. At the same time, having embraced and disseminated the notion that the people, in the form of an organic social body, was the entity from which the government derived its legitimacy, the latter's viability was now contingent on its ability to demonstrate social support. Thus not only was continual mobilization of its constituents essential, any tension within the social realm must also be repressed or domesticated. And there was tension aplenty in Canton of the mid-1920s.

CHAPTER FIVE

The Riddle of Mobilization

> Today, following the union of people and government, one
> can no longer be neutral . . . you gentlemen must be deter-
> mined, must be asked to have faith in the revolution. . . .
> For humankind to have progress, we cannot but get rid of
> the obstacles opposing progress. [This process of] getting
> rid of the obstacles is revolution.
>
> — SUN YAT-SEN, 1924[1]

In early 1926, an American journalist, Hallett Abend, arrived in Canton. Like many other visitors to the city in this period, Abend was struck by the apparent sense of purposefulness among its inhabitants. "A great and an ancient people was rising in resentment and in violence;" Abend wrote, "something portentous was taking form, for good or ill, that could not be quelled." He found Canton filled with "vivid life" and "stirring purpose." "There was," he added, "vitality and endeavor."[2] Indeed, the course of events in Canton had taken some rather dramatic turns in the latter half of 1925. A local demonstration in late June of that year, which ended with British and French soldiers firing upon a mostly unarmed crowd, convulsed the city. Coming shortly on the heels of the May Thirtieth incident in Shanghai, of which more will follow, the incident reinvigorated the beleaguered Guomindang-led government. Seizing the opportunity, the Guomindang, with its Communist allies, harnessed the force of popular resentment and translated it into an anti-imperialist crusade, as symbolized by the Canton-

Hongkong Strike of 1925–26. Meanwhile, the Guomindang also formally established a National Government (*Guomin zhengfu*) in Canton in July 1925, with the avowed objectives of forging China into a modern nation and of liberating it by force from imperialism and warlordism. Its leaders spoke the language of mobilization, that is to say, of the awakening (*juewu*) and the movement (*yundong*) of the people. Society was in ferment.

It is to be expected that the modernist elites should speak of mobilization in what Ranajit Guha calls "the idiom of enthusiasm."[3] Although written in reference to India, Guha's recapitulation of the lyricism with which mobilization was generally represented in nationalist narratives deserves to be quoted at some length:

> Crowds turning up in their hundreds of thousands to listen spell-bound to their leaders; column after column of patriots parading through festooned streets singing nationalist hymns and calling on their compatriots to rally to freedom's flag, people coming forward to donate their properties, their savings and all other material resources to nationalist fighting funds, and giving up the security of home and employment in order to serve as activists in the nationalist cause . . . mobilization [was depicted] as that integrated will of the people which had presumably overcome the divisive effects of caste, class, gender and regional interests in its drive to forge the unity of the nation.[4]

The enduring image was that the populace, once aroused by their leaders, would simply coalesce as a force behind them. They would come together as an expression of the will of the nation. The fact that the people, once mobilized into political action, might actually subvert the intents of the mobilizers through the very act of organizing themselves was conveniently elided in such a portrayal. More importantly, by insisting upon mobilization as a matter of raising the consciousness of and organizing a largely inert mass of constituents, the elites drained the process of, again as Guha puts it, "the very real tension between force and consent."[5] They obscured, in other words, the disciplinary aspects of mobilization. Thus in the case of China, it was not that the Guomindang-led government faced a simple dichotomy between mobilization and control in terms of its strategy, as some scholars suggest.[6] Rather, it was that the process of mobilization itself was in many respects a disciplinary exercise. The social foundationalism of the Guomindang-led government meant that it would inevitably have to negotiate such tension in its mobilization of society.

As an illustration one can turn briefly to the May Day rally in Canton in 1925. Public display of solidarity was, of course, a ritual central to the mobilization process. It was a festive moment, with the sea of flags and banners, the imposing twenty-foot-high podium, and the cacophony of chanting and drumming from the crowd. Caught in the midst of such a spectacle, as a reporter discovered, one could not but be overwhelmed by the force of the occasion which generated a certain singular (*teyi*) feeling within the participants.[7] But it was also a carefully choreographed celebration, as it masked much of the disciplinary work which was conducted away from public view: the identification and demarcation of the various segments of constituents, the use of directed education and the controlled dissemination of information, the strategic allocation of organizers, and, last but not least, the selective deployment of coercive tactics.

Depending on one's perspective, then, the process of mobilization served either to impose the will of the elites on the people by dissolving the immediacy of popular political participation,[8] or to give organized direction to the often inchoate political expressions of the populace. It is indubitable, however, that for mobilization to be effective, the mobilizers had to tread a very fine line between the emancipatory and the disciplinary sides of the exercise. For social support to be demonstrated, the people had to be drawn into the political process. The very unpredictability inherent in such a democratization, however, also needed to be managed and brought under control. The mobilized had to appear to be organized and active participants for the cause. New political space was carved, then, even as the social realm was increasingly subjected to the intervention of the governing elites in the name of discipline and cohesion.

In the Canton of 1925, conditions were further complicated by the relatively weak position in which the Guomindang-led government found itself. The government was eager to play an instrumental role in staging the Canton-Hongkong Strike. In organizing the different classes of constituents for the anti-imperialist cause, it hoped to turn the strike into an emblem of support from society. There were government-sponsored rallies and demonstrations as well as financial and other material help for the strikers. Above all, the administration assisted the strikers in establishing their own organizational structure: the Strike Committee and the armed pickets. But there was tension between the government and the strikers from the beginning. It did not take long for the strike organization to become an alternative locus of power within the city; an organ which the government could neither dispense with nor control.[9] Even the strike's chief supporter, the Communist Party, conceded that its cadres could no longer effectively keep the strikers in line. The strike organization became increasingly defiant of the government. Within this context the Guomindang became increasingly dominated by its own military, as signaled by the emergence of Chiang Kai-shek, the head of the Whampoa Academy, from relative obscurity to become the most visible figure in Canton in the latter half of 1925.

The subsequent military crackdown on the strikers was achieved only at a significant cost. The strike organization, however unruly or even unpopular at times, was supposed to be the societal embodiment of the anti-imperialist struggle. Its inception in 1925 was said to be a moment of the coming together of society for the cause of the nation. By undermining the strike organization, the government exposed the tension within the mobilization process, revealing the fissures within the social body to the public gaze. Discipline was restored only with the use of overt coercion. For the elites, "the idiom of enthusiasm" was increasingly replaced by the language of military regimen. Shortly thereafter the journalist Abend noticed a subtle but important change in his surroundings: the gradual dissipation of the air of surging purpose among the people of Canton. At the end of June 1926, on the eve of the launching of the Northern Expedition by the Guomindang, a moment when one might expect popular emotions to be running high, Abend described Canton as "a squeezed lemon. All the juice and flavor was gone. It was a city of apathy."[10]

THE POLITICS OF MOBILIZATION

Strictly speaking, the label "Canton-Hongkong Strike" (*shenggang dabagong*) for the event which lasted from June 1925 to November 1926 is something of a misnomer. The strike was in fact a walkout by Chinese workers in the British colony of Hong Kong. At its height more than 100,000 workers left their jobs.[11] Perhaps just over two-thirds of them returned to their native counties in Guangdong while the rest assembled in Canton with the material support of the Guomindang-led government.[12] The strike culminated in the severing of the hitherto close economic relationship between the two cities. The workers in Canton itself (with the exception of a small minority from the foreign enclave of Shameen), however, were not actively involved in the strike.[13] But they did provide considerable support, at least at the beginning, to the strikers.

The strike was initially called as a response to a shooting incident on May 30, 1925, in Shanghai, which led to a series of antiforeign protests around the country.[14] Those events, which have since been collectively canonized as the May Thirtieth Movement, have often been credited as a critical turning point for the fortune of the Guomindang and its government in Canton. It all started on May 15, when a worker named Gu Zhenghong, reportedly a Communist, was killed by a Japanese foreman in the course of a dispute at the Shanghai Nagai Wata Mills. The killing, which once again evoked the specter of imperialist domination, created a stir in the city.[15] A demonstration was held on May 30 to protest both the death of Gu and foreign privilege in general. As the crowd of perhaps two thousand, the majority of whom were students, gathered outside the Laozha Police Station on the famous Nanjing Road within the International Settlement, they were fired upon by a detachment of Sikh and Chinese constables under the command of a British officer. The result was eleven dead and some twenty injured.[16]

Unlike in similar incidents in the past, however, technological advances had by then made it possible for the images of the tragedy to be reproduced ad infinitum. The corpses of the martyrs and the funeral processions, the blood on the pavements, the sufferings of the injured, the commotion of the crowd and the landing of British troops in a show of force were all carefully captured by a Chinese crew in a documentary film. It was then run as a lead-in for the featured movie in cinemas in Shanghai (outside the International Settlement) and probably elsewhere. The film, entitled "The May Thirtieth Tide in Shanghai" (*Wusa Huchao*), included scenes such as close-up shots of a surgically extracted bullet held in the palm of a physician, accompanied by a caustic caption describing it as "an endowment of imperialism" (*diguo zhuyi de enci*).[17] In the major urban centers, the air was filled with repeated calls for an anti-imperialist struggle by all oppressed classes in China.

The immediate impact of the May Thirtieth incident on Canton, however, was tempered by another turn of local events. In early June, the metropolis was a battlefield between the Guomindang armies and rebel forces. Taking advantage of the fact that units loyal to the government were engaged in campaigns against the remnants of Chen Jiongming's forces in eastern Guangdong, the militarists Yang Ximin and Liu Zhenhuan of the so-called guest armies attempted to stage a coup in mid-May.[18] The insurgency was eventually put down on June 12 after loyal troops fought their way back to Canton. Even though the Russian adviser Cherepanov was correct in saying that "the Guangzhou [Canton] government had probably never enjoyed such solid support" as it did in its fight against the rebels, the challenge underlined the vulnerability of the Guomindang's position in its own backyard.[19] The popular enthusiasm also stemmed more from a widespread hatred of the oppressive outsiders—Yang and Liu being natives of Yunnan and Guangxi respectively—than from any lasting solidarity with the government. In fact, the vendetta against extraprovincials went to such an extreme following the rebels' defeat that the government had to intervene to halt a minipogrom, and to restrain local toughs from their random slaughtering of people with extraprovincial accents.[20]

The government's position in Canton at the time of the eruption following the May Thirtieth incident was thus rather precarious. Its sense of crisis was undoubtedly accentuated by the recent death of Sun Yat-sen. Sun left Canton in mid-November 1924 to head north for yet another attempt to negotiate with the northern militarists. He became, however, seriously ill, was bedridden by December, and passed away in Peking on March 12 at the age of 59. Sun's death deprived the Guomindang-led government of not only its animating and unifying force but also its dominant public face. However embattled in his final days, Sun, as the founder of the Guomindang, had always accorded his party a certain authority which could be traced back to his days as a pivotal figure in the republican movement of the late Qing. Indeed, shortly after his death, an editorial appeared in the semiofficial *Republican Daily*, suggesting that Sun be made into a "revolutionary god" (*geming zhi shen*) for the nation. Temples and lineage halls were the "symbol" (*xiangzheng*) of the collective life of the past, the author wrote, but they had been rendered useless in this age of "statism" (*guojia zhuyi*). Was it thus not dangerous, he asked rhetorically, that the people in this new age were deprived of a symbol with which to identify and rally around? A shrine should hence be created as a modern temple for the newly deified Sun. "Love the father of your nation just like your ancestors!" the author ended by exhorting the readers "to worship the revolutionary god just like the gods of the past!"[21]

The importance of Sun's symbolism aside, in view of the political makeup of the government in Canton in the mid-1920s, even more significant was the fact that Sun had also been responsible for pushing through the pact with the Soviets and the Chinese Communists over the vocal objections of some of his followers.[22] His death thus not only ignited a new contest for power within the Guomindang, but also aroused uncertainties regarding the future direction of the government and its project. The governmental reins, meanwhile, were supposed to be held by a triumvirate of Sun's closest followers—Hu Hanmin, Wang Jingwei, and Liao Zhongkai. Of the three, Hu was known to have reservations about the prolabor policies of the government as well as the strong influence of the Communists in Canton, while Liao was their most vocal supporter.

The political instability in Canton was made even more evident by the revelation that the troops which had just saved the regime from the rebels still remained to be reorganized into a unitary force.[23] They were, in any event, soon to be sent off to continue their task of consolidating control over the rest of the province. Threatened with rebellion and conscious of the faltering support for the government, the Guomindang administration was quick to try to reassure the inhabitants of the city that reform would be forthcoming. Editorials in the *Republican Daily* soon carried a series of articles of self-criticism. Promises were made in June that the many miscellaneous forms of taxation, particularly levies imposed upon daily necessities such as sugar and wheat, would be abolished. The widely loathed Bureau of Guarantee of People's Properties, whose operation undoubtedly contributed to the Merchant Corps incident, was closed. Censorship of news was to be rescinded.[24]

It is within this context that the role of the Guomindang in the Canton-Hongkong Strike must be grasped. During the rebellion of the guest armies, some labor organizers from Canton had made their way to Hong Kong to ascertain the conditions there. Despite their low expectations, they were pleasantly surprised to find that several local unions, notably those with workers employed by foreign enterprises, actually expressed willingness to go on strike as a gesture of solidarity with the protests in Shanghai.[25] Following the defeat of the rebels, therefore, the labor organizers immediately tried to organize a strike in Hong Kong against the British administration. There were, however, two problems. First, even those initial backers of the effort in Hong Kong voiced their uneasiness over the issue of the livelihood of the workers during the strike. Second, of particular concern to the organizers was the attitude of the stevedores and longshoremen, whose support was crucial if the strike was to have a definitive impact on Hong Kong.

The stevedores had several unions, the largest of which, the Tongde, claimed a total membership of about ten thousand. Then there was the Jixian, the Hong Kong branch of which commanded a following of another three to four thousand. There were still other smaller labor associations among the longshoremen. To bring the economic life of the port of Hong Kong to a halt, the participation of these workers was critical. The organizers had spent quite a bit of effort negotiating with the Tongde in early June, but the response of its leadership was lukewarm at best. The reservations of the stevedores stemmed to a significant extent from the potential cost of the strike, as they were reluctant to use their own funds for the purpose.[26]

The position of the post-Sun government in Canton was thus of crucial importance. With the example of the Hongkong Seamen's Strike of 1922, even those within the government who were most wary of worker militancy, such as Hu Hanmin, must have recognized the potential lifting effect of such a political strike on their tottering fortunes and authority. Accordingly, assurance of assistance from the government was granted by Hu and Liao Zhongkai on June 14.[27] The promise of sustenance from the Guomindang-led government eradicated the final obstacle to the strike. On June 19, workers began to leave their jobs in the colony and to head toward the border in throngs. Two days later labor leaders in Hong Kong issued a list of primarily political demands to the colonial government: freedom of assembly, speech, publication, and strike; equality before the law for Chinese and non-Chinese; the granting of electoral rights to Chinese workers; and the elimination of mandatory residential segregation.[28] A Communist internal report puts the number of strikers gathered in Canton at 37,000 (excluding those who had returned to other parts of the province).[29] They were joined by most of the two thousand Chinese service employees from the foreign enclave of Shameen in Canton. The largest contingent of strikers consisted of seamen and stevedores.

Although there were undoubtedly pressure tactics from the labor organizers, Governor Stubbs's observation that "except for intimidation there would be no strike" merely revealed his characteristic obstinacy.[30] While it could hardly be described as spontaneous, the strike, once commenced, took on a certain momentum of its own. Even workers who were still organized in the old-style guild (such as the shipyard workers) and many nonunionized laborers joined the walkout, apparently without direction from the strike leadership.[31] Still, it was a local replay of the May Thirtieth incident which provided the critical impetus for the strike.

As another show of solidarity, the city was set, on June 23, for an anti-imperialist demonstration. Tens of thousands (estimates vary from twenty to seventy thousand) of students and workers turned up for an assembly at a parade ground in the eastern section of the city at midday.[32] After a series of speeches were given by various government luminaries, a procession was formed, with the demonstrators carefully identified and divided by social segment or class, to march through the heart of the city. At the very end of the contingent were about two to three thousand soldiers and Whampoa cadets, some of whom were armed. Although the rally was orderly, emotions clearly ran high that day. It was a festival of social solidarity, a celebration of the coming together of society against the imperialists. The crowd was chanting enthusiastically as placards and flags flew in the air, displaying slogans such as "Down with imperialism" and "Abolish extraterritoriality." The demonstration was to end with a protest parade along a stretch to the west of the Bund about 50 yards across from the island of Shameen, which housed the foreign settlement. For its part, the foreign community had sealed off all access to the three-thousand-foot-long by one-thousand-foot-wide area of the island. The area was also fortified with sandbags and barbed wire entanglements behind which both British and French marines as well as volunteers were deployed. With the shadow of the May Thirtieth incident looming in the background, both sides seem to have been bracing for trouble. In doing so, they ensured that it would occur.

By about 2:40 P.M., most of the demonstrators had already marched past Shakee Road across from Shameen when the column of cadets approached. Exactly what happened next will perhaps never be known. Nor is the dispute in the final analysis particularly significant. Each side, needless to say, accused the other of first opening fire. What is consequential is that the exchange resulted in at least 52 deaths and 117 wounded on the Chinese side.[33]

The student segment of the procession marching along the Bund during the June 23, 1925, demonstration.

Flags and banners add to the festive atmosphere of an "anti-imperialist" rally in Canton in June 1925.

The fact that the marines were sheltered behind sandbags clearly gave them an advantage over the Chinese scrambling for cover, and the British and French marksmen certainly did not seem to discriminate among their targets. Of the 52 fatalities, 20 were known to be civilians, including 4 minors under the age of 16. A woman whose occupation was listed as unknown was also killed. There were 23 cadets and soldiers as well as a militiaman among the dead, although apparently not all of them were armed. On Shameen, a Frenchman was killed and eight others were injured.[34]

The incident shook the city. One of the toughest talking of the Guomindang leaders, incidentally, was Chiang Kai-shek, whose proposals in the aftermath of the shooting included preparations for taking part of Hong Kong and Shameen by force.[35] Riding on the tide of antiforeign feeling, the government decided to adopt a hard line, albeit one which fell short of engaging the powers with force, and which was more a symbolically charged gesture of defiance than a carefully planned strategy. On June 29, the party's Merchant Bureau summoned representatives of the four merchant associations, the rice trade, and the department stores to organize the Committee for Severing Economic Relations with the Outside World (*Duiwai jingji jue-*

Some of those killed on June 23, 1925, were put on display by the Canton government.

jiaohui).[36] The objectives were to prohibit any further imports and to restore the autonomy of Canton's financial system by forbidding the use of foreign, namely Hong Kong, currency.[37] The dependence of Canton on Hong Kong as an entrepôt port, particularly for its rice supply, led to the formation of the Committee for the Maintenance of Food Supply (*Liangshi weichihui*) to explore alternatives.[38] Caught up in the outburst of anger and bitterness which swept the city in the weeks after the incident, the merchants were initially rather compliant in contributing to the effort. In any case, they were hardly in a position to demur after being accused of harboring "unpatriotic" motives in the rebellion of 1924.[39]

Unlike previous boycotts, then, the boycott of Hong Kong in 1925 was more than just a protest. Its purpose was to free Canton economically from the clutches of the British colony, and to regain, as it were, its independence.[40] A government proclamation in early July, for instance, heaped all the blame for the putative backwardness of the city on Hong Kong. It declared that the colony was an obstacle (*dusai*) to the prosperity of Canton. Although Canton might seem vibrant (*chongfan*) on the surface, the pronouncement stated, it actually suffered from the dumping of foreign goods on its soil.[41] On July 9, the thirteen-member Strike Committee (*bagong weiyuanhui*), which had been established a week earlier to coordinate the strike effort, announced, with the support of the Guomindang-led government, that it was going to carry out a blockade of Hong Kong. All land and sea traffic to the colony from the Chinese side of the border must be halted as of that date. The blockade was to be enforced by teams of pickets (*jiuchadui*) formed from the ranks of the strikers.[42]

This quest for autarky, however appealing emotionally, proved to be patently unrealistic for Canton. Ever since the late nineteenth century, the economic well-being of the city had been tied to a southern economic network dominated by Hong Kong. The dislocation of the extensive endogenous marketing systems of the Qing meant that Canton's economic links with the interior of the country, save the immediate neighboring provinces, had often become tenuous. As the Communist Deng Zhongxia remarked in retrospect, the blockade initially sealed off supplies not only to Hong Kong but to Canton itself.[43] The threat of a complete cessation of rice imports from southeast Asia, for instance, was enough to cause widespread concern in the city and to send the price of the staple soaring.[44] Similarly, the supply of both coal and fuel oil, which were crucial for the operation of many industrial and commercial enterprises, was running dangerously low despite some provision of the latter from the Soviet Union.[45]

By August, it became clear that modifications must be made if Canton's economic life was not to be paralyzed by the punitive blockade against Hong Kong. Accordingly, on August 14, the Strike Committee unveiled its plan to issue "special permits" (*texuzheng*).[46] Merchants were required to submit their merchandise for inspection by the strike pickets. Upon determining that the goods were not British products, the picket would grant the merchant a special permit upon payment of a fee. The idea was that trade could then be resumed with other foreign countries, isolating the British in the process. The task of verifying the source of merchandise, however, was not always easy. The fact that many of the pickets were barely literate certainly did not facilitate the exercise.

In fact, the merchants lobbied for the abolition of the special permit even as the system was being established. In a meeting with the Strike Committee on August 17, the merchant organizations submitted that the special permit system would only disrupt the flow of trade without being an effective means of enforcing the boycott. The merchants argued that it would also be a corrupt system, benefiting the few with special access to those in charge of enforcement.[47] The Strike Committee initially insisted on retaining the system, although it promised to speed up the process of issuing permits.[48] It was not until the Guomindang-led administration, fearful of further adverse effects on commerce and thus on the financial condition of the government, intervened that the strikers relented and eliminated the scheme on August 28.[49] The movement of goods to and from Canton continued to be subject to inspection by the pickets, and British products (or merchandise shipped in British bottoms) remained targets for confiscation. But the merchants no longer needed to apply for permits in order to move their inventories. The relaxation of rules revived Canton's economy. By early September, American, French, Dutch, and Japanese traders began to move into the city from Shameen, as the latter remained blockaded.[50] Their transport networks helped to reestablish Canton's commercial links with the outside world, often diverting goods to and from the city through Shanghai. Statistics from the Maritime Customs recorded upward trends in the latter half of 1925.[51] A British official from Hong Kong who visited Canton in December found the city "to be in a very prosperous state." "There was a large number of ships in the harbour," he reported, "the shops were bright and prosperous looking."[52]

The recovery, to be sure, should not be exaggerated. Since the Canton harbor remained inaccessible to ships above 12.4 feet in draft most of the year, such vessels had to be discharged at Whampoa (about 40 kilometers downriver) and their cargo transported to the metropolis by small boats and junks.[53] The sudden influx to Whampoa of commodities hitherto imported through Hong Kong clearly overwhelmed Whampoa's modest port facilities. Delays and piracy were rampant. The cost of freight handling greatly increased, which fueled inflation and a rise of some 30 percent in the cost of living in Canton.[54] Still, by 1926 commercial life in Canton had regained a degree of normalcy.[55]

CONTESTING THE GOVERNMENT

In the words of Governor Cecil Clementi of Hong Kong, the strike organization, with its roving teams of pickets, had become an "imperium in imperio" in Canton shortly after the boycott commenced in early July.[56] If Clementi's language seems hyperbolic, it was nonetheless clear that the relationship between the Strike Committee and the Guomindang-led government was fraught with ambiguities. The strikers were sustained primarily by the extra household levies (*fangjuan*) imposed by the government, although they also received contributions from merchants and émigré communities.[57] The pickets were also armed by the government and trained by Whampoa officers and cadets.[58] But the government's initial tolerance and support were provided with good reason, as the dependence was in many ways mutual. The formation of the pickets, for example, was hailed as a potent symbol of social mobilization. More important, the pickets' presence enabled the regime, which was threatened by hostile forces from many directions in mid-1925, to maintain control over its own base while dispatching its army to other fronts.[59] The claim made by a contemporary, that the Guomindang-led government and the pickets relied on each other for survival (*xiangyi-weiming*) in the summer of 1925, was not an exaggeration.[60]

The problem, insofar as the government was concerned, was that the pickets were not always willing to subject themselves to direction and discipline. Nor were they, in fact, even effectively controlled by the Strike Committee, which was dominated by labor organizers and workers who were members of the Communist Party. Contrary to the historian Jean Chesneaux's claim that "the strike seems on the whole to have been conducted with great integrity and efficiency,"[61] an internal report of the Communists confirms the complaints voiced in many different quarters about the pickets' activities. The Communists conceded that "illegal activities such as extortion, corruption, misuse and abuse of power [*yishixing-xiong*] were inevitable" on the part of the pickets. Worse still, the head of the pickets, Huang Jinyuan, was said to have connived at (*zongrong*) the misconduct of his followers. The result was "such lax discipline that there was no way to stop crimes being committed by the pickets even as one witnessed them."[62]

There were altogether some two thousand pickets, arranged into five divisions. The basic unit of organization, *ban*, consisted of twelve men. Three *ban* would then form a team, and three teams would join into a detachment. Four detachments would make up a division. The head of the unit at each level was usually a worker, although a Communist member was also assigned for education and indoctrination (*xunyu*).[63] The decentralized structure, not to mention the need for the pickets to spread throughout the city and indeed along the border with Hong Kong to carry out their task, meant that each *ban* or team enjoyed substantial autonomy. From August 1925 onward, the pickets were also organized into "coastal patrols" (*qichuandui*), with jurisdiction over both foreign and domestic vessels coming in and out of Canton.[64] Otherwise they manned checkpoints and were endowed with the authority to inspect and confiscate merchandise, to maintain public order, and, more ominously, to arrest "lackeys" (*zougou*).[65] Given that the accused would then be sent to the strike organization's own special court, which in turn could issue any sentence short of execution, it is small wonder that the pickets were widely feared. Echoing Clementi's assessment, the Communist Deng Zhongxia asserted that the Strike Committee "amounted to a government with absolute power."[66]

Almost as soon as the picket teams were formed, there were rumbles regarding the exploits of their members among the inhabitants of the city. With the whole city then virtually under the occupation of armed pickets, however, the complaints were often phrased more in the form of pleas than of protests. The native banks, for example, were quick to affirm their support for the ban on the use of foreign currency, while urging a halt to the practice of random searches of premises by the pickets.[67] The merchants pointed to the fear of robbers who disguised themselves as representatives of the strike organization simply to ransack the shops. Indeed, along the Pearl River delta area, the line between pickets and pirates became so blurred that the Strike Committee had to issue a proclamation stating that the former should be properly identified by the possession of an authorization letter.[68] It was a dubious assurance, no doubt, to those whose cargoes were often examined by two or three different teams of armed men, all of whom claimed to be equally legitimate.[69] After repeated protests against extortion, arbitrary detention of vessels, and unwarranted interference by the pickets, the staff at the Maritime Customs in Canton finally went on a five-day strike in

February 1926.[70] Only after the government promised that the customs would not be further hindered in carrying out its duties did the staff resume their operations.[71]

How the reach of the pickets extended beyond the inspection of merchandise can be illustrated by the example of the partial opening of Shameen in late 1925. The resumption of external trade in late summer quickly revealed that much of the urgently needed capital, frozen in deposits with the foreign banks in Shameen, remained inaccessible. Furthermore, by September, funds for the strike, most of which came from the earlier household levies totaling C$400,000, were running out. Contributions from émigré communities were also decreasing.[72] Although another round of levies was imposed, it was clear that other measures would have to be taken to allow the merchants access to their funds, if only to ensure that they would continue to supply "loans" to the regime.[73] A system of special passports was accordingly devised to enable local depositors to withdraw their savings from the foreign banks in Shameen.

To effect a withdrawal, the depositor first had to go to the bureau of commerce to apply for a passport by filing the name of the bank and the amount involved. The bureau would then calculate the mandatory "guarantee fee," set at 1 percent of the withdrawal amount, required from the depositor to contribute to the strikers. The depositor would have to pay the fee at the Central Bank, and return to the bureau with the receipt to receive the passport. To validate the passport, the bureau pasted it with a C$3 stamp. The depositor then had to register with the inspection branch of the strike organization, that is, the headquarters of the pickets. After making all the rounds to the different institutions, the depositor could finally present his passport to the team of pickets guarding the entrance to Shameen. After making the withdrawal, the depositor was again subjected to inspection by the pickets upon his exit. The amount withdrawn had to be the same as the figure registered in the passport. After he was cleared, the depositor was required to make one more trip to the bureau of commerce to cancel his passport.[74] It hardly needs pointing out that there were numerous opportunities for abuse, particularly on the part of the pickets, throughout these cumbersome procedures. Yet, despite the difficulties, over C$5 million was reportedly retrieved from the Shameen banks.[75]

Considering the nature of the strike-boycott, the fact that there was friction between the strikers and the other inhabitants of Canton was hardly surprising. According to a Communist report, the merchants were, for example, fearful of the political dominance of the strikers. They were angry even though they did not dare to speak out (*gannu er buganyan*).[76] Even the government's control over the pickets was, as a British official put it, limited to little more than exercising the occasional restraint.[77] The Guomindang-led government had committed itself to the strike as a sign of a unified people fighting against imperialism. Even though the pickets were in many ways a creation of the governing elites, the latter quickly found themselves no longer able to bring the mobilized strikers under their direction and control. Indeed, T. V. Soong (Song Ziwen), who assumed the duty of head of the treasury to sort out the financial mess of the government in late 1925, observed then with some resignation that the government in Canton "would not last a single day, if it shot down the strike pickets."[78]

MANAGING THE RANKS

For the some 37,000 strikers from Hong Kong congregated in Canton, life was not always easy. They were, to be sure, fed by the government and housed in various temples or lineage halls, but otherwise they received little income and were simply idle and bored.[79] Some joined the picket teams. Another contingent was formed to construct a new road between Whampoa and Canton, with the aim of facilitating the movement of goods and of bringing independence to the metropolis. The group was dispatched with much fanfare. A rousing speech was delivered by Liao Zhongkai on the significance of the construction, which "promised to bestow wealth on the 30 million people of Guangdong."[80] The progress of the plan, however, did not exactly fulfill expectations. Many of those who showed up for work were turned away due to a shortage of tools.[81] A few stretches were completed, but they did not produce any discernible impact on transportation during this period.

For most of the strikers, then, gainful employment in Canton was the only way to relieve both poverty and boredom. It is certainly an understatement that their entry into the market was not welcomed by the local unions and their labor force. Surplus labor was a chronic problem in Canton in the mid-1920s. A survey by the municipal government in 1926 classified over 20 percent of the unionized workers as "unemployed" (60,744 out of a total of 290,628).[82] As has been shown, violent clashes among workers, stemming mostly from contests for control of jobs and scarce resources, were in any event endemic in the laboring world of Canton. The sudden injection of thousands of Hong Kong workers simply fueled the already considerable tension.

Take the dispute over the supply of tenders for the transportation of goods from larger vessels into Canton, for example. According to an organization of longshoremen in Canton, the Wanheguan, which had joined the Seamen's Union in 1924, its members were unloading a shipment of rice on the Pearl River in August 1925 when they were attacked by about 30 "pickets" armed with rifles.[83] The assailants allegedly injured three workers, severed the hawsers, and commandeered the tenders. In a hearing before the Strike Committee, the justification for the attack given by the "pickets," which were made up of striking stevedores from Hong Kong led by a fellow named Huang Yao, was that they had the contractual right to the transportation of all shipments of rice from southeast Asia. Their representative also argued that since the workers were on strike from Hong Kong, they should be entitled to make a living in Canton. That was the reason Huang and his followers had set up their own organization, the Rong'anguan, in August. The crew from Canton, on the other hand, contended that the agreement between the rice traders and the Hong Kong workers pertained only to cargoes imported via the colony. At the hearing, the Strike Committee, mindful of the possible repercussions on the support of local unions for the strike, admonished the strikers for not taking advantage of the provisions from the strike organization. It urged them not to use "making a living" as an excuse to compete for jobs with the local labor force.[84]

The intervention of the Strike Committee and subsequently of the government clearly failed to resolve the problem, however. As late as October, the two groups were still embroiled in conflict. Huang Yao and his followers actually issued a public threat to owners of tenders, warning them of dire consequences if they colluded with the Wanheguan. Irrespective of the kind of cargo, according to the announcement, the tender owners must first clear the job with Huang's organization. The workers there, it said, vowed to carry on their struggle against the Wanheguan.[85]

Such clashes were common. Indeed, the strikers were not always the aggressors. On October 17, for instance, a group of striking stevedores (from the Jixian) was attacked by armed members of a local organization (the Bozai) while working upon the request of the Strike Committee.[86] The two groups had apparently clashed several times earlier. The local union defended itself by asserting that the vessel in question had engaged in smuggling to supply Hong Kong, and that its members had refused to service the ship as a result. It maintained that hoodlums, who did not identify themselves, commandeered the tenders to unload the merchandise aboard the said vessel. By apprehending the "hoodlums," its members were therefore merely trying to prevent abuses of the strike-boycott.[87] The real problem, however, appears to have originated in a dispute between the shipping company and the local union, which led to a suspension of work by the latter. The Strike Committee, anxious to sustain the commercial revival of Canton, authorized the strikers from Hong Kong to take over the task. As the two unions tried to settle their differences in street brawls,[88] the Strike Committee decided to impose its own brand of justice by declaring that the leader of the local union, by instigating the dispute, must have been "acting under the direction of the imperialists."[89]

The majority of the conflicts between strikers and local laborers involved stevedores and longshoremen, who made up a substantial proportion of the striking population.[90] As the Communist cadres pointed out, the support of these transport workers was critical for the success of the strike.[91] They were both strategically and numerically significant. Many of them were active in the strike organization, serving as officials and pickets. Their frequent bloody clashes were thus clearly a cause for concern. In an attempt to ameliorate such an atmosphere of strife, the Strike Committee issued a desperate plea in August 1926: "We, the Canton-Hongkong strikers cannot, first, bear to see the internecine fights [zixiangcansha] between those who belong to the same class. Second, we are afraid that the conflicts will affect our strike and the foundation of the revolution. With our utmost sincerity, we want to offer a word of advice to the dear workers in Canton: Stop fighting with each other today, secure the foundation for the revolution."[92]

SUPPRESSING THE MOBILIZED

With the benefit of hindsight, Chiang Kai-shek's rise to supreme power within the Guomindang can be traced to the particular local conditions in Canton in 1925, especially in the aftermath of the assassination of Liao Zhongkai on August 20. Liao, together with Hu Hanmin and Wang Jingwei, assumed the reins of government in Canton after Sun's death. Liao and Wang Jingwei were also regarded as champions of the so-called left wing of the party, which supported the prolabor policies and the alliance with the Communists. The impact of Liao's untimely death at the hands of an assassin thus quickly reverberated through the whole regime. In particular, a group of associates of Hu Hanmin, including his younger cousin Hu Yisheng, were immediately implicated.[93] While Hu was known to have had his differences of opinion with Liao and Wang, his responsibility for the whole affair has never been clearly established. Still, he was forced into exile to the Soviet Union in mid-September.[94] Hu's departure would seem, at first glance, to have put Wang Jingwei in a position of unrivaled leadership of the government. As it turned out, it was Chiang Kai-shek who emerged as the chief beneficiary of the realignment of power in Canton.[95]

Significantly, Chiang, who assumed the post of commander of the city's garrison shortly after Liao's assassination,[96] moved rapidly to take advantage of the political fallout to consolidate his control over the military. A group of officers of the Guangdong Army, which hitherto was a major source of support for the Guomindang-led regime, were accused, probably with some justification, of colluding with associates of Hu Hanmin in a plot to seize control of the government.[97] In a shrewd maneuver, using the insubordination of the officers as a pretext, Chiang succeeded in forcing the commander of the Guangdong Army and his chief military rival, Xu Chongzhi, to retire to Shanghai in mid-September.[98] With the Guomindang's young but developing party army (dangjun) already under his charge, Chiang had clearly then established himself as the undisputed military leader of the regime.

While Chiang's stock was undoubtedly rising, few at the time would have expected a rupture between Chiang and Wang in the leadership. In an internal report filed in October 1925 evaluating the attitudes of the different military commanders, the Communists gave Chiang one of the highest rec-

Wang Jingwei (center with armband) preparing for a rally on a typically slogan-bedecked platform in 1925.

ommendations. Chiang was, according to the report, "very sympathetic" toward the workers and the strike.[99] Chiang's position, however, changed with the successful completion of the second expedition against the remnants of Chen Jiongming's units in eastern Guangdong in December 1925, when many of the victorious government forces were brought back to the Canton area. Their return obviously reduced the regime's dependence on the armed pickets to secure the city. Chiang, moreover, was reportedly unhappy about the influential role of the Russians in the government by January 1926, if indeed not earlier.[100] A British official reported in the beginning of February that "it is quite likely that Chiang might quarrel with the Bolshevists in the near future without outside influence."[101] Still, if there was tension between Chiang and Wang, it was not until the Zhongshan gunboat incident in March that there was any overt sign that Chiang might have his own agenda in mind.

There is little agreement among historians with regard to the Zhongshan gunboat incident, a rather bizarre episode involving the apparently irregular movements of a naval vessel. Tien-wei Wu, for example, argued some time ago in favor of the theory of a Communist plot, a view shared by the official history of the Guomindang.[102] On the other hand, Kitamura Minoru, in line with the position held by most historians of the People's Republic, suggests that Chiang actually initiated the episode himself in a bid for power.[103] The always judicious Martin Wilbur, citing the lack of conclusive evidence, wrote that "possibly each side was planning action against the other."[104] The contemporary Chen Gongbo offered yet another interesting view: The whole affair was inspired by a group of anti-Communists within the Guomindang, notably C. C. Wu (then the mayor of Canton), who planted the idea of a Communist plot against Chiang in the latter's head, exploiting Chiang's suspicious nature in order to create an open break between the military and the left-wing faction.[105]

The gunboat *Zhongshan* was commanded by a Communist, Li Zhilong. It was allegedly found to have engaged in unauthorized maneuvers to and from Whampoa, the home of Chiang Kai-shek, on March 18 and 19, 1926. Whether that was part of a conspiracy to kidnap Chiang or merely an excuse employed by the latter for the crackdown, the incident was followed by a show of force by Chiang and his supporters. On March 20 and 21, Chiang ordered the arrest of, in addition to Li, all the Communist political workers and representatives within the army, including the main garrison force for Canton. Just as important, guards were sent to seize the headquarters of the strike organization. Its leaders, many of whom belonged to the Communist Party, were disarmed and arrested.[106] The corps of Russian advisers was also put under house arrest.[107] What is most striking, and astonishing to many contemporaries, was the complete absence of resistance. That symbol of social mobilization and anti-imperialist struggle—the strike organization—was seemingly suppressed with nary a whimper from its constituents. Within the course of a day, Chiang was in effective control of the city and the government. Wang Jingwei was humiliated and went into temporary self-imposed exile shortly afterward.[108] For all intents and purposes, Chiang Kai-shek was now the head of the regime.

As it turned out, Chiang merely used this occasion to oust his rivals, and to test the strength of the strike organization and its allies. He was a shrewd enough politician to realize that, as a military man, he still needed time to consolidate his newly dominant position in the Guomindang and the government. He could also ill afford at that critical juncture to be completely deprived of the financial and military support of the Russians. Thus most of those who were held in custody in connection with the incident were released by Chiang several days later. In an interview with reporters, Chiang denounced "rumors fabricated by imperialist lackeys and scoundrels." He described himself as "the most enthusiastic supporter of the strike and the most fervent opponent of imperialism." He attributed the detention of the Soviet advisers to "misunderstanding on the part of subordinates" and praised the Soviet Union as "the center of the world revolution of which the national revolution in China is a part."[109] Still, Chiang's actions clearly spoke louder than his words. He began to initiate a series of measures designed to limit the activities of the members of the Communist Party within both the military and the government.[110] Furthermore, the power of the labor unions was curbed, and they were prohibited from keeping their own armed squadrons.[111] Pickets were no longer allowed to enter premises freely to carry out searches and arrests.[112]

Why did the strike leadership refrain from openly challenging Chiang's assault? The most obvious answer is that they were caught completely by surprise, and that Chiang commanded superior military forces. Still, some Chinese Communists blamed the Soviet advisers, who decided on a conciliatory policy toward Chiang in order to preserve the Comintern strategy of a united front for the "national revolution."[113] For their part, the Soviets, adopting an orthodox Marxian perspective, attributed the problem to the Chinese Communists' failures in organizing working class support. There were only about three hundred Communists among the laboring population of Canton. Within the supposedly Communist-led Council of Workers' Deputies, there were actually less than 100 party members among the 1,400 representatives. Even in the critical railroad sector in which the Communists had invested much of their organizational work, there were only twelve party members among the hundred-odd deputies.[114]

But the problem obviously extended beyond the issue of recruitment for the party. Particularly interesting are the findings of the Soviet Bubnov Commission, whose members were visiting the metropolis during the incident. Bubnov noted that the "main shortcoming [of the unions] was that they were unaware of the life of the masses, did not know how to get hold of their daily interests, and were hardly concerned with the economic struggle."[115] He also chastised the pickets for taking upon themselves police functions which were not within their purview, and the Chinese Communists for paying too much attention to military work.[116] As modernists of a Marxian strain, the Soviets and their Chinese allies quite naturally focused their analyses on the working class as the social foundation of political power. Assuming the knowability of the interests of the working class as a discrete segment, their official diagnosis was to reduce the problem of mobilization to a matter of the want of better strategy and information, even as the multiple and often contradictory interests of the workers seemed to suggest that they could hardly be encapsulated under the rubric of "class."

Members of the Guomindang, too, believed in the instrumentality of social mobilization to their project. Unlike the Communists, the Guomindang claimed to stand for the interests of all classes. For several years, the Guomindang had classified, sponsored, and sanctioned numerous social organizations, and the Canton-Hongkong Strike was supposed to represent the successful mobilization of the different classes for the cause of the nation. The problem for the Guomindang government, however, was that it found itself increasingly unable to effect the discipline necessary for its project. It was hampered in its ability to direct, mobilize, and organize the realm of the social. During the strike, the pickets, shielded by their arms and privileged position as the bearers of an anti-imperialist struggle, defied government authority and degenerated into unfettered bands of bullies who terrorized the lives of many local inhabitants. Taking advantage of the situation, Chiang Kai-shek emerged to rein in the strike with an old-fashioned threat of brute and superior force. In doing so, however, he laid bare the fragility of the heralded new social foundation of the political order. Despite the unpopularity of the pickets, the Canton-Hongkong Strike itself remained an emblem of anti-imperialism, making visible the quest for a cohesive society-and-nation. As the people of Canton—workers, merchants, and others—watched as the military repression continued, something was clearly lost. The atmosphere of the city could no longer be captured through "the idiom of enthusiasm," as Abend noted. The cost for domesticating a mobilized social realm could be high indeed.

SOCIETY IN LIMBO

By the summer of 1926, with the launching of the Northern Expedition by the Guomindang, many of the strikers were dispatched to the army to serve as transport workers. But their treatment at the hands of the military, as testified in the official account, was dismal. A government order revealed that not only were the workers malnourished, but their death toll was made unnecessarily high by the lack of medical attention in cases of disease or injury. Many workers were, moreover, left stranded in the difficult terrain of northern Guangdong when they were no longer needed, or simply dismissed en route with almost no provisions.[117] In its decree, the government implored Chiang and his officers at the front to treat the workers humanely, to allow them access to the army's medical corps, and to provide them the wherewithal to return home once their duties were discharged.[118]

In many respects, the fate of those workers who traveled with the army signaled the way in which the whole strike organization was subsequently discarded by the government. The activities of the strike organization were curtailed even before the strike itself was finally called off at the end of September. A decree was issued in August, for example, which restricted the right to bear arms to soldiers and policemen.[119] The measure was adopted as an official attempt to reduce the level of violence in the frequent clashes among workers, although it also clearly aimed to curb the authority of the pickets. The order was probably honored more in its breach than in its observance due to the difficulties of enforcement. Still, it sent an unmistakable message to the people that the days of the strike were numbered. Then came the decision of September 30 to lift the blockade of Hong Kong. The way in which the longest strike-boycott in Chinese history came to an end was a stark contrast to the elaborate fanfare that had marked its inception sixteen months earlier. The pickets were quietly withdrawn from their checkpoints, as communication with Hong Kong was resumed in early October of 1926.[120]

However, since the end of the strike-boycott was known in the parlance of the government as simply "a change in strategy" (from mandatory boycott to voluntary boycott),[121] some facilities of the strike organization, such as dormitories and canteens, remained in operation for a core of strikers. The latter's number fluctuated in the thousands.[122] They were active in enforcing the antiforeign boycotts which were periodically staged by the remnants of the strike organization. These workers were described derisively in a British report of 1927 as "professional boycotters." "The pickets," according to the report, "are put into a uniform and are paid so much a day in addition to the 'squeeze' they can make by surreptitiously releasing 'enemy' goods, while the [strike] committee take [sic] the lion's share of the money derived from the sale of the confiscated cargo." The author then suggests wryly that boycott "is a highly profitable business conducted by a gang of unscrupulous ruffians, who however work in with the officials and clothe their actions and sentiments with the language of patriotism."[123] The fact that the source of such an unflattering portrayal was a hostile Western official should no doubt give us pause, although the assertion that by then the remnants of the strike organization existed primarily for its own sustenance seems not unreasonable.

In Canton, there was hardly any popular reaction to the end of the strike, nor indeed to Chiang Kai-shek's purge in April 1927. Chiang led the Guomindang's military campaign and left Canton to head north at the end of July 1926. He reached Nanjing and Shanghai almost exactly eight months later, in late March. With the success of the expedition and the control of the industrial and economic center in the Shanghai area, Chiang now felt secure enough to finish what he started in Canton against the labor organizations and their Communist supporters. The purge began in Shanghai on April 12, 1927. It was carried out in Canton by the local military commander Li Jishen three days later. The operation went smoothly enough. The initial curfew imposed to facilitate searches and arrests was lifted in less than 24 hours.[124] The pockets of struggle put up by small bands of Communist-led workers were quickly suppressed.[125] About a hundred of those who resisted were killed, with another two to three hundred injured. Over 60 Communists were reportedly executed.[126] The headquarters of 43 local unions were attacked, and over two thousand people associated with the labor movement were captured.[127]

As the Communists observed, the working masses did not show much reaction (*wu ruohe biaoshi*) in the immediate aftermath of the repression.[128] Although many of the detainees were released after a few days, the first protest strike, which was called on April 22, produced only spotty (*lingsui*) support.[129] Perhaps as a result of the weakness of the resistance, the government response to the protest consisted of only twenty-odd arrests on the day, plus about a dozen more afterward.[130] The postpurge government did not, however, abandon the theme of the mobilization of society. In fact, it was careful to reiterate the rhetoric of commitment to "the masses."[131] The new reorganized administration included committees on both mass movement and propaganda.[132] Yet, although strikes were still possible, an order was issued on April 23, declaring all strikes which took place without prior consultation with the government to be "counterrevolutionary."[133]

One of the new government strategies to invigorate the flagging energy of its social constituents was to design periodically a list of ten to twenty official slogans (*kouhao*). They were to be displayed throughout the metropolis in order to create an ambiance of popular engagement. The message of the slogans, however, changed erratically throughout the months as it reflected the shift of power in the uneasy relationship between the local military commander Li Jishen and Chiang Kai-shek, and especially the entangled conflicts between Chiang and Wang Jingwei for supremacy within the fledgling national government.

Wang, who left for Europe after the Zhongshan gunboat incident, returned to China in early April of 1927. With Chiang's turn against the Communists, Wang and his supporters took charge of the new national headquarters at the city of Wuhan, pledging initially to continue the alliance forged in Canton.[134] It was, however, a difficult partnership. The Wuhan regime, wanting in both resources and military support, was justifiably suspicious of the Communists' ultimate intention. Thus it, too, decided to sever ties with the Communists in July. Yet, even as Chiang and Wang had technically reconciled over the issue of the Communists, their rivalry continued and reverberated around the country. With each contestant for power claiming to be the more authentic and worthy leader of the Guomindang, the slogans in Canton became little more than a caricature of political discourse. Thus in celebrating the anniversary of Chiang's assumption of the command of the Northern Expedition, the official slogans in July included "Generalissimo Chiang is the most loyal and faithful disciple of Zongli [Sun Yat-sen]," "Down with imperialism," "Generalissimo Chiang is the revolutionary leader who provides the strongest support for the welfare of peasants and workers," and more than a dozen others.[135] Following the arrival of Wang in Canton in late October, however, there was a different, though equally long, list of slogans circulating in the metropolis. It now comprised slogans such as "To put into practice comrade Wang Jingwei's ideas on saving the party," "To wipe out those party purgers who perpetrate corruption in the guise of being loyal and faithful," and other thinly veiled attacks on Chiang and his followers.[136]

Under such circumstances, attempts to instigate another round of anti-foreign boycotts in the summer of 1927 were halfhearted at best and hardly engaged the people of Canton. For example, an anti-Japanese boycott, which was started in June as a gesture of protest against Japanese military intervention in northern China, was, as one contemporary noted, "never very rigidly carried out."[137] There was also the brief revival of the anti-British boycott in November. The endeavor, however, was really sustained for no more than ten days.[138] The British authorities, to be sure, presented their usual combination of protest and threat. But it was the position of Wang Jingwei which turned out to be decisive. Deducing perhaps from the waning enthusiasm in the streets of Canton that the strike organization could no longer serve as an effective medium to generate support for his bid for power, Wang withdrew his blessing for the boycott.[139] A plan to disband finally the remnants of the strike organization was unveiled in mid-November, just before Wang left for Shanghai for another round of negotiation with Chiang Kai-shek.[140] It was vigorously carried out by Wang's military associate, Zhang Fakui. The remaining facilities of the organization were closed down. A hard core of strikers reacted by engaging in a burst of incendiarism. According to a Communist report, following a protest meeting held on November 26, the strikers set fire to ten different spots around the city, destroying over two hundred shops in the process.[141] By the end of November, even the anti-Japanese and anti-British "boycott societies" were rendered defunct by the government.[142]

Overall, in light of the ferment of the previous years, what is most striking about the events of 1927 in Canton is surely the apathy of society. In retrospect, it seems hard to avoid the conclusion that the much touted "social mobilization" of the Guomindang and the Communists was little more than a *political* creation. The organization of the numerous mass associations had more to do with the elites' perception of the social body than with the actual nature and working of the realm of the social. As a result, with the change in political direction many of them simply melted away. When the remain-

The dead being removed in the aftermath of the Canton Uprising of December 1927. The banner on the cart bears the name of the famous Fangbian Hospital.

ing strikers tried to ignite a popular revolt by resorting to a spate of bomb throwing in August, all they achieved was to force the military commander Li Jishen to travel in armored vehicles.[143] There was, to be sure, still a core of resisters, mostly Communists and their sympathizers, who created enough disruptions periodically for a westerner to note "the sight of soldiers patrolling the streets of the city with their fingers on the triggers of pistols."[144] But their attempts to seek wider support within the city remained largely fruitless.

Thus it was clearly wishful thinking when the Guangdong Provincial Committee of the Communist Party stated, on the eve of the hastily organized and ill-fated Canton Uprising in December, that while "our strength is not great, we believe that we definitely will have the support of the masses after the start of the rebellion." The coming revolt, the committee continued, "will definitely have an impact on the armies of the enemies and lead to their disintegration."[145] As it turned out, the uprising was an exercise in sheer

folly. A soviet was established in the city for about 48 hours on December 11–13, but at a rather high price. While indiscriminate killing and looting were practiced by both sides, it was the rebels who bore the brunt of the losses. Over two hundred members of the Communist Party perished, and more than two thousand who were involved in the uprising lost their lives.[146] Destruction was extensive, particularly as fire spread uncontrollably throughout the city. Over a thousand houses, for example, were reportedly destroyed in a single district, and a large section of Yonghan Road, a major thoroughfare of the new downtown, was completely gutted.[147] The death toll was raised still higher as a result of the subsequent "white terror." A contemporary official report put the number of executions carried out by government forces by December 20 at 5,700.[148]

THE UNFINISHED PROJECT

The turn against the Communists does not mean, however, that the Guomindang government, under the putatively conservative direction of Chiang Kai-shek, had abandoned its social foundationalism, or its self-appointed mission to reconstruct society-and-nation. In Philip Kuhn's words, "[Chiang] was enough a man of his time to be affected by the prevailing conviction that popular mobilization was an essential ingredient of modern nationhood."[149] Following the establishment of Chiang's Nanjing government in 1928, public rallies and demonstrations continued to be a regular part of the Guomindang repertoire, as were the various movements aimed at reconstituting the fiber of the citizenry.

The experience in Canton, however, taught Chiang's Guomindang the problems of constructing and managing the social body. It was clear that the organization of the various segments or classes of society did not in itself ensure cohesion. Once drawn into the political process, organizations of the constituents of society often took on lives of their own, charting trajectories that defied expectation. Thus instead of being instrumental in the quest for a cohesive society-and-nation, social mobilization actually brought into sharp focus the heterogeneity in social forms, constantly threatening to undermine the disciplinary regime of the government. In Nanjing, Chiang's prescription was to lay the blame for the lack of social cohesion at the door of the Communists, citing the latter's malignant influence as the cause. In doing so, the Guomindang government sought to manage and police the constituents of society, at times with an iron hand, under the cover of a crusade against the Communists. Caught between the need to generate and demonstrate support from society and the demand to maintain discipline, the Guomindang throughout the Nanjing period was never able to negotiate successfully such tension within its mode of governance.

The Communists, on the other hand, underwent intense debates within the party regarding the meaning of the events in Canton.[150] For them, the immediate concern following the debacle of December in Canton was where to put the blame. "Canton," according to a postmortem carried out by the Provisional Politburo of the Central Committee of the Chinese Communist Party, "is the cradle of the Chinese national revolution. Millions of oppressed people [in Canton] have joined this anti-imperialist revolution. It is there [that the impact of the revolution] has been most deeply and widely felt."[151] It was therefore not by chance, the report went on, that "it was in Canton the working class rose for the first time to seize political power" during the uprising. The anti-imperialist struggle had prepared the workers to play a leading role. Years of party work in Canton meant that the Communists "had formed a blood bond with the working class . . . and knew every desire of the working masses."[152] The failure of the uprising was thus primarily a case of a burgeoning movement, led by the working class, being overwhelmed by the naked force of reaction.

The fact that the Communist Central Committee or the Comintern would defend the decision to revolt is not surprising.[153] What is more interesting is the source of the most stinging rebuke of the report's claims: the post-uprising provincial party leadership in Canton. In their own resolution, the local cadres were scathing in their criticism. Either the Central Committee was misinformed, the resolution suggests, or it was a simple case of intellectual hypocrisy or "boasterism" (*chuiniupi zhuyi*).[154] The cadres then sought to refute the Central Committee's report point by point. "Although a small fraction of the working masses had struggled vigorously on several occasions, they were suppressed by the reactionaries" by the time of the uprising. True, the leadership of the revolt tried hard to incite the masses and to stage strikes, but the people were "completely unable to rise up" (*wanquan buneng qilai*). The so-called masses, in fact, "never exceeded 10,000 or 20,000 people from the beginning to the end." Furthermore, "not only did the working masses not join the fighting, there were only four to five hundred people at the mass meetings." The leaders of the soviet were appointed by the party rather than elected by the masses as claimed. The few female participants in the uprising were not workers. In fact, the cadres maintained that many workers actually provided assistance to the other side.[155] Nor was the 2,000-member Red Guards (*chiweidui*) a highly disciplined force as the Central Committee asserted. The guardsmen were almost impossible to command during battles. According to Nie Rongzhen, who was one of the directors of the military operation, only former pickets (from the Canton-Hongkong Strike) within the guards were effective. Although many others were eager to get hold of a rifle, some simply went home after the weapons were issued. Others were unable to handle the firearms, or were prone to disobey orders.[156] The local party leaders ended by saying that they would refrain from contradicting still further other claims which were made "to deceive ourselves and the masses." They stated bluntly, however, that their own observations were based on facts, and demanded that the Central Committee revise its findings accordingly.[157]

To be sure, the harsh verdict of the Guangdong party reflected in part the desire of its new leader, Li Lisan, to purge the local party apparatus of some of its old guard in order to facilitate his "reforms."[158] The thrust of the resolution was, however, in line with reports filed by other cadres who had participated in the uprising.[159] Indeed, the resolution clearly forced the Central Committee onto the defensive. In subsequent exchanges, the party headquarters criticized the provincial branch for the latter's erroneous "spirit" (*jingshen*), but was forced either to concede outright or simply to evade the substantive points raised by the local cadres.[160] The central leadership admitted, for instance, that many of its assertions were exaggerated or existed only on paper. It also granted that the labor movement in Canton had always been fragmented, modifying its position to allow just "some" worker support for the revolt.[161] These concessions did not, however, prevent the Central Committee from requesting a revision of the provincial report in accordance with the "fundamental spirit" of the party center. The previous provincial resolution was to be nullified (*quxiao*), eliminated from the orthodox account of the event.[162]

Despite the controversy, at the end the lesson for the Communists was clear. Guided by the Comintern, what emerged in their findings was the re-iteration of a rather crude Marxian orthodoxy, that is, the reduction of the problem of social mobilization to a matter of class. As in the case of other Communist-led revolts in China in the latter part of 1927, the Canton Uprising was to be represented as a result of the sharpening of class conflict, symbolizing the widespread discontent of the workers regarding the oppression of the bourgeoisie, warlords, and imperialists. To reconstruct society-and-nation, then, society must be rid of those classes which stood in the way of the people coming together as one. A cohesive society was to be achieved through the violence of class warfare. It seems superfluous to point out that such a verdict could only lead to perpetual cycles of overt repression and vi-olence, as the Communists repeatedly tried to reconfigure the social body by force. One could perhaps hear an echo of Liang Qichao who, eager to con-struct a modern and cohesive polity, once spoke of the necessity of the use of coercion. Or of Sun Yat-sen, who evoked the image of the necessary de-struction of obstacles in the path to progress. Sadly, it was left to the most ruthless of the modernists—the Communists—to try to complete, however tenuously, the task.

Epilogue

Our different fragments of history from Canton reveal, in addition to some of the drama and texture of life in early-twentieth-century China, a particular logic that exists between the realms of the political and the social in the modern era. As the twentieth century draws to a close, this might be an opportune moment to reflect briefly upon the legacy of modernist politics. By establishing the social realm as its foundation, modernist politics transforms the political community from the province of a privileged few to the domain of the people. The mobilization of the hitherto disenfranchised into the political arena ushers in a new world of mass democratic practices. The exact institutional forms of government might differ, ranging from the liberal democracy of the West to the people's democracy found in many parts of the postcolonial world. Yet, despite their differences, these governments invariably face a similar question: how to mobilize the people to become participants in the political process, while at the same time successfully negotiating often conflicting social interests and containing the masses within a manageable rubric for governance.

It was often said in the past that the answer to the above conundrum lay in nationalism. Recent writings have challenged this simple notion of nationalism as an almost inevitable and omnipotent force that, in modern times, serves to bind the newly mobilized together into distinct national groups. Indeed, as seen through a social history of late Qing and early republican Canton, the term "nationalism" hardly does justice to the multidimensional working of the myriad factors that enable or undermine, at times simultaneously, the project to construct a cohesive polity. To ask, for instance, whether the merchants or workers of Canton were nationalistic is to confine the multiplicity of forces that shaped their everyday experience to a straitjacket. Merchants actively participated in national construction and antiforeign boycotts, and yet turned against a government espousing anti-imperialism as its core political platform. Workers took the lead in rallying support in the struggles against foreign oppressors, and yet engaged in a seemingly interminable process of destructive behavior that ultimately called into question their role in the whole political enterprise.

By the same token, the mechanisms instituted by the government both to mobilize and to manage its constituents were also rather more layered, and were often riddled with contradictions and uncertainties. Emancipatory practices turned out to be the flip side of repressive strategies. The people were elevated to the center of the political stage only to be disciplined to become the orderly citizens of a bounded society-and-nation. The violence might be raw, and the tactics unpolished, in Guomindang-led Canton of the 1920s. As a sample of a mode of governance, however, our case study is undoubtedly representative of the productive tension generated by the privileging of the social as the basic premise of political practice.

When Li Liangfu of the Guangdong Merchant Association for the Maintenance of Public Order invoked the name of society in 1912, he most likely had little more than a vague notion of a constellation of elite civic organizations in mind. Nevertheless, the injection of the idea of the social as a discrete object—a locus of activities which were clearly distinct and often in opposition to those of the state—signified an important reconceptualization of the nature of a political order as well as its mode of governance. The introduction of "society" into the political discourse, however tentatively, meant the legitimacy of the ruling regime was no longer conditioned simply on the mandate of Heaven or checked by the remonstrances and protests of its various subjects. Rather, the regime now had to entertain the notion of representing a collective will of its people that found embodiment in society, even though most late Qing civic leaders were short on specifics regarding how this society was to come about. The turmoil and rapid pace of change in just about every sphere of life in turn-of-the-century China, however, provided further impetus for its elites to come under the sway of the contemporary political discourses of the West. They were increasingly convinced that new ways of instituting a cohesive collectivity among their compatriots must be found for their country to survive. In particular, a regenerated China must be constructed with its people as active constituents. A new social body of citizens would become the animating and legitimating force of a new polity.

To those searching for clues as to how exactly such a transformative process would take place, the answer was often found in the newly articulated fields of knowledge, such as sociology, that sought to address specifically the conditions of modernity. By the time the Guomindang and the Communists formulated their project in Canton in the 1920s, their modernist vision meant that these new governing elites no longer considered society as simply an amorphous site where people somehow came together, but as an actual organic entity with its own internal relations and patterns that lay at the foundation of a new nation. Despite their differences, both parties held that the key to uncovering those relations was to identify and recognize the interests of the various classes or segments which constituted the social body. The organization and mobilization of such interests, then, would provide a concrete way of drawing the people into the political process. By facilitating the physical transformation of Canton, the Guomindang-led government hoped to foster the material milieu conducive for its construction of this modern, disciplined, and well-ordered society of citizens. They were quick to find out, however, that the realm of the social was too complex, protean, and unpredictable to be either reduced to systematic ordering or contained within its mobilization strategy.

The Guomindang-led government, to be sure, faced grave challenges on many fronts. Militarists constantly threatened its tenuous hold on Canton, to say nothing of its struggle to establish the necessary fiscal and administrative apparatus for governance. But if the government's critical conflict with the merchant community of Canton in 1924 was driven by an obvious need for funds, its handling of the crisis was revealing with regard to its conceptualization both of the social and also of the relationships between the political and the social realms. Unlike previous regimes which controlled Canton since the early days of the Republic, these new governing elites were not simply interested in crushing the opposition. To bolster their claim of constructing a cohesive society, it was imperative for their government to demonstrate—to be seen to have—the support of its constituents. The integrity of their vision of an organic society was to be maintained through the production of a taxonomy of the body social. A classification scheme of the different classes and segments was produced: Some were embraced as legiti-

mate constituent parts of the body while others were rejected as alien elements deemed injurious to its health. And it was politics rather than, say, the
Marxian notion of the relations of production that determined the boundaries between the different classes. The violence waged against those segments which stood in the way of the government's construction of a
bounded and ordered society was not so much engendered by class conflict
(which the Guomindang officially renounced). Rather, it was rendered necessary by the quest to sustain the modernist foundational myth of the
Guomindang-led regime: that its political project was supported and legitimized by the collective will of a unified society-and-nation.

The government's problems, however, did not stop with the marginaliza-
tion of its opponents. Its primary mission, after all, was to organize and mobilize its social constituents for national construction. The workers, with
their history of organized activities, were promoted by the governing elites
as the symbol of a newly mobilized society. But the goal of turning a multiplicity of labor organizations into a discrete class or social segment proved to
be elusive. The politicization of labor did lead to growing militancy and
assertiveness among the workers. That did not, however, translate into a successful campaign of social mobilization for the government. Not only did increased organization result in more widespread internecine warfare within
the laboring world, the workers also used their enhanced political muscle to
resist as much as to assist the designs of the elites. Like many other modernist governments, the Canton regime soon learned that, for all its pretense
and organizational efforts to serve its own political purpose, it was in the end
impossible to direct or control the results of such a process or, indeed, to reduce the social realm to an easily manageable scheme.

The inability of the Guomindang-led government to fulfill its own
promise of laying a social foundation for its power was concealed, temporarily at least, by the fervor generated in the initial phase of the Canton-
Hongkong Strike in the summer of 1925. As time went on, however, the
symbolic coming together of society-and-nation in opposition to imperialism was replaced by the everyday tyranny of the strike pickets. Instead of
subjecting themselves to the management of the government, the mobilized
in this instance posed a clear challenge to both the authorities and the other
segments of society that included many of the workers. Once again, as in
1924, governmental order and discipline had to be restored through the use

of violence. But if the decimation of the rebellious Merchant Corps could be explained as cleansing the body social of counterrevolutionaries, the suppression of the pickets exposed the fracturing of society-and-nation in the aftermath of mobilization. As a result, the Guomindang, now under the direction of Chiang Kai-shek, resorted to quasi-militaristic regimentation as the way to impose discipline in the social realm. The Communists, meanwhile, affirmed their belief in class violence as the sure conduit for maintaining the integrity of the social whole.

One of the legacies of modernist politics is that a range of mechanisms for molding and manipulating the realm of the social is available to political authorities. The unsettled nature of the political order in China during much of the twentieth century, for example, dictated that the Guomindang and the Communists fashioned modes of intervention in the social arena that were often unrelenting and violent. That does not mean, however, that similar issues of modern governance are pertinent only to polities in flux (or only to those undergoing "revolutionary" conditions). Rather, governments which operate under more stable conditions have the luxury of developing, over a period of time, more deliberate and mediated mechanisms for their ordering of society, as in the case of the liberal democracies of the West.

Yet, many of us in the West (and particularly in the United States) are prone to regard society simply as a discrete sphere that shields us from the intrusion of governmental authorities or the state. The process of organizing the social realm is seen as an adequate guarantee in itself of freedom against the reach of the government, with the logic of domination and power embedded within such social organizations left largely unexplored. We tend to think, in other words, of social mobilization only in emancipatory terms: the empowerment of the excluded and disenfranchised, the assertion of private interests, the expression of the will of the common people. What is lost in these celebrations of society is a crucial distinction between the realm of the social as what it really is, an arena of infinite plurality of activities, and the constructed social body that is a product of political practice in which the governing elites often have assumed, either directly or indirectly, an instrumental role. It is the intervention of politics, for example, which sustains the representation of society as an objectified and organic body, with its own internal components neatly differentiated in terms of classes or segments (or for that matter races or ethnic groups). In the contemporary United States, the categorization of its body of citizens into various constituent parts based on ethnicity, class, or regional grouping is consistently reinforced by the political practices of the elites as well as by government rules and regulations.

Such representation, arbitrary as it might be, in turn serves as a guide for the government to organize and manage the people, who have been mobilized to join the political process. The representation is disseminated, manipulated, and unceasingly reconfigured for the government's own political purpose with the full backing of its apparatus. To say that the representation is arbitrary is not to deny, of course, that social relations are unequal and that there are genuine points of division and conflict. Nor is it to argue that governmental intervention always creates negative effects. Rather, it is to emphasize that social relations are also multilayered, ambiguous, and open-ended, and cannot be easily reduced to a constructed scheme of classification of distinct groups or segments. Thus to engage in a true emancipatory project and to reassert the autonomy of the social, it is not sufficient just to establish organizations along the by now familiar lines of class, gender, ethnicity, or professional affinities, independent of the political authorities. Instead, one would be well advised to begin by reassessing and deconstructing our conventional understanding of the nature of the body social and our notion of representation, and by seeking in the process a radical reconceptualization of the relationships between the political and the social realms.

Character List

Aiyu　愛育

bagong weiyuanhui　罷工委員會
ban　班
bang　幫
banzhuang　辦莊
baogong　包工
baoshouzhuyi　保守主義
Bi Changyan　畢昌言
boduo　剝奪
Bozai　駁載

Cai Chang　蔡昌
caizheng tongyi　財政統一
Cen Bozhu　岑伯著
Cen Chunxuan　岑春暄
Changdi　長堤
Changtaihou　昌泰厚
Chaoan　潮安
Chen Bingkun　陳炳焜
Chen Dachu　陳達初
Chen Duxiu　陳獨秀
Chen Gongbo　陳公博
Chen Heyun　陳鶴雲

Chen Huipu　陳惠普
Chen Jiongming　陳炯明
Chen Lianbo　陳廉伯
Chen Lianzhong　陳廉仲
Chen Xianzhang　陳顯章
Chen Yannian　陳延年
Chen Yaozu　陳耀祖
Chen Yubo　陳玉波
Chen Zhujun　陳竹君
Cheng Tiangu　程天固
chihua　赤化
chiweidui　赤衛隊
chongfan　衝繁
Chongzheng　崇正
chuiniupi zhuyi　吹牛皮主義

dadao　打倒
Dai Jitao　戴季陶
dangjun　黨軍
daoyan　導演
Daxin　大新
dazibenjia　大資本家
Deng Fengchi　鄧鳳墀
Deng Huaxi　鄧華熙

Deng Yusheng　鄧雨生

Deng Zhongxia　鄧中夏

difanggongshi gaibuganshe　地方公事概不干涉

diguo zhuyi de enci　帝國主義的恩賜

dingshoufei　頂手費

Dongdi　東堤

dongjiangpai　東江派

Dongshan　東山

Duiwai jingji juejiaohui　對外經濟絕交會

duli　獨立

dusai　堵塞

Fangbian　方便

fangbiansuo　方便所

fangjuan　房捐

Feng Qiang　馮強

fengqiangxie　馮強鞋

fengqijishu xishangyiyi　風氣既殊習尚亦異

fenhui　分會

Foshan　佛山

fu yu zhengzhi sixiang　富於政治思想

fushang　富商

fushuwu　附屬物

gaizao　改造

ganhua　感化

gannu er buganyan　敢怒而不敢言

Gao Yuhan　高語罕

geming zhi shen　革命之神

Gong Xinzhan　龔心湛

gongde　公德

gonghe minguo　共和民國

gonghui　工會

gongjia　公家

Gongren daibiao xiehui　工人代表協會

gongshe　工社

gongtou　工頭

gongtuanjun　工團軍

gongzhong yulun　公眾輿論

guafen　瓜分

Guangdong jieyan zonghui　廣東戒煙總會

Guangdong jiqi gongren weichihui　廣東機器工人維持會

Guangdong qishierhang shangbao　廣東七十二行商報

Guangdong shanghui lianhehui　廣東商會聯合會

Guangdong weichi yingyehui　廣東維持營業會

Guangdong xiongdi gongsi xiangjiao-chang　廣東兄弟公司橡膠廠

Guangdong zonggonghui　廣東總工會

Guangji　廣濟

guanguo　官國

Guangzhou minguo ribao　廣州民國日報

Guangzhoushi pudi weichihui　廣州市鋪底維持會

Guangzhoushi shanghui　廣州市商會

Guangzhoushi shangye weichihui 廣州市商業維持會

guankou　館口

Guo Xianzhou　郭仙洲

guofu　國父

guojia zhuyi　國家主義

guomin shehui　國民社會

Guomin zhengfu　國民政府

guozu tuanti　國族團體

hanru　寒儒

Haopanjie　豪畔街

hedaqun　合大群

Honam [Henan]　河南

Hou Guiping　侯桂平

Hu Hanmin　胡漢民

Hu Xianglin　胡湘林

Hu Yisheng　胡毅生

Huaiyuanyi　懷遠驛

Huang Hansheng　黃漢聲

Huang Huanting　黃煥庭

Huang Jinyuan　黃金源

Huang Yao　黃耀

Huaxian　花縣

hufa　護法

Huiai　惠愛

huiguan　會館

Huiyang　惠陽

Huzhu zongshe　互助總社

Jian Jinglun　簡經綸

Jian Zhaonan　簡照南

jianshangtangu　奸商貪賈

jianshu　堅樹

jie　界

jieji　階級

Jieji yu fenye　階級與分業

jingji　經濟

jingshen　精神

jinhua　進化

jinjiebukewenyi　今皆不可問矣

Jiqi shangwu lianyi gonghui　機器商務聯益公會

jiqi wanneng　機器萬能

jiqiju　機器局

jiuchadui　糾察隊

Jiushantang　九善堂

Jixian　集賢

juebuneng yu na shehui xiangrong 決不能與那社會相容

juewu　覺悟

juewu zhongli de yudi　絕無中立的餘地

julebu　俱樂部

Kaiping　開平

Kang Youwei　康有為

kejun　客軍

kezhang　課長

kouhao　口號

kulibang　苦力幫

laocheng　老城

Li Fulin　李福林

Li Henggao　李蘅皋

Li Jieqi　李戒欺

Li Jishen　李濟深

Li Liangfu　黎亮夫

Li Lisan　李立三

Li Yaofeng　利耀峰

Li Zhilong　李之龍

lianfang zongbu　聯防總部

Liang Dingfen　梁鼎芬

Liang Qichao　梁啓超

Liangshi weichihui　糧食維持會

Liangyue Guangren　兩粵廣仁

lianjietuanti　聯結團體

liansheng zizhi　聯省自治

Liao Zhongkai　廖仲愷

liaojie　了解

lijin　釐金

Lin Yungai　林雲陔

lingsui　零碎

lingtu　領土

Liu Gongsu　劉公素

Liu Zhenhuan　劉震寰

Liu Zhongping　劉仲平

Long Jiguang　龍濟光

Lu Rongting　陸榮廷

Luo Jieruo　羅節若

Luo Shaoao　羅少翱

luohou　落後

Ma Yingbiao　馬應彪

maiguo wangmin　賣國罔民

maitai　賣檯

manwu biaozhun　漫無標準

maozei　蟊賊

mimoerhao　米磨二號

minchan baozheng　民產保證

minguo　民國

minjun　民軍

minquan　民權

Mo Rongxin　莫榮新

muzha　木榨

Nanhai　南海

nianmi　碾米

Nie Rongzhen　聶榮臻

niumanuli　牛馬奴隸

Ou Zansen　區贊森

Pan Shicheng　潘仕成

Pan Zhencheng　潘振承

Panyu　番禺

paoqile ta de jiejixing　拋棄了他的階級性

piaohao　票號

pingguijian zhijie, feibaigui zhili　平貴賤之階廢拜跪之禮

pingtiao zonggongsuo　平糶總公所

potianhuang zhi xinzhidu　破天荒之新制度

pudi　鋪底

pumian　鋪面

puwei　鋪位

qiangzhi zuzhi zhi guojia　強制組織之國家

qiangzhili　強制力

qianji　鈐記

Qiao Ming　巧明

qichuandui　騎船隊

Qingyuan　清遠

qishierhang shang　七十二行商

Qu Dajun　屈大均

Quanyue shehui shilu　全粵社會寔錄

qun　群

qunxue　群學

qunzhong　群眾

quxiao　取消

renyi jiehe zhi shehui　任意結合之社會

Rong'anguan　榮安館

sanjiangbang　三江幫

Sanshui　三水

Shakee [Shaji]　沙基

Shameen [Shamian]　沙面

shangbu weinüe　尚不為虐

shangdian　商店

shangmin xiehui　商民協會

shangtuan　商團

shanshi　善士

shantang　善堂

Shaoguan　韶關

shehui　社會

shehui de bingtai　社會的病態

shehui diaocha　社會調查

shehui guojia　社會國家

shehui jiaoyu　社會教育

shehui jinhua de dinglü　社會進化的定律

shehui juntuan　社會軍團

shehui zuzhi de quexian　社會組織的缺陷

shehuixue　社會學

shenggang dabagong　省港大罷工

shengshi　聲勢

shengyou　生油

shenshang　紳商

shirentuan　十人團

Shisanhang　十三行

shizhe　識者

shizheng gongsuo　市政公所

shizheng heshu　市政合署

shouquanyumin　受權於民

shuanghao　雙毫

Shuangmendi　雙門底

Shunde　順德

Song Ziwen　宋子文

Sun Dapao　孫大炮

Sun Fo [Sun Ke]　孫科

Tan Liyuan　譚荔垣

taoyan　討厭

texuzheng　特許證

teyi　特異

tongda guanmin gehe　通達官民隔閡

Tongde　同德

tongxiang　同鄉

tongyi puyequan　統一鋪業權

tongzhiquan　統治權

tuan　團

tuoli　脫離

Wang Jingwei　汪精衛

Wanheguan　萬合館

wanquan buneng qilai　完全不能起來

Wei Shengxuan　衞省軒

weihuzuochang　為虎作倀

weixie　諉卸

Wenlan　文瀾

Whampoa [Huangpu]　黃埔

woguo shehui suoyou yingshi erqi　我國社會所由應時而起

wu ruohe biaoshi　無若何表示

Wu Tiecheng　吳鐵城

Wuchan jieji yu wuye jieji　無產階級與無業階級

Wusa huchao　五卅滬潮

xian　縣

Xiangshan　香山

xiangyiweiming　相依為命

xiangzheng　象徵

Xianshi [Sincere]　先施

xiaoyang　小洋

Xie Kunyi　謝焜彝

Xie Yingbo　謝英伯

Xietonghe　協同和

Xiguan　西關

Xihaokou　西濠口

xijiangpai　西江派

xincheng　新城

Xing Ya　興亞

xingtonghuawai　形同化外

Xinhui　新會

xinmin　新民

xiuhao gongsuo　修濠公所

Xu Chongzhi　許崇智

Xuehaitang　學海堂

xunyu　訓育

Yan Fu　嚴復

Yang Weibin　楊蔚彬

Yang Ximin　楊希閔

Yangcheng ribao　羊城日報

yanghuo　洋貨

yi tongji de xingshi biaolie　以統計的形式表列

yiguan　夷館

yinhao　銀號

yiqunsixiang　益群思想

yishixingxiong　倚勢行兇

yitian liangzhu　一田兩主

Yongfeng　永豐

Yonghan　永漢

youzhi　幼稚

Yueshang weichi gonganhui　粵商維持公安會

Yueshang zizhi yanjiusuo　粵商自治研究所

Yueshang zizhihui　粵商自治會

yundong　運動

Zeng Xisheng　曾西盛

Zhang Binglin　章炳麟

Zhang Fakui　張發奎

Zhang Mingqi　張鳴岐

Zhang Nairui　張乃瑞

Zhang Renjun　張人駿

Zhang Songnian　張崧年

zhawei zongli　札委總理

zhe　哲

Zheng Guanying　鄭觀應

zhiwen　質問

Zhong Jinping　鍾覲平

Zhongshan　中山

zhongshu　中樞

zhuquan　主權

zichan guoyouzhi　資產國有制

zige　資格

zixiangcansha　自相殘殺

zizhi tuanti　自治團體

Zizhi yanjiushe　自治研究社

zongrong　縱容

zongzu　宗族

Zou Lu　鄒魯

zougou　走狗

zuge zhongcheng zhi lü　阻隔重城之慮

zuishimao zhi koutouchan　最時髦之口頭禪

zuzhi guojia zhi yaosu　組織國家之要素

Abbreviations

ATRR	Annual Trade Reports and Returns. The Maritime Customs, China.
GDA	*Guangzhoushi dang'anguan* (Guangzhou Municipal Archives).
GDTYS	*Guangdongqu dang, tuan yanjiu shiliao* (Research materials on the history of the [Chinese Communist] Party and Youth Corps in Guangdong).
GDWZ	*Guangdong wenshi ziliao* (Source materials on the history and culture of Guangdong).
GGLWH	*Guangdong geming lishi wenjian huiji* (Documents on the revolutionary history of Guangdong).
GMGR	*Guangzhou minguo ribao* (The Canton Republican Daily).
GQHSB	*Guangdong qishierhang shangbao* (The Guangdong Seventy-two Guilds News).
GQZ	*Guangzhou qiyi ziliao* (Source materials on the Canton Uprising).
GSG	*Guangzhoushi shizheng gongbao* (The Canton Municipal Government Gazette).
GSSDB	*Guangzhoushi shizhengting shehui diaochagu baogao* (Report of the Social Survey Section of the Canton Municipal Government), 1926.
GSTH	Zhang Yuanfeng, ed., *Guangzhoushi shehui tongji huikan* (Statistics on Canton Society), 1935.
GSTN	*Guangzhoushi shizhengfu tongji nianjian* (The statistical yearbook of the Canton Municipal Government), 1929.
GZWZ	*Guangzhou wenshi ziliao* (Source materials on the history and culture of Canton).
LDDGX	*Luhaijun dayuanshuai dabenying gongbao xuanbian, 1923/2–1924/4* (Selected bulletins from the headquarters of the Generalissimo [Sun Yat-sen]).

MSR   *Minsheng ribao* (The People's Livelihood Daily).

PRO/CO   Great Britain. Colonial Office. Archives, Public Record Office, London.

PRO/FO   Great Britain. Foreign Office. Archives, Public Record Office, London.

SDZ   *Shenggang dabagong ziliao* (Source materials on the Great Canton-Hongkong Strike).

SZSQJ   *Sun Zhongshan quanji* (Collected works of Sun Zhongshan [Sun Yat-sen]).

WYS   *Wusa yundong shiliao* (Source materials on the May Thirtieth Movement).

ZMSDZH   *Zhonghua minguoshi dang'an ziliao huibian* (Archival materials on republican history).

Notes

Introduction

1. Zhang Songnian, "Shehui," 1–2. Zhang, who was cofounder with Li Dazhao of the journal *Meizhou pinglun* (Weekly Commentary) in 1918, was also an editor of *Xinqingnian* (New Youth). Upon returning from France, Zhang went to Canton in early 1924, working at one point as a translator for Chiang Kai-shek at the Whampoa (Huangpu) Military Academy. He was a professor of philosophy at Qinghua University in the 1930s, and was involved in the formation of the Democratic League during the war years in the 1940s. He was also known as Zhang Shenfu. See *Minguo renwu dacidian* (Hebei, 1991), 911.

2. Schwartz, "Culture, Modernity, and Nationalism—Further Reflections," 222.

3. Regarding the issue of territorial integrity, one could hardly miss the barrage of official media materials in recent years, consisting of reports on the triumphant return of Hong Kong to the motherland, reports on the drive for "reunification" with Taiwan, and warnings against real or imagined secessionists in different parts of the country. Commenting on the unrest in Xinjiang, for instance, the government issued a typical statement accusing the protesters of "trying to overthrow the political power of the people and split the unity of the motherland." See the *New York Times*, 2/28/1997: A8.

4. "Constitution of the People's Republic of China," *Beijing Review* 25, no. 52 (1982): 18.

5. There are, of course, good comparative works such as Liah Greenfeld's *Nationalism: Five Roads to Modernity*. Even there, however, the concern, as in the case of many excellent earlier works by scholars such as Ernest Gellner and Anthony Smith, is more with the origin and typology of nationalism than with how it works.

6. See Anderson, *Imagined Communities: Reflections on the Origin and Spread of Nationalism*. Also Hobsbawm and Ranger, eds., *The Invention of Tradition*.

7. For a fine recent example of this genre of work, see Fujitani, *Splendid Monarchy: Power and Pageantry in Modern Japan*.

8. Thus I agree with Schwartz's suggestion that Prasenjit Duara overstated his case when the latter wrote that "[w]hat is novel about modern nationalism is not

political self-consciousness, but the world *system* of nation-states" (emphasis original). See Schwartz, "Culture, Modernity, and Nationalism," 221; Duara, "De-Constructing the Chinese Nation," 9.

9. In *Awakening China: Politics, Culture, and Class in the Nationalist Revolution*, John Fitzgerald provides a compelling account of the broad intellectual geneaology of the pursuit of unity in modern China. In contrast to Fitzgerald's approach, my problematic here focuses specifically on the process of constructing a cohesive body social and, more significant, on how that process unfolded in practice and its material consequences.

10. In Touraine's words, "reason would take control of not only scientific and technical activity, but also of the government of human beings as well as the government of things." Touraine, *Critique of Modernity*, 10.

11. Hobsbawm, *The Age of Empire, 1875–1914*, 273.

12. See, for example, Liang Qichao, "Shizhong dexing xiangfan xiangcheng yi" (1901), in *Yinbingshi wenji*, 5: 44; Sun Yat-sen, *Sanmin zhuyi*, 48.

13. Tang, *Global Space and the Nationalist Discourse of Modernity*, 68.

14. Woodside, *Community and Revolution in Modern Vietnam*, 54. For the evolution of the Western concept of society, see Williams, *Keywords: A Vocabulary of Culture and Society*, 291–95. Lydia Liu has recently compiled a useful list of what Woodside calls "innovative classicism": Japanese terms which were derived from classical Chinese, usually to render some Western concepts. Just like *shehui*, these terms were then reincorporated into the Chinese language with their newly coined meanings. Liu, *Translingual Practice: Literature, National Culture, and Translated Modernity—China, 1900–1937*, Appendix D (302–42).

15. Qian Mu, *Zhongguo lishi yanjiufa*, 33.

16. Sun Benwen, *Dangdai Zhongguo shehuixue*, 6.

17. Wong, *Sociology and Socialism in Contemporary China*, 10–12. According to Wong, the Christian colleges proved to be a particularly effective conduit for the spread of sociological knowledge. Yenching University, for instance, offered 31 courses on the subject in 1925.

18. Tao, "Shehui," 1.

19. Yeh, *The Alienated Academy: Culture and Politics in Republican China, 1919–1937*, 145.

20. This line of analysis has been most fruitfully developed in the works of Michel Foucault.

21. In their endeavor the elites were undoubtedly encouraged by the introduction of the new human sciences, covering areas ranging from economics to psychology, as they promised to open up new vistas to the social realm.

22. Foucault, "Governmentality," 100–101.

23. The Treaty of Nanjing was signed between the Qing and the British governments to end the Opium War. As part of its provisions, the defeated Qing govern-

ment was forced to open five "treaty ports"—Canton, Xiamen, Fuzhou, Ningbo, and Shanghai—to unrestricted British trade and residence.

24. Wilbur, *The Nationalist Revolution in China, 1923–1928*, 1.

25. Ming Chan, "A Turning Point in the Modern Chinese Revolution: The Historical Significance of the Canton Decade, 1917–27," 224.

26. See, for example, the discussion in "Symposium: 'Public Sphere'/'Civil Society' in China?"

27. As Etienne Balazs put it long ago, throughout Chinese history, "whenever national sovereignty was divided, and the power of the state and the ruling scholar-officials was consequently weakened, the middle class flourished as a result." The flourishing of nonofficial organizations, in other words, was not by itself a transformative phenomenon. See Balazs, *Chinese Civilization and Bureaucracy*, 44.

28. As the architectural historian Liang Sicheng pointed out, while Chinese cities, led by the capital, did have "plans" under the dynasties, the planners' concerns then were quite different from those of the European practice of "urban planning," which emerged in the nineteenth century. For example, to dynastic planners, the majesty of the imperial house was far more important than, say, the circulation of human and material resources. See Liang Sicheng, *Zhongguo jianzhushi*, 205.

29. Contrast this with Fitzgerald's *Awakening China* in which the author analyzes the discourse of "class" in this period primarily through the prism of "class conflict."

30. The term "organic solidarity" comes, of course, from Durkheim. See his *Division of Labor in Society*.

31. The argument that the first decade of the Republic was a most favorable and growing time for the indigenous entrepreneurs of China has been most forcefully put forward by Marie-Claire Bergère in *The Golden Age of the Chinese Bourgeoisie, 1911–1937*.

32. The issue of boundary-making is discussed in Duara, "De-Constructing the Chinese Nation," 20–25.

33. The latest and more sophisticated version of this argument is that of Fitzgerald, who suggests that the Communists, in their advocacy for class struggle, simply tried to equate the interests of specific classes to those of the nation. See "The Misconceived Revolution: State and Society in China's Nationalist Revolution, 1923–26," 339; and *Awakening China*, 315–48.

34. See Dirlik, *The Origins of Chinese Communism*, chapter 7.

35. According to John Fitzgerald, "Nationalists and Communists, in particular, derived their different conceptions of the nation from distinctive historical and ethical conceptions of the world order within which the nation-state happened to find itself—in the one case a 'struggle for survival' among the races, and in the other a struggle for supremacy among international class formations," and that "the establishment of a rationale and a rhetorical framework for inserting *class struggle* into nationalism was the most significant development of China's national revolution"

(emphasis added). Fitzgerald, "The Nationless State: The Search for a Nation in Modern Chinese Nationalism," 90, 101. While cognizant of the Communist advocacy of "class struggle," the argument here, as the following pages will substantiate, is that, for both Guomindang members and Communists, their engagement with class analysis could not be simply reduced to either acceptance or rejection of the Marxian notion of conflict. Rather, the discourse of class in early-twentieth-century China must also be traced to the modernist idea of the division of labor *and* the possible formation of an organic social realm. Thus while Marx saw the division of labor as the harbinger of conflict, others from Fichte to Durkheim interpreted it as the necessary foundation for the construction of a new, cohesive, and viable modern social order. This latter view must be taken into account, I will suggest, if one is to explore the multilayered nationalist imagination of the Chinese modernist elites, including that of the Communists.

36. Touraine, *Critique of Modernity*, 16 (Touraine's emphasis).

37. For a useful discussion of this trend, see Esherick, "Ten Theses on the Chinese Revolution."

38. Friedman, *National Identity and Democratic Prospects in Socialist China*, 63–76.

39. As Chatterjee puts it, the nationalist discourse in the non-Western world, "even as it challenged the colonial claim to political domination . . . also accepted the very intellectual premises of 'modernity' on which colonial domination was based." See his *Nationalist Thought and the Colonial World: A Derivative Discourse*, 30. Also see his more recent attempt to retrieve an alternative sense of community which has been suppressed by the grand narrative of nationalism within the context of India, in *The Nation and Its Fragments*.

Chapter 1

1. Preface to *Yueshang weichi gonganhui tongrenlu*. Li was the director of the most powerful unofficial organization in early republican Canton, the Guangdong Merchant Association for the Maintenance of Public Order, founded shortly after the fall of the Qing in early 1912.

2. Kerr, *Canton Guide*, 2–3.

3. Turner, *Kwang Tung or Five Years in South China*, 23–24.

4. Schafer, *The Golden Peaches of Samarkand*, 15.

5. As the result of a rebellion against the Tang in the ninth century, in which 120,000 Moslems, Christians, and Jews were reportedly massacred in Canton, the commercial center of gravity shifted toward Quanzhou and the southeastern region during the Song-Yuan period. Not until the thirteenth century did Canton begin to regain its dominant position. See Loewe, *Imperial China: The Historical Background*

of the Modern Age, 236; Deng Duanben, *Guangzhou gangshi: gudai bufen*, 117–20; Xu Junming et al., *Guangzhou shihua*, 64–67.

6. As in many other centers of administration, the inhabitants of Qing Canton had spread well beyond its protective walls. Unless otherwise stated, whenever the word "city" is used to describe Qing Canton here, it refers to territories both within and in the immediate vicinity of the walled area, or Guangzhoucheng.

7. *Guangzhoushi yan'ge shilüe*, 18–19; Rhoads, "Merchant Associations in Canton, 1895–1911," 99.

8. Turner, *Kwang Tung*, 32.

9. While there was no statute barring outsiders from entering and residing in the walled city, local inhabitants clearly regarded the area within the wall as the "official section" of Canton.

10. Kerr, *Canton Guide*, 13; Turner, *Kwang Tung*, 34.

11. *Panyuxian xuzhi*, 9:11a. The compilers' sentiment probably also reflected the fact that part of the Nanhai section within the walls was the home of the bannermen.

12. For more information on Zheng's ideas and activities, see Hao, *The Comprador in Nineteenth-Century China: Bridge Between East and West*.

13. Faure, "What Made Foshan a Town? The Evolution of Rural-Urban Identities in Ming-Qing China," 24. Contrast Faure's position with that of Rowe as put forward in the latter's two volumes on Hankow. Also see Wakeman, "The Civil Society and Public Sphere Debate."

14. Qu Dajun, *Guangdong xinyu*, 17 [gongyu] (notes on buildings and structures): 475.

15. Shen, "Guangzhoushi Haopanjie he Datongjie de bianqian," 1–11. The demand for space at Haopanjie—home to the Shanxi-Shaanxi, Huguang, and Zhejiang merchants—was apparently so great that even the powerful Huizhou merchants were forced to move west to build their *huiguan*, as did their brethren from Ningbo. Kerr, *Canton Guide*, 7 and 11.

16. Xian, "Qingdai liusheng xiban zai Guangdong," 108; Naquin and Rawski, *Chinese Society in the Eighteenth Century*, 183.

17. The origin of the Thirteen Guilds and its genealogical link to the Cohong system are matters of some controversy. For different interpretations, see Liang Jiabin, *Guangdong shisanhang kao*; Wang Zongyan, *Guangdong wenwu congtan*, 177–84; Peng, "Qingdai Guangdong yanghang zhidu de qiyuan," and "Guangzhou shisanhang xutan." See also Qu Dajun, *Guangdong xinyu*, 15 [huoyu] (notes on commodities): 432; and Negishi, *Baiban seido no kenkyū*, 51–70. The latter contains some interesting information on the living arrangements for foreigners at the *yiguan*. See also Liang Tingnan, *Yuehaiguan zhi*, 29: 20a–27b. While many of the Cohong merchants were originally from Fujian province, they were migrants rather than sojourners and appear to have settled in Canton.

18. *Nanhai xianzhi*, 1872, 5: 19; Hunter, The *"Fan Kwae" at Canton*, 50–60.

19. Hunter, *"Fan Kwae"*, 40; Kerr, *Canton Guide*, 7; Rhoads, "Merchant Associations," 102.

20. *Guangzhoufu zhi*, 1879, 66: 23. An inscriptional record of the Wenlan can be found in Liang Jiabin, *Guangdong*, 410.

21. Gong Zhiliu, "Guangzhou Xiguan shishen he Wenlan shuyuan," 163; *Guangzhoufu zhi*, 1879, 66: 23; Liang Jiabin, *Guangdong*, 410.

22. For some of the details, see Hao, *The Commercial Revolution in Nineteenth-Century China*.

23. Shen, "Guangzhoushi Haopanjie," 4–5, 12–13.

24. Ou, *Guangdong zhi yinye*, 192–93; Zhou Siming, "Wushinianlai de Guangdong jinrong gaikuang," 21–22. *Sanjiangbang* merchants specialized in supplying Canton and the surrounding areas with products such as wheat, flour, or soybeans through a long distance trade network, taking advantage of the new transport and financial facilities introduced by westerners in the latter part of the nineteenth century. See Guo Zenong, "Guangdong sanjiangbang de xingqi, fanrong ji shuailuo," 56–70. For the background to the growth of the local silk industry, see Eng, *Economic Imperialism in China: Silk Production and Exports, 1861–1932*, chapter 2.

25. See, for example, the comments in *MSR*, 1912/6/4: 3, which point out how the devaluation of the local currency was having an adverse effect on the mercantile community due to the conventional practice of settling accounts with Western (Hong Kong) dollars. And with the instability of its government and currency during the early Republic, the Hong Kong dollar quickly became the *de facto* legal tender for commerce in Canton. It is unclear, however, whether the *yinhao* were supported by Western banks through the granting of short-term loans on credit, or "chop loans" (*zhekuan*), as was the case with the *qianzhuang* of Shanghai. But by the early twentieth century, with the final demise of the Shanxi banks and the full retreat of other extraprovincial financiers, the Hongkong and Shanghai Bank reportedly began to advance loans directly to the *yinhao*. See Pan Lupeng, "Huifeng yinhang yu Chen Lianbo caozong yinye de huodong," 17–18.

26. Ou, *Guangdong zhi yinye*, 190.

27. Li Benli, "Shunde cansiye de lishi gaikuang," 113–14; Li Weishi, "Guangdongsheng cansiye de maoyi ji qi shuailuo," 78–80.

28. Cheng Hao, *Guangzhou gangshi: jindai bufen*, 52.

29. A British report of 1920 stated that "Hong Kong is, for the total tonnage entered and cleared, by a very wide margin the greatest seaport in the world." The colony was described as "the distributing point of all the enormous trade of south China, and about 30 percent of the entire foreign commerce of China." See "British interests in China, 11/17/1920" (memo. by Ashton-Gwatkin), PRO/CO 129/470, 134.

30. *ATRR*, 1882: 338; 1898: 472.

31. Thus while according to a 1882 table a small amount of foreign rice had en-

tered the port of Canton, the item disappeared altogether in the 1893 chart. At the same time, rice imports from Hong Kong soared from 3,047 piculs (about 184,000 kilograms) to 404,146 piculs. The Maritime Customs sensibly began to group imports from foreign countries and Hong Kong together under the same heading from the late 1890s, although the total was still broken down into two separate columns in summaries. *ATRR*, 1882: 337; 1893: 453. For the mechanisms of transactions in the rice trade, see *Guangzhou zhi miye*, 38–42.

32. *Guangzhou zhi miye*, 38; Huang Xihui, "Guangzhoushi xiangjiao hangye shihua," 349.

33. *Nanhai xianzhi*, 1872, 5: 18; Cheng Hao, *Guangzhou*, 68; Wakeman, *Strangers at the Gate: Social Disorder in South China, 1839–1861*.

34. For a sampling of the conflict between locals and foreigners in nineteenth-century Canton, see Fairbank et al., eds., *The I.G. in Peking: Letters of Robert Hart, Chinese Maritime Customs, 1868–1907*, nos. 433, 435, 436, 451.

35. Wakeman, *Strangers*, 85, 95–96.

36. *Ibid.*, 161.

37. Joanna Handlin Smith, "Benevolent Societies: The Reshaping of Charity during the Late Ming and Early Ch'ing," 309–37. According to Fuma Susumu, it was the *tongshanhui* of the late Ming which laid the foundation for the flourishing of the *shantang* during the Qing. Fuma, "Dōzenkai shōshi."

38. In late nineteenth-century Canton, for example, state-run charities included separate homes for old people, infants, women, lepers, and the blind. Kerr, *Canton Guide*, 29–33.

39. *Nanhai xianzhi*, 1910, 6: 10b.

40. According to Smith, for example, "the benevolent societies expressed widespread public beliefs that wealth could serve noble causes and a spirit of civic pride." Joanna Handlin Smith, "Benevolent Societies," 331. A writer in a local gazetteer, however, preferred to persuade his readers by suggesting that success for one's descendants could be gained by an accumulation of good deeds. *Nanhai xianzhi*, 1910, 20: 13b–14a.

41. John Henry Gray, *Walks in the City of Canton*, 20. For information on the geographical distribution of the various trades, see Kerr, *Canton Guide*.

42. *Guangzhoufu zhi*, 1879, 131: 26–27; Arthur Hummel, *Eminent Chinese of the Ch'ing Period* (Washington, D.C., 1943), 605–6.

43. *Guangzhoufu zhi*, 1879, 131: 27; *Nanhai xianzhi*, 1910, 6: 10b; Hummel, *Eminent Chinese*, 606; Li Huichuan, "Guangzhou ge gongyi shetuan gaikuang," 199. It seems that Pan's case was dramatic but not atypical. Most descendants of the Cohong families had reportedly become impoverished by the turn of the century (Wakeman, *Strangers*, 100). Liang Jiabin, a descendant himself, disputes the claim by tracing several others who succeeded in acquiring degrees or bureaucratic posts (*Guangdong*, 413–14). They seem, however, to be the exceptions rather than the rule.

44. *Nanhai xianzhi*, 1910, 6: 10b.

45. Ibid., 20: 12a–12b. For Zhong's "gentry-merchant" partner, Chen Ciren, see 20: 11a–12a.

46. *Guangdong qishierhang shangbao nianwu zhounian jinianhao*, 20; *Nanhai xianzhi*, 1910, 6:10b.

47. Li Huichuan, "Guangzhou ge gongyi," 199.

48. *Nanhai xianzhi*, 1910, 6: 11a; Deng Yusheng, *Quanyue shehui shilu chubian*, 1: 1a and 1: 5a–10b.

49. *Nanhai xianzhi*, 1910, 6: 10b–13a; Li Huichuan, "Guangzhou ge gongyi," 195–208.

50. Deng Yusheng, *Quanyue*, 2: 1a; Li Henggao and Yu Shaoshan, "Yueshang zizhihui yu yueshang weichi gonganhui," 21.

51. A reprint of the proclamation can be found in Deng Yusheng, *Quanyue*, 2:1a–1b.

52. See Benedict, *Bubonic Plague in Nineteenth-Century China*, 133–137.

53. Deng Yusheng, *Quanyue*, 2: 1a; Lu, "Guangzhou de fangbian yiyuan," 139–40. It was likely that the group consisted of merchants most immediately affected by the deteriorating conditions outside the walls.

54. According to Lu Yu, a former employee of the Fangbian Hospital, initial funding for the institution came primarily from the following guilds: Jinsihang (silk), Sanjianghang (miscellaneous products), and Nanbeihang (medicine/herbs). Lu, "Guangzhou," 140. For details of the disputes in 1899, see Deng Yusheng, *Quanyue*, 2: 1a.

55. Ibid.

56. *Panyuxian xuzhi*, 1931, 12: 32b; Rhoads, "Merchant Associations," 105–6; Qiu Jie, "Xinhai geming shiqi de yueshang zizhihui," 377.

57. Contrast with Rhoads, *China's Republican Revolution: The Case of Kwangtung, 1895–1913*, 37; "Merchant Associations," 107.

58. *Pingtiao* had long historical precedents. The philanthropists were quite explicit in admitting that their charitable work here involved more than simple altruism, and that it was meant to forestall agitation and ensure social stability. See their petition in Deng Yusheng, *Quanyue*, 4: 1a.

59. Ibid., 4: 1a–2a.

60. Wakeman, "Civil Society," 121.

61. Sun Benwen, *Dangdai Zhongguo shehuixue*, 5; Wong, *Sociology and Socialism in Contemporary China*, 5.

62. Mizoguchi, "Chūgoku no kō, shi," 10: 78; Schwartz, *In Search of Wealth and Power: Yen Fu and the West*, 56–57.

63. Yan Fu, "Yuanqiang," 358. Also Wong, *Sociology*, 5.

64. Liang Qichao, *Yinbingshi wenji*, 5: 44. The phrase "a heap of sand" was, of course, later popularized by Sun Yat-sen.

65. Ibid.; "Xinminshuo," 12–13.

66. Liang Qichao, "Xinminshuo," 15.

67. Ibid., 14.

68. On this point, see Seligman, *The Idea of Civil Society*, 25–44.

69. In the words of Hannah Arendt, "society expects from each of its members a certain kind of behavior, imposing innumerable and various rules, all of which tend to 'normalize' its members, to make them behave." Arendt, *The Human Condition*, 40.

70. Liang Qichao, *Yinbingshi wenji*, 23: 42.

71. Li Liangfu's preface to *Yueshang weichi gonganhui tongrenlu*, 1912.

72. Li Henggao and Yu Shaoshan, "Yueshang zizhihui," 21; Wang Yunsheng, *Liushinianlai Zhongguo yu Riben*, 5: 159.

73. Wang Yunsheng, *Liushinianlai*, 5: 159–60.

74. Deng Yusheng, *Quanyue*, 1: 2a–2b and 3:1a.

75. For details of the boycott and the railway company dispute, see Ding You, "Yijiulingwunian Guangdong fanmei yundong," 8–55; Rhoads, *Republican Revolution*, 83–94; He Yuefu, "Guangdong shishen zai Qingmo xianzheng zhong de zhengzhi dongxiang," 35–36.

76. The two leaders of the Boycott Committee responsible were the *jinshi* Jiang Kongyin and the resident manager of the chamber of commerce, Wu Jieming. Rhoads, "Nationalism and Xenophobia in Kwangtung (1905–1906): The Canton Anti-American Boycott and the Lienchow Anti-Missionary Uprising," 166; *Republican Revolution*, 87.

77. *Zhonghua minguo kaiguo wushinian wenxian*, [ser.1], 16: 648–60; He Yuefu, "Guangdong shishen," 35–36; Rhoads, *Republican Revolution*, 93–94.

78. Qiu Jie, "Xinhai geming shiqi de yueshang zizhihui," 376. Qiu makes the mistake here of identifying Chen Huipu and Chen Jijian as two different persons.

79. Deng Yusheng, *Quanyue*, 4: 3b–4a.

80. Deng Yusheng, *Quanyue*, 5: 1a–8a. It is interesting to note how the place of each successive meeting ascended in accordance to the hierarchy of social institutions (Fangbian-Aiyu-Wenlan) in Canton, and each meeting was attended by more senior officials than the one before.

81. Ibid., 5: 4b.

82. There were 44 active officials, 14 *jinshi*, 49 *juren*, 27 *gongsheng*, and 7 *shengyuan*. He Yuefu, "Guangdong shishen," 38.

83. Deng Yusheng, *Quanyue*, 6: 4a.

84. Ibid., 6: 2a; Li Henggao and Yu Shaoshan, "Yueshang zizhihui," 29.

85. The number for *shangdian* is taken from a 1909 survey. Cited in Qiu Jie, "Guangdong shangren yu xinhai geming," 364.

86. The *Guangdong Seventy-two Guilds News*, while not tied to any particular organization, gained a reputation as the mouthpiece of the merchants. The *Goat City Daily*, on the other hand, was believed to be close to the gentry establishment. The fact that its editor was active within the Merchant Self-Government Association should guard us from overstating the differences between gentry and merchant

organizations in late Qing Canton. For more information, see Shen Qionglou, "Qingmo minchu Guangzhou baoye zayi"; Shen Qionglou and Lu Dunweng, "Cong Qingmo dao kangzhan qian de Guangzhou baoye."

87. Wang Yunsheng, *Liushinianlai*, 160; Shen Qionglou, "Qingmo minchu," 250.

88. The Daxin Bank was founded by a group of returned émigrés around 1909. It folded, however, shortly after the collapse of the Qing apparently as a result of mismanagement. "Guangzhoushi shangban yinhang diaocha," 1926, 20.

89. These biographical fragments are culled from the following sources: Li Henggao and Yu Shaoshan, "Yueshang zizhihui," 21–26; *Yueshang zizhihui hanjian chubian*; Deng Yusheng, *Quanyue*; Qiu Jie, "Xinhai geming shiqi," 376–77.

90. Deng Yusheng, *Quanyue*, 6: 5a; Xu Jifeng, *Zou Lu yu Zhongguo geming, 1885–1925* (Taipei, 1981), 32.

91. Li Henggao and Yu Shaoshan, "Yueshang zizhihui," 25.

92. Deng Yusheng, *Quanyue*, 6: 1b–3a.

93. *Yueshang zizhihui hanjian chubian*, 11a–12a.

94. Ibid., 18b–19b, 50a–52b.

95. Rhoads, *Republican Revolution*, 133.

96. For more information on these incidents, see Rhoads, *Republican Revolution*, 136–43; Deng Yusheng, *Quanyue*, 6: 1a; Wang Yunsheng, *Liushinianlai*, 146–63; *Dongfang zazhi*, 6:3 (1909), [jishi] (record of events) 19–23.

97. *Yueshang zizhihui hanjian chubian*, 18b–19b. Many old phrases acquired new meanings in the context of the late Qing.

98. Remer, *A Study of Chinese Boycotts*.

99. *Yueshang zizhihui hanjian chubian*, 6b; Rhoads, *Republican Revolution*, 139–40.

100. *Yueshang zizhihui hanjian chubian*, 52b–53b.

101. Ibid., 51b.

102. *Dongfang zazhi* 6:4 (1909), [jishi] (record of events) 53–60; 6:5 (1909), [jishi] (record of events) 127–34.

103. Chang P'eng-yuan, *Lixianpai yu xinhai geming*, 16. Also see the list of the members of the Guangdong Provincial Assembly in 302–6.

104. *Guangdong gaixuan ziyiju yiyuan guize biaoce huibian*, 1:13a.

105. Cited in Chang P'eng-yuan, *Lixianpai*, 15.

106. He Yuefu, "Guangdong shishen," 46.

107. Esherick, *Reform and Revolution in China: The 1911 Revolution in Hunan and Hubei*, 66–69.

108. He Yuefu, "Guangdong shishen," 46–47.

109. *Guangdong ziyiju choubanchu baogaoshu*, 2: 48a–54a. The election of the Provincial Assembly was a two-step process. A quota of 94 seats, for instance, was set for Guangdong. The registered voters were to elect 940, ten times the quota, in the

first round. Those elected would then elect the 94 assemblymen from within their ranks in the second round.

110. He Yuefu, "Guangdong shishen," 47; Rhoads, *Republican Revolution,* 160.

111. "Shanghai shangtuan xiaoshi," 86–90; Wu Guilong, "Qingmo Shanghai difang zizhi yundong shulun," 425, 427.

112. Li Henggao and Yu Shaoshan, "Yueshang zizhihui," 28; Qiu Jie, "Xinhai geming shiqi," 395.

113. "Guangdong duliji," 112–13.

114. Ibid., 114–15, 149.

115. Ibid., 118.

116. Cited in Qiu Jie, "Xinhai geming shiqi," 396.

117. "Guangdong duliji," 118–20.

118. As Liang Qichao put it, "the nation is like a company, while the dynastic government is just its business office [*shiwusuo*]." "Xinminshuo," 18. Free from such modernist notions, Chinese rebels in the past might have sought to overthrow the old dynasty and to create a new one themselves, but it would have made little sense for them to declare independence or to make the distinction between dynastic government and nation.

119. "Guangdong duliji," 128–29.

120. Hu Hanmin, *Hu Hanmin zizhuan,* 50.

121. "Guangdong duliji," 132, 136.

122. Comment of a contemporary cited in Bergère, "The Role of the Bourgeoisie," 268.

123. Qiu Jie, "Guangdong shangren," 395–96.

124. "Choushe Yueshang weichi gonganhui yuanqi" in *Yueshang weichi gonganhui tongrenlu,* 1912.

125. Liu Zhongping's preface to *Yueshang weichi gonganhui tongrenlu,* 1912.

126. Xie Kunyi's preface to *Yueshang weichi gonganhui tongrenlu,* 1912.

127. Li Liangfu's preface to *Yueshang weichi gonganhui tongrenlu,* 1912.

128. "Guangdong duliji," 146–47.

129. Hu Hanmin, *Hu Hanmin zizhuan,* 50–51.

130. Qiu Jie, "Guangdong junzhengfu chuqi de caizheng zhuangkuang," 194.

131. Ibid., 195–97.

132. The Qing first started circulating paper notes in Canton in 1909, which seems to have been readily accepted by the populace. The public's confidence, however, became increasingly shaken by 1911, particularly after the failed "April Uprising" staged by the republicans against the imperial government. There were periodic runs on the banks, forcing Governor-General Zhang Mingqi to mortgage a substantial loan from the foreign banks to weather the crisis. What the republicans did after taking over the province was simply to stamp the old notes with a new insignia and to let them circulate. Ou, *Guangdong zhibishi,* 1: 23–24; Qiu Jie, "Guangdong junzhengfu," 203.

133. Hu Hanmin, *Hu Hanmin zizhuan*, 50.

134. *MSR*, 1912/5/13: 5; Qiu Jie, "Guangdong junzhengfu," 201–2.

135. *MSR*, 1912/6/4: 3; 6/10: 4; 7/18: 4; 8/15: 4.

136. See the rather gloomy description in *MSR*, 1912/7/11: 4.

137. Qiu Jie, "Guangdong junzhengfu," 202–203.

138. Qiu Jie, "Guangdong shangren," 393–394.

139. "Zai Hubei junzhengjie daibiao huanyinghui de yanshuo, 1912/4/10," in *SZSQJ*, vol. 2, 335.

Chapter 2

1. Dai, "Geming! Hegu? Weihe?" 30. Dai Jitao (1891–1949), who also studied in Japan, was a close follower of Sun Yat-sen and was known as a leading theorist of the Guomindang.

2. Harvey, *The Condition of Postmodernity*, 249.

3. Ibid., 66. For a critique of such modernist conceptions of space, see Soja, "The Spatiality of Social Life: Towards a Transformative Retheorisation," and *Postmodern Geographies: The Reassertion of Space in Critical Social Theory*.

4. Ozouf, *Festivals and the French Revolution*, 126.

5. Harvey, *Condition of Postmodernity*, 16. The effort to "modernize" a city through redesigning and renovating its physical layout has been associated with the name of Baron Georges Haussmann who, during his tenure as the prefect of Seine (1853–1870), was responsible for reshaping a large part of Paris. See David P. Jordan, *Transforming Paris: The Life and Labors of Baron Haussmann*.

6. Sun Fo, "Dushi guihualun," 1, 13–14. For more detail on Sun's plan, see Tsin, "Canton Remapped." The compound *jingji* had long been used in classical Chinese texts. Its meaning then, however, was quite different from that of its modern usage. In classical texts, *jingji* was usually associated with the notion of *jingshi jimin*, that is, the administration of the realm. As in the case of *shehui*, this Chinese compound was first endowed with new meanings as a result of its appropriation by Meiji Japanese intellectuals, who used it to denote a novel Western concept. It is perhaps superfluous to note that the exercise of a new form of governmental power was mediated by the articulation of these terms.

7. "Guangzhoushi zanxing tiaoli," reprinted in Huang Yanpei, *Yisui zhi Guangzhoushi*, 3–16. Also Lai, "Sun Fo yu Guangzhoushi de jindaihua."

8. Sun Fo, "Dushi," 8.

9. Harvey, *Condition of Postmodernity*, 249.

10. Wakeman, *Policing Shanghai, 1927–1937*, 46.

11. That meant intervention in even the most intimate details of the lives of the people. For instance, in the words of Frank Dikötter, "[f]or the modernizing élites in Republican China, individual sexual desire had to be disciplined and evil habits

eliminated, and couples were to regulate their sexual behaviour strictly to help bring about the revival of the nation." See his *Sex, Culture and Modernity in China*, 2.

12. Foucault, "Governmentality," 100.

13. Liang Qichao, *Yinbingshi wenji*, 32: 70–71. Liang admitted that he then had access to only bits and pieces of *Addresses to the German Nation*.

14. Ibid., 32: 80. While the essay was meant to introduce Fichte to Chinese readers, Liang said explicitly in the preface that he freely interpreted and elaborated on Fichte's pronouncements with his own ideas (32: 71).

15. The Chinese compound for "class," *jieji*, is another one of those terms easily found in classical texts, and which has been endowed with new meanings in its modern usage. Philip Kuhn has suggested that the traditional usage of the term referred to social distance or rank rather than groupings, and that it was in the former sense that Liang Qichao first used the term in 1899 ("Chinese Views of Social Classification," 17–18). If that was true with Liang in 1899, it was clearly no longer the case by 1915. Indeed, following the Japanese usage of *kaikyū*, the term *jieji* was used increasingly by Chinese intellectuals after the turn of the century to denote the differentiation of social groups.

16. Liang Qichao, *Yinbingshi wenji*, 32: 84–88.

17. Durkheim, *Division of Labor*, 68–87.

18. See Hu Hanmin, "Jieiji yu daode xueshuo," *Jianshe*, 1:6 (1920), 1–18; Lin Yungai, "Jieji douzheng zhi yanjiu," *Jianshe*, 2:6 (1920), 1–16.

19. *Guangzhou bainian dashiji*, 1:142; Ernest P. Young, *The Presidency of Yuan Shih-k'ai*, 140–42. The "Second Revolution" refers, as mentioned earlier, to the failed attempt of Sun Yat-sen and his supporters to oust Yuan Shikai from the presidency in 1913.

20. *Guangdong junfashi dashiji*, 45, 49.

21. Ibid., 65, 70.

22. The old Guangxi clique should be distinguished from its successor which emerged in the mid-1920s. The latter, the new Guangxi clique, played a significant role in the reorganized Guomindang's military campaign to the north (1926–28), was responsible for reconstructing the province of Guangxi in the 1930s, and was active in the politics of Guomindang China (1928–49). The new clique's most famous leaders were Li Zongren and Bai Chongxi.

23. Li Jiannong, *Zhongguo jinbainian zhengzhishi*, 507–508.

24. Liao, *Shuangqing wenji*, 1: 384.

25. Enclosure dated 1922/3/16 in "Alston to Curzon, 1922/3/24," PRO/FO 405/236/219 [F 1597/84/10], 845. Beilby Alston was the head of the British Legation in Peking; Marquess Curzon of Kedleston the foreign secretary in London.

26. Writings on Chen tend to be fiercely partisan, as shown by two 1922 publications: an anti-Chen account by Li Shuixian, *Chen Jiongming panguoshi*, and a hagiography titled *Chen Jiongming lishi* published under the pen name "Dongyue fusheng." Other sources include a Hong Kong publication *Chen Jingcun xiansheng*

nianpu (1957), which contains a copy of a letter addressed to Wu Zhihui by Chen clarifying the latter's conflict with Sun Yat-sen, and *Youguan Chen Jiongming ziliao* (1965), issued by the Guangdong Academy of Social Sciences in mimeographed form. Few of Chen's own writings, with the notable exception of *Zhongguo tongyi chuyi*, written in the mid-1920s as an argument for "federalism," seem to be extant.

27. *Guangzhoushi yan'ge shilüe*, 73; Huang Yanpei, *Yisui zhi Guangzhoushi*, 10–13; Lin Zhijun et al., "Chen Jiongming pan Sun, liansheng zizhi ji minxuan xianzhang," 168–75, 190–93.

28. Gao Yuhan, *Guangzhou jiyou*; Huang Yanpei, *Yisui*.

29. Winston Hsieh, "The Ideas and Ideals of a Warlord: Ch'en Chiung-Ming (1878–1933)," 234.

30. Report on Southern Expedition against the North dated 1921/12/15, enclosed in "Alston to Curzon, 1921/12/19," PRO/FO 405/236/129 [F 559/84/10], 440.

31. Whether the revolt against Sun took place on direct orders from Chen or as a result of initiatives taken by his subordinates is still a matter of debate. For a rather colorful blow-by-blow account of Sun's exit from Canton attributed to Chiang Kai-shek, see *Sun dazongtong Guangzhou mengnanji*. Also see *Sun Zhongshan nianpu* (Beijing, 1980), 294–98.

32. Wang Jingyu, ed., *Zhongguo jindai gongyeshi ziliao*, 2:1, 626–29.

33. *Guangzhou zhinan*, 455; Edward Bing-shuey Lee, *Modern Canton*, 62.

34. *Guangzhoushi dianli gongsi ershi nianlai zhi gaikuang*, 5–9; *Guangzhou zhinan*, 456; Edward Bing-shuey Lee, *Modern Canton*, 51. The change in the denomination of the currency from tael to yuan was a result of the Qing government's decision to circulate paper notes from about 1908 onward. Ou, *Guangdong zhibishi*, 1: 1–4.

35. For some of Sun Yat-sen's ideas on the role of the department store in national reconstruction, see John D. Young, "Sun Yatsen and the Department Store: An aspect of national reconstruction," 33–45.

36. Edward Bing-shuey Lee, *Modern Canton*, 14–15.

37. Xiao, "Guangzhou Xianshi gongsi saduonian de shengshuai," 127–29.

38. Ni Xiying, *Guangzhou*, 33.

39. See Wellington K. K. Chan, "Personal Styles, Cultural Values, and Management," 70–78.

40. Xiao, "Guangzhou Xianshi gengsi," 131–34.

41. Chen Xingwu, "Ma Yingbiao yu Xianshi gongsi," 125.

42. Ibid., 131.

43. Xiao, "Guangzhou Xianshi gongsi," 129; Chen Xingwu, "Ma Yingbiao," 132.

44. Ni, *Guangzhou*, 33–34. The original Daxin store was burned down during the Japanese occupation.

45. Ibid., 13. Although the avowed purpose of the new municipal council was to modernize the city, most members of the government, which in 1918 was still in the grips of the so-called Guangxi clique, were probably more interested in a share of the

wealth than in the welfare of the city. By claiming jurisdiction over municipal affairs, they could then monopolize matters from the sale of "public properties" (such as land belonging to the bannermen or temples) to the imposition of various fees and levies. Functions assumed by the municipal authority, moreover, could be farmed out to merchants and others for profit.

46. Kerr, *Canton Guide*, 1.

47. Edward Bing-shuey Lee, *Modern Canton*, 4.

48. *GSTN*, 257.

49. Xiao, "Guangzhou Xianshi gongsi," 127; Chen Xingwu, "Ma Yingbiao," 132. Both stores were located on Huiai zhonglu (now Zhongshan wulu). The Huiai shangdian, however, did not last long; it was closed by the early 1930s.

50. For a description of how each street in Xiguan was characterized by a specific trade, see Ni, *Guangzhou*, 41–43. There were, of course, some newer and larger stores in Xiguan, particularly along Shibafu (Eighteenth Ward). But in general, as Ni pointed out, the whole area had a rather "old-fashioned" air to it. Indeed, Xiguan still possesses a somewhat distinct ambiance even today.

51. Ni, *Guangzhou*, 39.

52. In an attempt to reduce the number of conflicts between pullers and passengers over fares, the municipal government introduced and tried to enforce a system of regulated routes with designated stops for the rickshaws in Canton. See *Guangzhoushi caizhengju renli shouche chezhan jiamubiao*; *Guangzhoushi shizheng baogao huikan*, 352.

53. See "Guangzhoushi renli shouche chengche guize" and "Chefu changxu zhuyi zuolie tiaoli," in *Guangzhoushi caizhengju renli shouche chezhan jiamubiao*, 1927.

54. *GSTN*, 446.

55. Ibid., 446, 454.

56. Whether it is the case of a municipality or a nation, boundary lines defined in relation to other "equal" entities are essential to the modernist notion of space. To borrow the words of Thongchai Winichakul, "the concept of a nation in the modern geographical sense . . . requires the necessity of having boundary lines clearly demarcated. A map may not just function as a medium; it could well be the creator of the supposed reality." See his *Siam Mapped: A History of the Geo-Body of a Nation*, 56.

57. "Guangzhoushi zanxing tiaoli," reprinted in Huang Yanpei, *Yisui*, 3–4.

58. Ibid., 17–21.

59. The six bureaus were finance, public security, health, public works, public utilities, and education.

60. Huang Yanpei, *Yisui*, 23–24. Also Lai Zehan, "Sun Fo yu Guangzhoushi," 90.

61. Reprinted in Huang Yanpei, *Yisui*, 46.

62. Ibid., 45–48. Yet as late as 1929, the new central government building was

still not built. An official report then stated that the lack of a *shizheng heshu* had rendered the administrative and supervisory tasks of the government rather difficult, and that its construction was an extremely urgent matter. See *GSTN*, 1929, 454.

63. *Guangzhoushi shizheng baogao huikan*, 1924, 220.

64. The figure for London is cited in Dray-Novey, "Spatial Order and Police in Imperial Beijing," 905. Dray-Novey also cites the ratio for nineteenth-century New York (1 for 800) and Paris in the late eighteenth century (1 for 193). According to Dray-Novey, the ratio of policeman to residents in nineteenth-century Beijing [Peking] could be as high as 1 to 30, which, if true, would surely make it by far the most heavily policed city in the world at the time.

65. "Guangzhoushi zanxing tiaoli," reprinted in Huang Yanpei, *Yisui*, 8, 49. Also Lai, "Sun Fo yu Guangzhoushi," 95. For comparison, see Wakeman, *Policing Shanghai*, 43–59. The 12 wards were apparently changed to 40 later, as a proposal was made to reduce the number to 30 in 1929. See *GSTN*, 1929, 461.

66. Robert Storch, "The Policeman as Domestic Missionary: Urban Discipline and Popular Culture in Northern England, 1850–1880."

67. "Guangzhoushi zanxing tiaoli," reprinted in Huang Yanpei, *Yisui*, 8. Lai, "Sun Fo yu Guangzhoushi," 93.

68. "Guangzhoushi zanxing tiaoli," reprinted in Huang Yanpei, *Yisui*, 9.

69. *GSTN*, 459.

70. Lai, "Sun Fo yu Guangzhoushi," 94. For a discussion of the use of public lectures as a medium to "educate" the people in early-twentieth-century China, see Li Xiaoti, *Qingmo de xiaceng shehui qimeng yundong*, 59–147.

71. See Nord, *Paris Shopkeepers and the Politics of Resentment*, 22–23, 96. In Canton, for instance, those who engaged in specialty trades (silk products, jewelry, and so forth) or long distance wholesale of staples were less affected by the department stores than others which competed directly with the *grands magasins*.

72. This is not to say, of course, that there was not any "worker," or *gongren*, in China previously. It is rather to suggest that in the early Republic there was a new sensibility toward the positioning of workers in the realm of the social, the result of which was to elevate them to the center of the public discourse on the construction of society-and-nation.

73. Chen Zhen, ed., *Zhongguo jindai gongyeshi ziliao*, 4:1, 95. The top three cities were Shanghai (3,485), Tianjin (1,224), and Canton (1,104). Unfortunately, the definition of "factory" in the survey is unclear.

74. Ibid.

75. *GSTH*, 47.

76. *Guangzhou zhi xinxing gongye: xiangjiao ye*, 5; Huang Xihui, "Guangzhoushi xiangjiao," 346–47.

77. Zeng Yangfu, *Guangzhou zhi gongye*, 119.

78. Huang Xihui, "Guangzhoushi xiangjiao," 347.

79. Zeng Yangfu, *Guangzhou zhi gongye*, 119–120.

80. Huang Xihui, "Guangzhoushi xiangjiao," 350.

81. *Guangzhou zhi xinxing gongye*, 5; Zeng Yangfu, *Guangzhou zhi gongye*, 120.

82. Ibid.

83. Huang Xihui, "Guangzhoushi xiangjiao," 351.

84. In the mid-1930s, the average capitalization for a match manufactory was C$31,000 in comparison to close to C$67,000 for the latex industry. Both figures, however, are likely to be underestimates due to the tendency of Chinese entrepreneurs to underreport their assets. Zeng Yangfu, *Guangzhou zhi gongye*, 44–45, 124–25.

85. Li Yaofeng, "Huiyi sishi nianjian Guangzhou diqu de huochai gongye," 1.

86. Zeng Yangfu, *Guangzhou zhi gongye*, 39. It is unclear, however, whether the growth in match manufacturing was made possible, as in the case of some other industries, by the temporary retreat of Europeans during and immediately after the First World War. For the match industry, the principal foreign competitor was Japan, which actually expanded her economic activities in China during this period. Thus while the volume of match imports fell, there was at the same time an increase in the number of Japanese-owned match manufactories in China.

87. Huang Fushan, "Jiefang qian Guangdong huochai gongye gaimao," 167.

88. Ibid.

89. Li Yaofeng, "Huiyi sishi nianjian," 5–7.

90. Ibid., 12–15.

91. Ibid., 15–16.

92. "Guangzhoushi shangban yinhang diaocha," 20–23; Ou, *Guangdong zhi yinye*, 75–94.

93. Zeng Yangfu, *Guangzhou zhi gongye*, 123–25.

94. Ibid., 182.

95. *Guangzhou zhi miye*, 23–24; Zeng Yangfu, *Guangzhou zhi gongye*, 183, 204.

96. Liao, "Zhongguo renmin he lingtu zai xinguojia jianshe shang zhi guanxi," in *Shuangqing wenji*, 275, 277, 291.

97. Zeng Yangfu, *Guangzhou zhi gongye*, 145.

98. Ibid., 56.

99. Huang Fushan, "Jiefang qian Guangdong," 172–73. The match manufacturers, incidentally, were reputedly the best-organized group among the new industrialists. Zeng Yangfu, *Guangzhou zhi gongye*, 42–43.

100. Gao, *Guangzhou jiyou*, 201.

101. Ibid., 219.

102. Enclosure in "Alston to Balfour, 1922/7/10," PRO/FO 405/237/28 [F 2646/2646/10], 44.

103. For more on the nature of *bang*, see Quan, *Zhongguo hanghui zhidushi*, 121–49, 187–96. Also Zhou Yumin and Shao Yong, *Zhongguo banghuishi*.

104. Perry, *Shanghai on Strike: The Politics of Chinese Labor*, 87.

105. Huang Shaosheng, "Wusi yundong zai Guangzhou," 17–18. The purpose of

the demonstration in Peking on May 4, 1919, was to protest the terms of the Versailles treaty which recognized the Japanese claim to the rights previously held by Germany in the Chinese province of Shandong.

106. Zheng Yanfan, "Wo zai wusi yundong de yixie jingli," 33–34.

107. There were several strikes later in 1919, which were organized by Sun Yat-sen's followers who were active in labor organization. While some May Fourth rhetoric was adopted, those strikes were carried out primarily in conjunction with the Guomindang's struggle to oust the old Guangxi clique from Canton rather than in direct response to the May Fourth incident. See Liu Yongming, *Guomindang ren yu wusi yundong*, 363–73.

108. Gao, *Guangzhou jiyou*, 201.

109. Enclosure in "Giles to Macleay, 1924/10/16," PRO/FO 228/3140, 773. Bertram Giles was acting consul-general in Canton; James Macleay the head of the British Legation in Peking.

110. Li Yaofeng, "Wo shi zenyang canjia shangtuan de," 95.

111. Zeng Yangfu, *Guangzhou zhi gongye*, 54–55.

112. Ibid., 133–34.

113. "Diyici guonei geming zhanzheng shiqi de Guangdong funü yundong," 158.

114. See, for example, "Guangzhou gonghui yundong de baogao, 1926 xia."

115. Christina Kelley Gilmartin, for example, mentions "the disdain of many male Communist labor organizers in Guangzhou [Canton] for the very idea of organizing women or working with the women's movement" in this period. See Gilmartin, *Engendering the Chinese Revolution*, 164.

116. "Diyici guonei geming zhanzheng shiqi de Guangdong funü yundong," 157–58; Gilmartin, *Engendering the Chinese Revolution*, 153.

117. Perry, *Shanghai on Strike*, 39.

118. Ibid., 251.

119. For an incomplete list of labor organizations (85) in Canton in the early 1920s, see Huang Yanpei, *Yisui*, 52–59. Also Li Zonghuang, *Guangdong guanchaji*, 192–202.

120. Huang Yibo, *Guangdong zhi jiqi gongren*, 8–9.

121. Ma Chaojun, ed., *Zhongguo laogong yundongshi*, vol. 1, 135.

122. See Chapter 4 for more details. Also Perry, *Shanghai on Strike*.

123. Enclosure in "Barton to Macleay, 1923/7/6," PRO/FO 228/3140, 335–36.

124. Ibid.

125. "Guangzhou gonghui yundong de baogao, 1926 xia," 321–22.

126. Li Zonghuang, *Guangdong guanchaji*, 193.

127. "Denham to Alston, 1922/7/25," PRO/FO 228/3140, 164. On the history of the SY, see "Report on the Communistic Movement of Youth in China" in Wilbur and How, eds., *Missionaries of Revolution: Soviet Advisers and Nationalist China, 1920–1927*, 472–78.

128. "Guangzhou difang meiyue tuanyuan tongjibiao, 1922/1–7, 10–12." It is

surely not coincidental that the two summer months without reports were vacation time for students.

129. "Canton Intelligence Report: December Quarter, 1921," PRO/FO 228/3276, 391; "CIR: March Quarter, 1922," FO 228/3276, 420. Also see Kimura, *Chūgoku rōdō undō shi nempyō*, 26–73.

130. "Canton Intelligence Report: March Quarter, 1922," PRO/FO 228/3276, 420.

131. See, for example, Kimura, *Chūgoku rōdō undō shi nempyō*, 26–73.

132. Gao Yuhan, *Guangzhou jiyou*, 212.

133. Deng Zhongxia, *Zhongguo zhigong yundong jianshi, 1919–1926*, 37.

134. For a brief genealogy of the term "imperialism" (*diguo zhuyi*) in modern Chinese history, see Wu Yannan et al., *Qingmo shehui sichao*, 44–57.

135. The official demands of the seamen, first forwarded to the employers in September 1921, included wage increases and recognition of the union's right to participate in both the hiring process and contract negotiation. As they were rebuffed, the seamen reiterated their wage demand in November and again in January of 1922. Only when the shipowners refused thrice even to negotiate wage increases did the men go on strike.

136. See, for example, "Zai Guomindang yuesheng zhibu chenglihui shang de yanshuo, 1921/2/1," in *SZSQJ*, vol. 5, 460.

137. Cited in Ming K. Chan, *Labor and Empire: The Chinese Labor Movement in the Canton Delta, 1895–1927*, 291. Also there was no negative reference to imperialism in a Guomindang proclamation in August 1922. Wilbur and How, eds., *Missionaries of Revolution*, 98.

138. Enclosure dated 1922/3/11 in "Jamieson to Curzon, 1922/3/14," PRO/FO 405/236/207 [F 1496/927/10], 791.

139. While it is a modernist credo that society (and by extension nation) is always amenable to systematic dissection and classification, for those in the modernist camp who subscribe to the notion of class struggle, as the Communists did, there is an obvious tension between the discourse of class (with its implication for conflict) and the discourse of nation (with its emphasis on unity). The Chinese Communist Party was still in its infancy in 1922. How the Communists subsequently dealt with such tension will be addressed in Chapter 5.

140. Zhang Hong, *Xianggang haiyuan dabagong*, 1–11.

141. "Jamieson to Curzon, 1923/3/14," PRO/FO 405/236/207 [F 1496/927/10], 790.

142. Ibid.; also Ming K. Chan, *Labor and Empire*, 292.

143. Zhang Hong, *Xianggang haiyuan dabagong*, 43.

144. Enclosure in "Colonial Office to Foreign Office, 1922/5/25," PRO/FO 405/236/249 [F 1866/927/10], 920.

145. Enclosure in "Alston to Curzon, 1922/3/6," PRO/FO 405/236/? [F 1529/927/10], 802. The source of the information was supposed to be a letter

by a seaman in Canton to his relatives in Shanghai. The letter was paraphrased by the British consul-general in Shanghai, E. H. Fraser.

146. Ma Chaojun, *Zhongguo laogong yundongshi*, vol. 1, 180–81; Ming K. Chan, *Labor and Empire*, 278–79.

147. Annex (F) to enclosure in "Colonial Office to Foreign Office, 1925/5/25," PRO/FO 405/236/249 [F 1866/927/10].

148. Enclosure in "Colonial Office to Foreign Office, 1922/3/9," PRO/FO 405/236/181 [F 1000/927/10], 678. The figures are taken from Stubbs's report on the incident. Deng Zhongxia, on the other hand, maintained that four were killed instantly, "hundreds" were wounded, and two later died as a result of injuries. Deng Zhongxia, *Zhongguo zhigong*, 58.

149. The consul-general, James Jamieson, described the shooting as "the most unfortunate incident" in his report in "Jamieson to Curzon, 1922/3/14," PRO/FO 405/236/207 [F 1496/927/10], 791.

150. Even as the seamen won wage increases, there were only vague promises from the employers regarding possible new ways of hiring. No arrangement was actually made to allow the union to participate in the process.

151. Enclosure in "Jamieson to Curzon, 1922/3/14," PRO/FO 405/236/207 [F 1496/927/10], 795; Zhang Hong, *Xianggang haiyuan*, 69.

152. Enclosure dated 1922/3/18 in "Colonial Office to Foreign Office, 1922/5/25," PRO/FO 405/236/249 [F 1866/927/10], 916–17.

153. Huang Yanpei, *Yisui*, 59.

154. "Yu gongren daibiao tanhua, 1922/5/24," *Youguan Chen Jiongming ziliao*, irregular pagination.

155. "Zai Guomindang yuesheng zhibu chenglihui, 1921/2/1," in *SZSQJ*, vol. 5, 460.

156. Dirlik, *Origins of Chinese Communism*, chapter 7.

157. "Zai Guangzhoushi gongren daibiaohui de yanshuo, 1924/5/1," in *SZSQJ*, vol. 10, 148–49.

Chapter 3

1. The Whampoa Academy, modeled on the command schools of the Soviets, was established with the aim of providing junior officers of the new Guomindang army with not only military but political training. It began enrollment in May 1924. See Landis, "Training and Indoctrination at the Whampoa Academy"; and Hazama, "'Sendai seisaku' to kōho gunkō."

2. *GMGR*, 1924/9/11: 1. For the nature of "warlord" factions such as Fengtian and Zhili, see Ch'i, *Warlord Politics in China 1916–1928*, 36–76. For an argument for the critical significance of the second Fengtian-Zhili war in Chinese history, see Waldron, *From War to Nationalism*.

3. According to Chiang Kai-shek, it was he who realized the paramount importance of retaining the Canton base at that critical juncture and wrote to Sun urging his return. See *Jiang Jieshi nianpu chugao*, 247. Another prominent Guomindang member, Zou Lu, maintained that Chiang too wanted to abandon Canton, and it was Chiang's main military rival, Xu Chongzhi of the Guangdong army, who organized the attack on Xiguan. Zou Lu, *Zhongguo Guomindang shigao*, 1095. A telegram sent by Chiang to Sun, dated October 10, 1924, seems to confirm Chiang's claim that he advocated the crushing of the Merchant Corps, although Chiang's plan for himself then remains unclear. He stated explicitly that the task of suppression should be entrusted to Xu and another military commander, Li Fulin. For the text of the telegram, see *ZMSDZH*, vol. 4, 789.

4. *The Hongkong Daily Press*, 1924/10/17: 7.

5. A text of the Merchant Corps' appeal for support from émigré communities as far away as Vancouver and New York can be found at the GDA. For Sun's reply to the public protest of Cantonese organizations in Shanghai, see *GMGR*, 1924/10/27: 3. Also see Wilbur, *Sun Yat-sen: Frustrated Patriot*, 263.

6. "Giles to Macleay, 1924/10/28," PRO/FO 371/10935 [F117/117/10]. Also Wu Tiecheng, *Wu Tiecheng huiyilu*, 134–35; and Cherepanov, *As Military Adviser in China*, 98–99.

7. See the Guomindang's proclamation "Jinggao Guangzhou shimin, 1924/10/18" deposited at the GDA. Also the *Hong Kong Daily Press*, 1924/10/17: 7; 10/18: 5.

8. See Laclau, *New Reflections on the Revolution of Our Time*, 91. Also Bhabha, *The Location of Culture*, 139–70.

9. Wu Tiecheng, *Wu Tiecheng huiyilu*, 133.

10. "Yu waiguo jizhe de tanhua, 1924/9," in *SZSQ J*, vol. 11, 40.

11. Li Yunhan, *Cong ronggong dao qingdang*, 332.

12. *Shuangshi* (1924), 3–4, 18.

13. See the report delivered at the Second Party Congress of the Guomindang on 1926/1/7, in *Zhongguo Guomindang diyierci quanguo daibiao dahui huiyi shiliao*, 209–10. Also *Shangmin yundong* (1926), 1: 13–14.

14. Ma Chaojun, *Zhongguo laogong yundongshi*, vol. 2, 320; Li Boyuan and Ren Gongtan, *Guangdong jiqi gongren fendoushi*, 97–98.

15. Bergère, *Golden Age*, 231.

16. Chesneaux, *The Chinese Labor Movement, 1919–1927*, 249.

17. "Jinggao Guangzhou shimin," deposited at the GDA.

18. In Laclau's words, "the 'totality' does not establish the limits of 'the social' by transforming the latter into a *determinate* object (i.e. 'society'). Rather, the social always exceeds the limits of the attempts to constitute society" (Laclau's emphasis). *New Reflections*, 91.

19. Cheng Tiangu, *Cheng Tiangu huiyilu*, 89.

20. Ibid., 49.

21. *Yuesheng shangtuan yuebao* [zhuanji] (biography) (August 1919), 1–3.

22. *Who's Who in China* (1925), 123–24; Chen Tianjie, "Wo suo zhidao Chen Lianbo de ji jian shi," 183.

23. For more on the Nanyang Tobacco Company, see Cochran, *Big Business in China: Sino-Foreign Rivalry in the Cigarette Industry, 1890–1930.* According to Cochran, "after Nanyang became identified with the national goods movement, sales soared in Canton" (69). It is also interesting to note that when Nanyang tried to expand into the lower Yangzi area and north China in 1916–17, its efforts were initially less than successful. Jian Zhaonan was reportedly shocked that "none of the people in the interior know what national goods (*guohuo*) are or why they are significant" (73).

24. *Yuesheng shangtuan yuebao* (August 1919); Cochran, *Big Business in China*, 66; Chen Guo, "Guangzhou shangtuan panbianhou de Chen Lianbo," 87–88.

25. Li Yaofeng, "Wo shi zenyang canjia shangtuan de," 95. As was increasingly the case in the 1920s, Li and Luo did not actually join the corps themselves but sent two junior staff members as their representatives instead.

26. "Chengjiao Sun Zhongshan de Yuesheng gejie huanyinghui huiyuan mingdan, 1912," in Huang Yan and Li Boxin, eds., *Sun Zhongshan cangdang xuanbian*, 481–82.

27. "Yueshang shangtuan huanying Sun Zhongshan songci, 1912/5/2," in ibid., 490.

28. Li Liangfu et al., "Yueshang weichi gonganhui huanying Sun Zhongshan songci, 1912," in ibid., 488.

29. Ibid., 489.

30. On this point, see Schoppa, "Province and Nation: The Chekiang Provincial Autonomy Movement, 1917–1927." Also Duara, *Rescuing History from the Nation*, 177–204.

31. Li Liangfu et al., "Yueshang weichi gonganhui," in Huang Yan and Li Boxin, eds., *Sun Zhongshan*, 489.

32. "Yuesheng shangtuan huanying Sun Zhongshan songci, 1912/5/2," in Huang Yan and Li Boxin, eds., *Sun Zhongshan*, 491.

33. *MSR*, 1912/7/8: 5; 7/29: 4.

34. *MSR*, 1912/8/15: 5.

35. Cited in Jerome Ch'en, *China and the West*, 302.

36. The "crisis" involved primarily the posturing and maneuvering for power by the various Beiyang militarists following the death of Yuan in 1916, punctuated by yet another dissolution of the National Assembly and Zhang Xun's attempt to restore the Manchus and the monarchy. See Li Jiannong, *Zhongguo jinbainian zhengzhishi*, 474–542.

37. *GQHSB*, 1917/5/1: 3.

38. *GQHSB*, 1917/6/19: 3.

39. *GQHSB*, 1917/7/11: 3.

40. *GQHSB*, 1917/7/14: 3.

41. *GQHSB*, 1917/6/12: 3.

42. "Yanqing Guangdong shangjie renshi shi de yanshuo, 1918/2/22," in *SZSQ J*, vol. 4, 344–47.

43. "Canton Intelligence Report: March Quarter, 1922," PRO/FO 228/3276, 410.

44. Ibid. The British consul-general in Canton, James Jamieson, was present at the inauguration.

45. See, for example, Li Guoqi, *Minguoshi lunji*, 353.

46. Lai, "Sun Fo yu Guangzhoushi," 101.

47. "Submission by Yang Ximin to Sun Yat-sen, 1923/3/6," in *LDDGX*, 14.

48. *Zhonghua minguo huobishi ziliao*, vol. 1, 727.

49. "Submission by Ye Gongchuo to Sun Yat-sen, 1923/8/5," in *LDDGX*, 135. Also see the report in *GMGR*, 1923/9/19: 2.

50. *Zhonghua minguo huobishi ziliao*, vol. 1, 908–9.

51. "Zhengli sheng yinhang zhibi banfa zonggang, 1923/8/10," and "Submission by Ye Gongchuo and Liao Zhongkai to Sun Yat-sen, 1924/2/?," in *LDDGX*, 135–37, 336–37.

52. "Intelligence Report: Political Summary for the December Quarter, 1923," PRO/FO 228/3276, 534.

53. *GMGR*, 1923/12/25: 3, 6.

54. *GMGR*, 1924/1/7: 3.

55. When Song Ziwen tried to simplify the structure of taxation in late 1925, he reportedly abolished over 70 miscellaneous levies. Li Guoqi, *Minguoshi lunji*, 369.

56. See *Guangdong gongbao*, no. 3196 (1923/7/9), 1–2. Also "Order no. 389, 1923/12/17," in *LDDGX*, 256.

57. *Guangzhoushi shizheng baogao huikan*, 1924, 40–60.

58. Qin Qingjun, "Beifa zhanzheng shiqi de Guangdongsheng caizheng," 164–65.

59. *Guangzhoushi shizheng baogao huikan*, 1924, 28–29.

60. For more on the campaigns against religion in early-twentieth-century China, see Duara, *Rescuing History*, 86–113.

61. *GSG*, no. 88 (1923/8/6), 18.

62. *GSG*, no. 88 (1923/8/6), 18; *GMGR*, 1923/8/7: 6.

63. See "Order no. 19 (1924/1/12)," in *LDDGX*, 297.

64. Zhou Ruisong, "Yijiuersinian Guangzhou de minchan baozheng," 132–33; Pan Jueqiu, "Wo suo zhi de Guangzhoushi minchan baozhengju," 137–38, 141–42.

65. *Guangzhoushi shizheng baogao huikan*, 1924, 30.

66. See, for example, the petition submitted by the Association of Chambers of Commerce in *GMGR*, 1923/10/18: 6–7.

67. See "Yijue xiuzheng Guangzhoushi minchan baozheng tiaoli," in *Guangdong gongbao*, no. 3333 (1923/12/19), 4–6. Also "Queding minye zhizhao tiaoli," in *LDDGX*, 297–99.

68. Pan Jueqiu, "Wo suo zhi de," 138–45.

69. Zhou Ruisong, "Yijiuersinian Guangzhou," 135–36. Also *Guangdong gongbao*, no. 3196 (1923/7/9), 1–2.

70. "Stubbs to Secretary Devonshire, 1923/5/9," PRO/CO 129/480, 111.

71. After an unsuccessful attempt on the life of the governor-general of French Indochina (by a Vietnamese) at the concession area of Shameen in June 1924, members of the foreign community decided to control access to their enclave. Shameen is a tiny island on the Pearl River, which was linked to the city by two small bridges. A system of photographed passes, to be carried by every Chinese, was instituted. The result was a protest strike staged by the Chinese employees on the island. The strike, supported by the Guomindang, began in July and lasted for about a month. The strikers, who gained a partial victory, ranged from police constables and clerks to domestic workers.

72. "Zhongguo Guomindang diyici quanguo daibiao dahui xuanyan, 1924/1/23" in *Zhongguo Guomindang diyierci quanguo daibiao dahui huiyi shiliao*, 85.

73. Yokoyama Hiroaki, "Kanton seiken no zaisei hippaku to Son Bun seiji," 37–38.

74. "Guangzhoushi shangdian gezhong de xiguan," 38.

75. Ibid., 38–39, 43–44.

76. While many native banks theoretically granted loans "on trust" without requiring formal collateral, their "investigators" usually carried out a detailed assessment of the business conditions of the applicant to determine his "trustworthiness." The possession of shop bottom right was thus an important asset in establishing one's credentials with the bank. The new banks which came into existence in the early Republic, moreover, were likely to demand security for loans. See Ou, *Guangdong zhi yinye*, 75, 78.

77. *GMGR*, 1923/8/3: 6. The registration system had already been put in place under Chen Jiongming's administration. See *Guangdong gongbao*, no. 2874 (1922/2/20), 9–11.

78. *GMGR*, 1923/10/18: 6.

79. Edward Bing-shuey Lee, *Modern Canton*, 13.

80. *MSR*, 1912/5/21: 3; Lai, "Sun Fo yu Guangzhoushi," 92.

81. *Guangdong gongbao*, no. 2874 (1922/2/20), 7.

82. *GMGR*, 1923/8/28: 6.

83. *GSG*, no. 109 (1924/1/1), 5.

84. See, for example, the letter to the chamber of commerce from the municipal government in *GSG*, no. 131 (1924/6/2), 6.

85. Ibid., 9.

86. The plan was subsequently codified into a set of regulations. See "Guang-

zhoushi qingli pudi dingshou banfa" and "Guangzhoushi qingli pudi dingshou dengji jianzhang," in *Guangzhoushi tudiju dengji ji zhengshui fali huiji.*

87. *GMGR*, 1924/3/29: 7; 4/2: 3.

88. In a 1933 survey on the capitalization of 19,698 shops in Canton, 55.5 percent were said to have been capitalized at less than C$1,000, 18 percent at C$1,000–C$2,000, 15 percent at C$2,000–C$5,000, 7 percent at C$5,000–C$10,000, 4 percent at C$10,000–C$50,000, and 0.5 percent at over C$50,000. Out of the 97 shops in the last category, 52 were native banks and jewelry stores. In contemporary local usage, "small shops" usually referred to those with a capitalization of less than C$5,000 (88.5 percent), although there were undoubtedly cases of underreporting. *GSTH*, 49.

89. *GMGR*, 1924/5/23: 2.

90. *GQHSB*, 1924/5/10: 5.

91. Ibid.

92. *GQHSB*, 1924/5/16: 5.

93. *GMGR*, 1924/5/27: 3.

94. *GQHSB*, 1924/5/27: 3; *GMGR*, 1924/6/10: 7.

95. *GMGR*, 1924/5/27: 3. Although the newspaper did not give full identifications but simply stated that certain scoundrels named Chen and Zou headed the meeting, it is clear that it was referring to Chen Lianbo and Zou Dianbang, another prominent figure in the native banking sector.

96. *GQHSB*, 1924/5/31: 6; *GMGR*, 1924/5/31: 9.

97. *GMGR*, 1924/7/4: 3.

98. *GMGR*, 1924/7/24: 6; Liang Langqiu, *Guangzhou shangyun yan'geshi*, 6.

99. *GMGR*, 1924/7/24: 6.

100. The Merchant Corps of Canton itself (excluding the suburb of Honam) consisted of close to four thousand recruits plus about two thousand reserves. The strength of the corps in the surrounding areas varied greatly. The Foshan unit, one of the largest outside Canton, was made up of about 1,600 corpsmen. The Jiangmen corps, on the other hand, claimed at most 600 followers. See "Guangdong kouxiechao," *juan* 1: 94; Zhang Junqian and Chen Guo, "Foshan shangtuan jianwen," 43; Huang Dingsan and Zhu Liyu, "Yijiuersinian qianhou Jiangmen shangtuan huodong jianwen huiyi," 128.

101. "Jamieson to Waterlow, 1925/2/?," PRO/ FO 228/3009, 367. S. P. Waterlow was the head of the Far Eastern Department at the Foreign Office in London.

102. *GMGR*, 1924/8/14: 3.

103. According to an antigovernment source, the permit was initially granted by Xu Chonghao, brother of the Guomindang military leader Xu Chongzhi. "Guangdong kouxiechao," *juan* 1: 8.

104. The manifest of the shipment listed 4,850 rifles (with 1,500,000 rounds of ammunition), 4,331 Mauser pistols (with 2,060,000 rounds), and 660 miscellaneous revolvers (with 164,000 rounds). It was also believed to include an undeclared vol-

ume of about a hundred machine guns, mountain guns, and parts for two airplanes, which does suggest supplies for forces other than the corps. "Extract from China Command Intelligence Diary, 1st–31st August, 1924," PRO/ CO 129/485, 470.

105. Acting Consul-General Giles was informed that Chen Lianbo had apparently remitted about C$1,100,000 to Chen Jiongming to encourage the latter to make an advance on Canton, a transaction considered by Giles to have been "money wasted." "Giles to Macleay, 1924/11/3," PRO/FO 228/3008, 131.

106. *GMGR*, 1924/8/21: 3; "Guangdong kouxiechao," *juan* 1: 17–20.

107. *GMGR*, 1924/8/8: 7; 8/12: 3.

108. *GMGR*, 1924/8/14: 3.

109. There were, for example, the attempts at reaching a settlement made by two officers of the Yunnan Army, Fan Shisheng and Liao Xingchao. "Guangdong kouxiechao," *juan* 1: 46–65.

110. *Who's Who in China*, 121–22.

111. *Who's Who in China*, 124; "Tan Liting de huiyi," 59.

112. "Guangdong kouxiechao," *juan* 1: 23–24.

113. The letter, dated the 21st day of the 7th moon [1924/8/21], can be found at the GDA.

114. The flier, deposited at the GDA, bears the name of Lu Chinan et al. I have not been able, however, to find further information on Lu.

115. This account of the commercial strike is based primarily on the reports in *GMGR*, 1924/8/26 through 8/30.

116. *GMGR*, 1924/8/27: 7.

117. "Tan Liting de huiyi," 58.

118. *GMGR*, 1924/8/22: 3; 8/26: 8.

119. Lin Fang, "Wo canjia shangtuan de jingguo," 99. Lin's family owned a small shipyard in the Honam area. Also "Guangdong kouxiechao," *juan* 1: 94.

120. Enclosure no. 1 [Sun to Stubbs, 1923/12/4] in "Governor Stubbs to Secretary Devonshire, 1923/12/19," PRO/CO 129/481, 504.

121. Cited in Wilbur, *Sun Yat-sen*, 252.

122. Proclamation of 1924/9/1, *Geming wenxian*, vol. 10, 52.

123. See the series of orders from Sun to Chiang Kai-shek at Whampoa, dated from 1924/8/23 to 9/12, to distribute the weapons to the various military commanders. *ZMSDZH*, vol. 4, 775, 779–81.

124. For conditions of the settlement, dated 1924/10/9, see *ZMSDZH*, vol. 4, 786.

125. The antigovernment "Guangdong kouxiechao" reports that one worker and four cadets were killed, and three corpsmen were injured. In addition, many bystanders were forced to seek refuge in the Pearl River (*juan* 1: 81–82). On the other hand, a progovernment source, *Shuangshi*, provides what it describes as an incomplete list of 6 dead, 41 injured, and about a dozen unaccounted for, none of whom belonged to the Merchant Corps. The Russian adviser Cherepanov claimed in his

memoir that twenty were killed and as many wounded. It is possible that Cherepanov's figure came from the final death toll. Cherepanov, *As Military Adviser in China*, 97.

126. "Guangdong kouxiechao," *juan* 1: 82; according to Cherepanov, about 2,700 rifles, 1,000 pistols, and 330,000 rounds of ammunition were not returned to the corps. *As Military Adviser*, 97.

127. Sun seemed to have some difficulty making up his mind about what to do. On October 11, he established a revolutionary committee, with the apparent intention to suppress the Merchant Corps. Meanwhile, however, he was also urging Chiang Kai-shek and others to abandon Canton and join him in Shaoguan. See *Jiang Jieshi nianpu chugao*, 247–48; Wilbur, *Sun Yat-sen*, 261–62.

128. Wilbur, *Sun Yat-sen*, 250.

129. "Stephen to Jamieson, 1923/10/10," enclosed in PRO/CO 129/485, 374.

130. Minute by Jamieson, dated 1923/10/11, in PRO/ CO 129/485, 374.

131. "Foreign Secretary Curzon to Colonial Secretary Devonshire, 1923/12/19," PRO/CO 129/482, 204; "Stubbs to Jamieson, 1923/7/21," PRO/CO 129/482, 253.

132. "Stubbs to Devonshire, 1923/1/7," PRO/CO 129/479, 167.

133. "Stubbs to Secretary Amery, 1924/12/31," PRO/ CO 129/485, 472–474. Stubbs did eventually, just before the end of his tenure as governor in October 1925, get involved in financing, albeit indirectly, an attempt at a coup d'état against the Guomindang-led government during the Canton-Hongkong Strike. See "Governor Clementi to Secretary Amery, 1926/9/24," PRO/CO 129/498, 692–95.

134. "The Guomindang's people's rights," according to the proclamation, "are such that they seek to fit the present needs of the revolution in China, and are different from the 'so-called natural human rights' [*suowei tianfu renquan*]." See "Zhongguo Guomindang diyici quanguo daibiao dahui xuanyan, 1924/1/23," in *Zhongguo Guomindang diyierci quanguo daibiao dahui huiyi shiliao*, 85, 86–87.

135. *Geming wenxian*, vol. 10, 52.

136. See the Guomindang's proclamation on the commercial strike, dated 1924/8/29, in *Geming wenxian*, vol. 10, 50.

137. "Jinggao Guangzhou shimin," deposited at GDA.

138. *GMGR*, 1924/8/18: 6–7.

139. *GMGR*, 1924/8/20: 7.

140. *GMGR*, 1924/8/29: 8.

141. *GMGR*, 1924/9/1: 7; 9/22: 3.

142. The government forces, according to Cherepanov, consisted of 2,000 policemen, 800 Whampoa cadets, 500 cadets from the Yunnan Military School, 220 cadets from the Hunan School, and two armored trains with 250 men. *As Military Adviser*, 97. Wu Tiecheng, on the other hand, did not even mention the Worker Militia in his memoir, and emphasized the role of units loyal to Xu Chongzhi and Li Fulin as well as his own police force. *Wu Tiecheng huiyilu*, 134–35. However, the historian Jean Chesneaux, following the official narrative, dismissed the "mercenar-

ies" as not reliable and the Whampoa cadets as not strong enough, and wrote that "[t]he government was therefore in crying need of additional military support, and this need was met when the Workers' Delegates' Conference formed a 'Labor Organizations' Army.'" Chesneaux, *Chinese Labor Movement*, 249.

143. *GMGR*, 1924/10/30: 6; 10/31: 6.

144. Hu Hanmin, "Jieji yu daode xueshuo," 1.

145. See, for example, Liang Qichao, "Xinminshuo," 81.

146. Dai, "Geming! Hegu? Weihe?" 10–11.

147. *GMGR*, 1925/10/16: 10.

Chapter 4

1. Liang Qichao, *Yinbingshi wenji*, 42: 1–2.

2. *GMGR*, 1926/5/3: 10.

3. Hunt, "Introduction: History, Culture, and Text," in Hunt, ed., *The New Cultural History*, 17. Also see her *Politics, Culture and Class in the French Revolution*, esp. Part I.

4. Cited in Li Xin, ed., *Guomin geming de xingqi*, 566–67.

5. Sun Yat-sen, *Sanmin zhuyi*, 48.

6. Ibid., 165.

7. Ibid., 160–61, 165.

8. Ibid., 179.

9. Despite the founding of the officially sponsored Merchant Association in early 1925 to rally support from the merchants, the government's relationship with the mercantile community remained, not surprisingly, strained after the Merchant Corps incident. Other associations, such as those organized for students or women, did not command the same kind of material resources or strategic importance to provide a critical foundation of support. There were, to be sure, attempts at organizing peasants. Yet while the Guomindang-led Canton government had by 1925 achieved some partial success in consolidating its rule in the rest of the province, its control in the hinterland remained patchy and often tenuous. Above all, by crushing the Merchant Corps, the government had placed the future of its project upon the continued viability of Canton as a base.

10. *GSSDB*, 2–3, 6–44.

11. Ming K. Chan, *Labor and Empire*, 9–10. Also see Chesneaux, *The Chinese Labor Movement*.

12. Luo Xing, "Diyici guogong hezuo shiqi Guangzhou gongren daibiaohui de yan'ge," 139–40.

13. Li Xianheng et al., *Chen Yannian*, 30–31, 40–41.

14. *GSSDB*, 8. The term for "literate" here is *shizi*, which literally means "can recognize characters." This, of course, covers a range stretching from those who

could barely write their own names to those who could, say, read a newspaper or compose a simple letter.

15. Ibid. The total number of rickshaw pullers in Canton in 1926 was estimated to be around eight thousand, of which one thousand were listed as unemployed. At the same time, the union claimed a membership of about seven thousand.

16. Faure and Siu, eds., *Down to Earth: The Territorial Bond in South China*, 209.

As many scholars have noted, human beings are quite capable of maintaining multiple levels of identity. For example, one could easily identify oneself as a member both of a locality or an ethnic group and of a nation. Thus Bryna Goodman argues, for instance, that *tongxiang* or native-place sentiments in China were not necessarily always in conflict with the nationalist project. In certain contexts, they could actually facilitate the construction of the latter. See Goodman, *Native Place, City, and Nation: Regional Networks and Identities in Shanghai, 1853–1937*. As indicated earlier, Sun Yat-sen himself mentioned briefly the use of lineages as building blocks for the nation, albeit to no avail. Yet, the fact is that for most of the political and intellectual elites who constituted the modernist leadership of twentieth-century China, local or regional sentiments were more often than not viewed with suspicion, as an obstacle to their effort to discipline the social realm. In the final analysis, local or ethnic ties were to be suppressed in the quest to get the people to come together as one.

17. Those from Canton belong to the *yue* dialectal group, while the Chaoan dialect is part of the *min* dialectal system. The latter has close affinity not only with the *min* dialect of neighboring Fujian Province, but also with the dialects of the Hainan and Leizhou areas within Guangdong. See Li Xinkui, "Guangdong min fangyan yingcheng de lishi guocheng."

18. Robert Young, *Colonial Desire: Hybridity in Theory, Culture and Race*, 27. Young uses these words while discussing the concept of hybridity.

19. Quan Hansheng, *Zhongguo hanghui zhidushi*, 192.

20. "Canton Intelligence Report: December Quarter, 1921," PRO/ FO 228/3276, 393.

21. *Guangzhoushi shizheng baogao huikan*, 1924: 345–47, 351–57. Vera Vladimirovna Vishnyakova-Akimova, a Soviet interpreter who went to Canton in early 1926, recalls in her memoir that the local rickshaw pullers were then apparently powerful enough to pressure the government to refrain from expanding the transit system. See Vishnyakova-Akimova, *Two Years in Revolutionary China, 1925–1927*, 189–90.

22. *Guangzhoushi shizheng baogao huikan*, 1924: 220; *Guangzhoushi nianyinian renkou diaocha baogao*, 1932. No exact figure is available for the early part of the century, although a 1909 survey counted 96,614 households (*hu*) in Canton (cited in Qiu Jie, "Guangdong shangren," 364). The figure of 600,000 is an estimate. Gilbert Rozman, using Qing Tianjin as an example, suggests that the mean household size of a large urban center (6.09 in the case of Tianjin) in China, with its concentration

of rich and shopkeeper households with servants and apprentices, tended to be larger than that of rural areas. See Rozman, *Population and Marketing Settlements in Ch'ing China*, 60–66.

23. "Canton Intelligence Report: December Quarter, 1922," PRO/FO 228/3276, 477.

24. *Guangzhoushi shehuiju yewu baogao.* Section 2, "gongshang xingzheng" (*administration of industries and commerce*), 68, 73–75.

25. Yu, ed., *Guangzhou gongren jiating zhi yanjiu*, 13–14.

26. The most famous portrayal of the life of rickshaw pullers was provided by Lao She in his novel, *Luotuo xiangzi*, which was set in Peking and published in 1937.

27. *Guangzhoushi shehuiju yewu baogao.* Section 6, "zongwu" (general affairs), 121.

28. Wang Qingbin et al., eds., *Diyici Zhongguo laodong nianjian*, section 2: 2–3; Quan Hansheng, *Zhongguo hanghui zhidushi*, 187–89.

29. Wang Qingbin et al., eds., *Diyici Zhongguo laodong nianjian*, section 1: 615–16; *Guangzhoushi shizheng baogao huikan*, 1924: 352–53.

30. Wang Qingbin et al., eds., *Diyici Zhongguo laodong nianjian*, section 1: 621.

31. *Guangzhoushi shehuiju yewu baogao.* Section 2, "gongshang xingzheng" (*administration of industries and commerce*), 72.

32. For a comparison of the working conditions of rickshaw pullers in different Chinese cities, see Wang Qingbin et al., eds., *Diyici Zhongguo laodong nianjian*, 1928, section 1: 613–24. Also Strand, *Rickshaw Beijing: City People and Politics in the 1920s*, 20–64.

33. "Zhonggong Guangdong quwei guanyu gongren yundong de baogao, 1925/10/10," 61.

34. See Quan Hansheng, *Zhongguo hanghui zhidushi*, 187–96.

35. *GMGR*, 1926/5/3: 10.

36. Ibid.

37. *GSTH*, 3.

38. "Huanan gongren yundong zhong de Gongchandang ren, 1925/1/9," 98–99.

39. Zeng Yangfu, *Guangzhou zhi gongye*, 81.

40. It might be noted that the mechanization of production in the oil-processing industry in republican Canton was in the end largely a failure. Out of the 37 enterprises in 1937, only 2 were fully mechanized. The reasons were complex, ranging from the shortage of capital to poor management, even though labor resistance had ceased to be a serious factor after 1927. Production costs of the machines also tended to be high relative to labor costs within the industry. Zeng Yangfu, *Guangzhou zhi gongye*, 18, 89–92.

41. There were only 21 female workers in the whole industry in Canton in 1937. Zeng Yangfu, *Guangzhou zhi gongye*, 104.

42. *GSSDB*, 13.

43. Zeng Yangfu, *Guangzhou zhi gongye*, 103–6.

44. Hou, "Dageming shiqi Guangzhou youye gongren de douzheng he Huaxian nongmin yundong," 147–48. Hou dated the strike to 1922, which was mistaken.

45. Luo Hequn and He Jinzhou, *Liu Ersong*, 35.

46. Perry, *Shanghai on Strike*, Part I.

47. Hou Guiping, "Dageming shiqi," 144–46. Zeng Xisheng apparently became a renegade later and supported the suppression of the Communists in 1927.

48. In a report filed by the Guangzhou branch of the Communist Youth Corps, the cadres put the UOPW at the top of a list of unions to which they had paid special attention. Those organizations shared the characteristics of not only being unions for important industries, but of having a large number of young workers as well. "Tuan Guangzhou diwei gongnongbu baogao, 1925/7/21," 311.

49. Hou Guiping, for instance, was at one point accused by other workers of favoring his *tongxiang* from Huaxian. Although the union initially asked for a raise of C$1.50 (per day per *muzha*) and a compensation sum of C$25 (per *muzha*), at the end it had to settle for 80 cents and C$5 respectively. Hou Guiping, "Dageming shiqi," 147–48.

50. "Tuan yue quwei guanyu Guangdong gongnong zhuangkuang de baogao, 1924/3/6," 354.

51. See, for example, *GMGR*, 1926/8/5: 11.

52. Wu Jin, "Jiefang qian Guangzhoushi siying jiqi gongye gaikuang," 73–78.

53. Liang Moyuan and Xue Zemin, "Xietonghe jiqichang huigu," 1–3. Despite occasional setbacks, Xietonghe went on to expand and employed two hundred workers by 1937. See Zeng Yangfu, *Guangzhou zhi gongye*, 28.

54. A word should be said about the arsenal in Canton. In the mid-1920s the arsenal employed 1,800 workers and at first sight appears to be *the* modern enterprise. Yet the workers there, despite occasional stirrings, remained at best a force marginal to the labor movement. Why? It is possible that the crucial significance of the arsenal to the government meant that the authorities were particularly sensitive to any potential disruptions there. But three more reasons can be suggested. First, the arsenal was actually located in the countryside about 30 kilometers north of the city. About three hundred of its workers were labeled "natives," presumably so-called minorities, with another six hundred being local rural inhabitants from the surrounding villages. Few of them went to the city for more than a couple of days a month. As a result, the whole place had the air of a rural community where urban influence was limited. Second, work within the arsenal was fragmented into six autonomous units with extensive use of contract labor, making coordination between them extremely difficult. Third, the general skill level of the workers was rather low. If this sounds strange for an arsenal, it is because "arsenal" is a misnomer here. In the 1920s the factories there were merely centers for the basic work of assembling imported ammunition and weapons. They did not manufacture hardware. Although the senior staff were engineers and skilled machinists, the majority of the workers were often little more than casual hands who lived in constant fear of losing their jobs to

the large rural labor pool. See "Zhonggong Guangdong quwei guanyu gongren yundong de baogao, 1925/10/10," 45–46. Also Wu Weiyong, "Guangdong bingqi zhizaochang gailüe," 19–20.

55. *GSSDB*, 13, 35. These are no doubt only approximate figures, but the large gap between the two groups is unmistakable.

56. Vishnyakova-Akimova, *Two Years in Revolutionary China*, 233; *GSSDB*, 13. The latter puts the top income of the machinists at C$500, which might apply to a very select group of owner-machinists. *GSSDB*, 35.

57. The machinists changed the name of their union from *Guangdong jiqi gongren weichihui* to *Guangdong jiqi zonggonghui* in January 1926. The change from the more traditional nomenclature *weichihui* to *zonggonghui* was meant to give the organization a more modern flavor as well as a more inclusive claim on all machinists.

58. *GSSDB*, 35.

59. Vishnyakova-Akimova, *Two Years in Revolutionary China*, 233.

60. Liu Yongming, *Guomindang ren yu wusi yundong*, 368–69. Also Huang Yibo, *Guangdong zhi jiqi gongren*, 2–20.

61. Zeng Yangfu, *Guangzhou zhi gongye*, 82.

62. Ibid., 34.

63. "Guangzhou gonghui yundong de baogao, 1926 xia," 328.

64. Ibid.

65. "Guangdongqu qunzhong yundong zhuangkuang, 1923/11," 56.

66. "Zhonggong Guangdong quwei guanyu gongren yundong de baogao, 1925/10/10," 62–63; "Guangzhou gonghui yundong de baogao, 1926 xia," 328–29.

67. "Guangzhou gonghui yundong de baogao, 1926 xia," 328–29. It has also been suggested that Changtaihou's decision to mechanize its production, which led to mass dismissals, was prompted by workers' demands for better wages and working conditions. See Luo Daming et al., "Dageming shiqi Guangdong gongyun qingkuang de huiyi," 154.

68. As late as May, the UOPW still denied any knowledge of the allegedly missing persons. *GMGR*, 1925/5/22: 7.

69. *GMGR*, 1925/5/29: 6; 5/30: 6.

70. *GMGR*, 1925/7/8: 6.

71. "Zhonggong Guangdong quwei guanyu gongren yundong de baogao, 1925/10/10," 72. It is also interesting to note that in a semiofficial biography of Liu Ersong, then a pivotal figure in both the Communist Party and the labor movement in Canton, the authors chose to emphasize his role in the UOPW strike in 1923. The union's conflict with the machinists in the mid-1920s was not even mentioned. See Luo Hequn and He Jinzhou, *Liu Ersong*.

72. "Guangzhou gonghui yundong de baogao, 1926 xia," 328.

73. "Zhonggong Guangdong quwei guanyu gongren yundong de baogao, 1925/10/10," 72.

74. *Ibid.*, 73.

75. *GMGR*, 1925/5/13: 7.

76. "Guangzhou gonghui yundong de baogao, 1926 xia," 329–30. The machinists were apparently able to turn the incident into a campaign on their own behalf, even setting up offices in Hong Kong and southeast Asia to collect donations for their "plight." See Luo Daming et al., "Dageming shiqi Guangdong gongyun," 155.

77. "Zhonggong Guangdong quwei guanyu gongren yundong de baogao, 1925/10/10," 73.

78. The labor organizers later actually arranged a "reconciliation party" for the two unions. It was, however, little more than a symbolic gesture, as the causes of their antagonism remained unresolved. *GMGR*, 1925/12/10: 11.

79. See, for example, Wang Jianchu and Sun Maosheng, *Zhongguo gongren yundongshi*, 95. For a Guomindang view, see Ma Chaojun, *Zhongguo laogong yundongshi*, vol. 2, 347.

80. Perry, *Shanghai on Strike*, 215, 251. One might question, in the absence of "class consciousness," whether the divisions amongst the workers could be described as "intraclass."

81. Deng Zhongxia, *Zhongguo zhigong yundong jianshi*, 85. For a study of the Jinghan strike, see Takatsuna Hirofumi, "Chūgoku tetsudō rōdō undō no hatten to sono kōzō," 26–42.

82. Xing Bixin et al., eds., *Dierci Zhongguo laodong nianjian*, section 1: 6, 92. The Canton municipal survey of 1926 listed 3,850 workers for just two of the three lines, of whom 2,870 were estimated to be literate (*GSSDB*, 8). These figures presumably included those employees who resided along the routes as well.

83. *GMGR*, 1925/6/15: 7; Li Fu, "Huiyi Guangzhou tielu gongren de geming douzheng," 7; Luo Daming et al., "Dageming shiqi Guangdong gongyun," 164–65. The railroad workers had good reason to be resentful of the guest armies, as the latter were particularly notorious for arbitrarily appropriating the resources of the railroads and for subjecting workers to impressment.

84. Ling Hongxun, *Zhongguo tieluzhi*, 219–20; Cheng Hao, *Guangzhou gangshi*, 119.

85. Ling Hongxun, *Zhongguo tieluzhi*, 221. Also Rhoads, *China's Republican Revolution*, 63.

86. Ling Hongxun, *Zhongguo tieluzhi*, 224, 232–33.

87. See He Huaimin, "Guangshao duan tielu yunshu hangye," 62–66.

88. *GSSDB*, 8.

89. Xing Bixin et al., eds., *Dierci Zhongguo laodong nianjian*, 1932, section 1: 6–7.

90. *Ibid.*, 124. The remainder of the group was made up of 20 workers between the ages of 15 and 19, 38 between 50 and 59, and 10 who were over 60.

91. Wang Qingbin et al., eds., *Diyici Zhongguo laodong nianjian*, section 1: 59. It

also appears that workers at the carpentry shop were paid on a daily rate, while others, with the exception of unskilled laborers, received monthly stipends.

92. "Zhonggong Guangdong quwei guanyu gongren yundong de baogao, 1925/10/10," 51.

93. Ibid., 52, 65–66.

94. By late 1925, regulations were enacted forbidding, in theory at least, the election of management personnel and contractors as officials of the unions at the Canton-Shaoguan and the Canton-Sanshui lines. See "Zhonggong Guangdong quwei guanyu gongren yundong de baogao, 1925/10/10," 66.

95. Ibid., 53.

96. "Guangzhou gonghui yundong de baogao, 1926 xia," 334–37.

97. The offer of resignation, submitted by Chen Gongbo, was not accepted by the government (*GMGR*, 1925/9/14: 3). Chen, who was briefly a member of the Communist Party, joined the Guomindang in early 1925. In his memoir Chen recalls how at that time Canton was afflicted with daily strikes and incessant conflicts between the unions. See Chen Gongbo, *Kuxiaolu: Chen Gongbo huiyi, 1925–1936*, 46.

98. *GMGR*, 1925/9/14: 3.

99. *GMGR*, 1925/9/10: 3.

100. "Guangzhou gonghui yundong de baogao, 1926 xia," 336.

101. *GMGR*, 1925/9/14: 3.

102. *GMGR*, 1925/9/16: 6.

103. "Zhonggong Guangdong quwei guanyu gongren yundong de baogao, 1925/10/10," 55–56; *GMGR*, 1925/9/14: 3.

104. *GMGR*, 1925/9/16: 6; 9/22: 11.

105. *GMGR*, 1925/9/23: 3.

106. "Guangzhou gonghui yundong de baogao, 1926 xia," 337.

107. Ibid., 321–46 (especially 341–45).

108. An all too familiar example of such mechanisms at work was the conflict between the Jinlun Weavers Union (JWU) and the Guangzhou Machine-Weaving Union (GMWU). In theory, the former was the home for the more traditional type of weavers, while the latter should have enlisted the workers in the mechanized weaving industry within the city. In practice, however, the boundary between the two was not always easy to draw. As the government found out, the GMWU simply took the membership list of the JWU and stamped it with its own emblem, thus claiming those on the list as members of the GMWU (*GMGR*, 1925/8/15: 6; 8/18: 11; 8/28: 10). JWU's answer was to send 70 of its own members, clubs in hand, to various mechanized workplaces to "persuade" the weavers there to join their organization. Those who demurred usually ended up in the hospital (*GMGR*, 1925/9/7: 11). The dispute was apparently still unresolved over a year later, as more fighting between the two unions was reported (*GMGR*, 1926/12/10: 10).

109. "Guangzhou gonghui yundong de baogao, 1926 xia," 344.

110. Ibid.

111. Ibid., 345. In 1924, the Guangdong branch of the Socialist Youth Corps had already warned that the Alliance of Labor Unions of Guangdong (*Guangdong gonghui lianhehui*), the predecessor to the Council of Workers' Deputies as an umbrella organization, was not "capable of becoming a substantive and active labor organization" (see "Yinianlai zhi tuan Yuequ, 1924/4/4," in *Ruan Xiaoxian wenji*, 130). Still, the assessment of the labor organizers was revealing, as on paper the position of the Council of Workers' Deputies seemed relatively secure. In 1926 there were only two other small blocs of workers of some significance in Canton: the Guangdong Workers' Federation (*Guangdong zonggonghui*) with about 27,000 members, most of whom belonged to traditional-style handicraft associations and, of course, the 12,000 members of the Machinists' Union.

112. "Guangzhou gonghui yundong de baogao, 1926 xia," 345–46.

113. Yu Qizhong, ed., *Guangzhou laozi zhengyi de fenxi*, 4–5.

114. Liang Qichao, *Yinbingshi wenji*, 42: 2.

Chapter 5

1. "Zai Guangzhou shangtuan ji jingcha lianhuanhui de yanshuo, 1924/1/14," in *SZSQJ*, vol. 9, 62.

2. Abend, *My Life in China, 1926–1941*, 33.

3. Guha, "Discipline and Mobilize," 71.

4. Ibid.

5. Ibid., 72.

6. See, for example, Fewsmith, *Party, State, and Local Elites in Republican China: Merchant Organizations and Politics in Shanghai 1890–1930*.

7. *GMGR*, 1925/5/4: 3.

8. In reference to early-twentieth-century India, Guha describes how Gandhi's plan to "evolve order out of chaos" represented a "strategy to replace a discipline specific to the subaltern domain by a discipline appropriate to the elite domain." While this is an important insight, Guha's concept of a binary opposition between "elite" and "subaltern" domains seems problematic. See "Discipline and Mobilize," 110.

9. Chesneaux, for example, describes the strike organization with his typical enthusiasm as "a kind of workers' government" or "Government No. 2." *Chinese Labor Movement*, 293.

10. Abend, *My Life in China*, 33.

11. *GMGR*, 1925/6/30: 7.

12. "Zhonggong Guangdong quwei guanyu shenggang bagong qingkuang de baogao, 1925/7," 29–30.

13. In 1925 there were about 1,500 to 2,000 Chinese employed within Shameen. *SDZ*, 126.

14. For general accounts, see Rigby, *The May 30 Movement: Events and Themes*, and Clifford, *Shanghai, 1925: Urban Nationalism and the Defense of Foreign Privilege*.

15. See the collection of contemporary reports and fliers in *WYS*, vol. 1, 551–80.

16. Clifford, *Shanghai, 1925*, 16.

17. *WYS*, vol. 1, 682–85.

18. *Guangzhou bainian dashiji*, 315–16.

19. Cherepanov, *As Military Adviser*, 148.

20. *GMGR*, 1925/6/20: 7.

21. *GMGR*, 1925/3/31: 2.

22. A group of Guomindang members who had long been opposed to the alliance with the Communists, for example, met in November 1925 in Peking to form the so-called Western Hill group, contesting the policies and authority of the Canton government. Meanwhile, even those Guomindang leaders who remained at the headquarters in Canton were far from being of one mind regarding the future of the regime, as subsequent events were to reveal.

23. In Wilbur's words, the first Guomindang campaign against Chen Jiongming—the "Eastern Expedition" which took place between February and April of 1925—revealed that "the command situation was confused, participating units were not organized on a common basis, communications were poor, and there was a deficiency of maps and geographical information." Wilbur and How, eds., *Missionaries of Revolution*, 145.

24. See *GMGR*, 1925/6/17: 2; 6/18: 2–3; 6/20: 4.

25. Support came from the tramway workers, employees of the "foreign business" sector, typesetters for Western publications, and, of course, the seamen. "Zhonggong Guangdong quwei guanyu shenggang bagong, 1925/7," 26–29.

26. Ibid., 28–29.

27. The labor organizers from Canton also remarked rather cryptically in their report that they had no choice but to acquiesce to the agreement reached by the six different unions of stevedores and longshoremen with the labor leadership in Hong Kong. Although the authors did not elaborate, one might hazard a guess that the agreement probably involved some kind of financial inducement for the workers to join the strike. "Zhonggong Guangdong quwei guanyu shenggang bagong, 1925/7," 28–29.

28. *SDZ*, 147–48.

29. "Zhonggong Guangdong quwei guanyu shenggang bagong, 1925/7," 30.

30. "Governor Stubbs to Colonial Secretary, 1925/6/26," PRO/ CO 129/488, 455.

31. "Zhonggong Guangdong quwei guanyu shenggang bagong, 1925/7," 29.

32. The sources used here to reconstruct the events of June 23 include *The Report of the Commission for the Investigation of the Shakee Massacre*, submitted by a group of nineteen civic leaders in Canton in the immediate aftermath of the conflict; *The Canton Incident of June 23rd: The Truth*, prepared by the British authorities to give their side of the story; and Qian Yizhang, *Shaji tongshi*. The figure of between

20,000 and 30,000 demonstrators was given in *The Truth*. Qian, on the other hand, reported that 50,000 to 60,000 people took part in the march. The estimate of 70,000 comes from Cherepanov, *As Military Adviser*, 155.

33. The details of the fatalities were given in *The Report of the Commission*, and were accepted by the British.

34. See Appendix B in *The Report of the Commission*. Also *The Truth*, vii–viii.

35. *GMGR*, 1925/7/6: 3.

36. *GMGR*, 1925/6/30: 3.

37. The call for a ban on the use of foreign currency and work for foreigners, as well as the use of foreign goods, also came up in the protests in Shanghai. *WYS*, vol. 1, 660–61.

38. *GMGR*, 1925/7/1: 6–7; 7/18: 6.

39. It is tempting to suggest that the merchants in Canton might have embraced the measures as an opportunity for the city to regain its premier position in the regional economy. There is perhaps a grain of truth to this assertion, although it certainly has to be carefully qualified. There were close economic and social connections between merchants of Canton and Hong Kong, and the demarcation between the groups was not necessarily always clear. They often invested in each other's enterprises, and mobility across the border was fluid. While the precise nature of the relationships depended ultimately on the particular sector of trade or even personal circumstances, the prospect of severing ties with Hong Kong would raise as much alarm as optimism among the merchants of Canton.

40. See, for example, the plan for the financial independence of Canton in *GMGR*, 1925/7/18: 6.

41. *GMGR*, 1925/7/6: 3.

42. *SDZ*, 281–82; Cai and Lu, *Shenggang dabagong*, 38–39.

43. Deng Zhongxia, *Zhongguo zhigong*, 235.

44. *GMGR*, 1925/6/30: 7.

45. See the reports in *GMGR*, 1925/8/26: 3; 9/3: 7.

46. *SDZ*, 288.

47. *GMGR*, 1925/8/18: 10.

48. *GMGR*, 1925/8/19: 7; 8/20: 7.

49. *SDZ*, 295; *GMGR*, 1925/8/28: 3.

50. See *GMGR*, 1925/9/3: 7; 9/15: 10; 9/16: 7. Also Cai and Lu, *Shenggang dabagong*, 55.

51. *ATTR*: Canton, 1925, 1–2.

52. "Enclosure (Diary of Visit to Canton by M. Fletcher, 1925/12/20–12/23) in Governor Clementi to Secretary Amery, 1925/12/24," PRO/FO 228/3586, 408. Cecil Clementi replaced Reginald Stubbs as the governor of Hong Kong in November 1925.

53. *Canton: Its Port, Industries and Trade*, 6.

54. *ATTR*: Canton, 1925, 5.

55. *GMGR*, 1926/1/26: 10.

56. The term was used by Clementi in his "Outline of Cantonese history from September 1911 to date," in "Clementi to Amery, 1926/10/12," PRO/CO 129/494, 405.

57. "Zhonggong Guangdong quwei guanyu shenggang bagong qingkuang de baogao, 1925/10," 87–88; Cai and Lu, *Shenggang dabagong*, 163.

58. "Zhonggong Guangdong quwei guanyu shenggang bagong, 1925/7," 32.

59. There were, for example, the forces of Chen Jiongming to the east, of Xiong Kewu to the north, and of Wei Bangping to the south. Wilbur and How, eds., *Missionaries of Revolution*, 173.

60. Deng Zhongxia, *Zhongguo zhigong*, 234.

61. Chesneaux, *Chinese Labor Movement*, 293.

62. "Zhonggong Guangdong quwei guanyu shenggang bagong, 1925/10," 84.

63. "Zhonggong Guangdong quwei guanyu shenggang bagong, 1925/7," 32.

64. Cai and Lu, *Shenggang dabagong*, 46.

65. "Zhonggong Guangdong quwei guanyu shenggang bagong, 1925/7," 32–33.

66. Deng Zhongxia, *Zhongguo zhigong*, 228.

67. *GMGR*, 1925/7/20: 7.

68. *GMGR*, 1925/8/18: 10.

69. *GMGR*, 1925/8/25: 7.

70. *GMGR*, 1926/2/24: 3.

71. *GMGR*, 1926/2/26: 3.

72. "Zhonggong Guangdong quwei guanyu shenggang bagong, 1925/10," 87.

73. *GMGR*, 1925/9/21: 10; 10/16: 10. For the government's negotiation with the merchants for loans, see *GMGR*, 1925/10/17: 7. More information on the fiscal policies and financial conditions of the Canton government in the mid-1920s can be found in Wang Zhenghua, "Guangzhou shiqi guomin zhengfu de caizheng," 511–44. Also Qin Qingjun, "Beifa zhanzheng shiqi de Guangdongsheng caizheng," 161–93.

74. The procedures followed by the depositors were described in *GMGR*, 1925/10/21: 10; 10/23: 10–11.

75. Close to C$2.5 million was said to have been withdrawn within the first five days of the "opening" of Shameen; see *GMGR*, 1925/10/21: 10. The figure of over C$5 million was given in "Guangzhoushi shangban yinhang diaocha," 22–23.

76. "Zhonggong Guangdong quwei guanyu shenggang bagong, 1925/10," 84.

77. "Clementi to Amery, 1925/12/24," PRO/ FO 228/3586, 401.

78. Ibid.

79. "Zhonggong Guangdong quwei guanyu shenggang bagong, 1925/7," 34.

80. *GMGR*, 1925/8/13: 3.

81. *GMGR*, 1925/8/25: 6.

82. *GSSDB*, 3–4.

83. See the submission by the Wanheguan to the Peasant and Labor Bureau in *GMGR*, 1925/8/26: 3.

84. Ibid.

85. *GMGR*, 1925/10/2: 11.

86. See the proclamation issued by the Jixian in *GMGR*, 1925/10/19: 11.

87. The Bozai's version of the event was reported in *GMGR*, 1925/10/20: 11.

88. *GMGR*, 1925/10/21: 11.

89. Ibid.

90. The Tongde, the largest organization of stevedores from Hong Kong, for example, was involved in yet another dispute over access to work in Canton. *GMGR*, 1925/12/9: 10.

91. "Zhonggong Guangdong quwei guanyu shenggang bagong, 1925/7," 29.

92. *GMGR*, 1926/8/11: 10.

93. Chen Gongbo, *Kuxiaolu*, 40–42; Li Yunhan, *Cong ronggong dao qingdang*, vol. 1, 382–92. Also Hu Hanmin's own account in "Hu Hanmin zizhuan xubian," 32–42.

94. *GMGR*, 1925/9/16: 3. Hu finally returned to Shanghai in April of 1926. Other senior members of the Guomindang who were also forced out of Canton following Liao's death included Zou Lu and Lin Sen; see Li Yunhan, *Cong ronggong dao qingdang*, 392.

95. Until he assumed the role of head of the Whampoa Military Academy in mid-1924, Chiang was a relatively obscure figure within the Guomindang. His new post, however, afforded him considerable power and visibility. As pointed out by his second wife, Ch'en Chieh-ju, "[f]or the first time in his life, Kai-shek [as head of Whampoa] figured prominently in the party and in Canton political life." Ch'en Chieh-ju, *Chiang Kai-shek's Secret Past*, 143.

96. *GMGR*, 1925/8/26: 3.

97. See the detailed report in *GMGR*, 1925/9/24: 2–3.

98. One could perhaps sense a shift of power when Wang Jingwei felt compelled to deny that he had been intimidated by Chiang into demanding Xu's departure. *GMGR*, 1925/9/24: 2–3. As might be expected, orthodox Guomindang historians tend to portray Wang Jingwei as the main instigator of the political turmoil following Liao's death. See, for example, Li Guoqi, *Minguoshi lunji*, 448–54.

99. "Zhonggong Guangdong quwei guanyu shenggang bagong, 1925/10," 84.

100. See, for example, the entry on 1926/1/19 in Chiang's "diary"; Mao Sicheng, ed., *Minguo shiwunian yiqian zhi Jiang Jieshi xiansheng*, 609. Also Zhang Guotao, *Wo de huiyi*, vol. 2, 503.

101. "Enclosure (Canton Consul-General Jamieson to the Foreign Office, 1926/2/2) in Clementi to Amery, 1926/2/10," PRO/ FO 228/3586, 428.

102. Tien-wei Wu, "Chiang Kai-shek's March Twentieth Coup d'Etat of 1926," 585–602.

103. Kitamura, "Kanton kokumin seifu ni okeru seiji kōsō to Shō Kaiseki no taitō," 132–139.

104. Wilbur and How, eds., *Missionaries of Revolution*, 253.

105. Chen Gongbo, *Kuxiaolu*, 77–78.

106. Wilbur and How, eds., *Missionaries of Revolution*, 252; Zhang Guotao, *Wo de huiyi*, vol. 2, 502.

107. See the account provided in Vishnyakova-Akimova, *Two Years in Revolutionary China*, 210–13.

108. *GMGR*, 1926/3/27: 3.

109. *GMGR*, 1926/3/27: 3.

110. Wilbur and How, eds., *Missionaries of Revolution*, 267–73.

111. *GMGR*, 1926/4/24: 10.

112. *GMGR*, 1926/4/27: 11.

113. This is, for example, the basic explanation given by Zhang Guotao. *Wo de huiyi*, vol. 2, 505, 514–15.

114. "Guangzhou gonghui yundong de baogao, 1926 xia," 346. The report's estimate of the number of workers in Canton (150,000) was substantially lower than the figure of unionized workers (290,628) provided in the municipal survey (*GSSDB*, 3). Neither document, however, includes a definition of "worker."

115. Cherepanov, *As Military Adviser*, 212.

116. Ibid., 213.

117. "Zhonghua minguo guomin zhengfu ling (no. 452), 1926/8/26," in *ZMS-DZH*, vol. 4, 974–75.

118. Ibid.

119. *GMGR*, 1926/8/10: 10.

120. *GMGR*, 1926/10/8: 3; 10/11: 7.

121. See the proclamation in *GMGR*, 1926/10/1: 10.

122. Little information is available on the background of those workers who remained in Canton. One source states that in mid-1927, there were only about six hundred striking seamen left in the metropolis ("Chen Quan, Zu Yi zhi Su Ji xin, 1927/7/2," 5). While some of the workers might have chosen to stay to continue the struggle, it is safe to say that many others had virtually no choice. By 1926, new workers from southeast Asia had taken over a large number of the jobs in Hong Kong (Cai and Lu, *Shenggang dabagong*, 142). Since the strike had not officially been settled with the colonial authority, many of the workers had little prospect of returning to their old positions or finding alternative means of livelihood. In Canton, they were at least assured of some provision of food and shelter.

123. "Acting Consul-General J. F. Brenan (Canton) to Minister M. W. Lampson (Head of the Peking Legation), 1927/9/21," PRO/ FO 228/3586, 120.

124. *GMGR*, 1927/4/16: 6.

125. *GMGR*, 1927/4/18: 3; 4/19: 4.

126. "Canton Political Report, June Quarter 1927," PRO/FO 228/3639, 163.

127. "Guangzhou gongren daibiao dahui baogao, 1928/1," 222.

128. "Chen Quan, Zu Yi zhi Su Ji xin, 1927/7/2," 7.

129. "Guangzhou gongren daibiao dahui baogao, 1928/1," 223; "Canton Political Report, June Quarter 1927," PRO/FO 228/3639, 163.

130. "Guangzhou gongren daibiao dahui baogao, 1928/1," 223.

131. See, for example, the decree on the protection of peasants and workers in *GMGR*, 1927/4/18: 4.

132. *GMGR*, 1927/4/18: 7.

133. *GMGR*, 1927/4/25: 3.

134. With the northward progress of the military campaign, the capital of the Guomindang's National Government was officially moved from Canton to Wuhan at the beginning of 1927.

135. *GMGR*, 1927/7/14: 2.

136. *GMGR*, 1927/11/14: 5.

137. "Canton Intelligence Report, April to September 1927," PRO/FO 228/3639, 186.

138. "Acting Consul-General Brenan to Minister Lampson, 1927/11/14," PRO/FO 228/3586, 234.

139. Ibid., 236–37.

140. *GMGR*, 1927/11/14: 5. Wang left with Li Jishen on November 15.

141. "Guangzhou gongren daibiao dahui baogao, 1928/1," 232. Also "Governor Clementi to Secretary Amery, 1927/12/1," PRO/FO 228/3586, 314.

142. *GMGR*, 1927/12/1: 9; "Canton Political Report, December Quarter 1927," PRO/FO 228/3826, 110.

143. "Guangzhou gongren daibiao dahui baogao, 1928/1," 225.

144. "Canton Political Report, September Quarter 1927," PRO/FO 228/3639, 197.

145. "Zhonggong Guangdong shengwei gei zhongyang de baogao, 1927/12/8," 186.

146. "Shengwei duiyu Guangzhou baodong jueyian, 1928/1–5," 208, 212. It is not entirely clear who comprises the over two thousand deaths. The resolution at one point describes them simply as "worker-and-peasant masses," but later labels them as "red guards" and "red soldiers," implying that they had been engaged in combat. The latter interpretation fits another figure of over five thousand executions in the week following the uprising, during which many who were not directly involved in the revolt were put to death by the government.

147. "Acting Consul-General Brenan to Minister Lampson, 1927/12/15," PRO/FO 228/3728, 9.

148. Letter dated 1927/12/20 in Rea, ed., *Canton in Revolution: The Collected Papers of Earl Swisher, 1925–1928*, 97.

149. Kuhn, "Local Self-Government under the Republic: Problems of Control, Autonomy, and Mobilization," 297.

150. See Thomas, *"Proletarian Hegemony" in the Chinese Revolution and the Canton Commune of 1927*, 37–74.

151. "Guangzhou baodong zhi yiyi yu jiaoxun, 1928/1/3," 243.

152. Ibid., 232.

153. There is still some debate as to who exactly was responsible for the fiasco in Canton. While Benjamin Schwartz suggested long ago that "there is much evidence that the events of Canton were inspired directly from Moscow" (*Chinese Communism and the Rise of Mao*, 105), Tso-liang Hsiao has taken the rather extreme position of arguing that the Communist leadership in Shanghai; the Comintern agent in China, Vissarion Lominadze (July to November 1927); and the Comintern itself all learned of the uprising from newspapers or telegraphic reports ("Chinese Communism and the Canton Soviet of 1927," 68–69, 72–73). In light of the available evidence, Hsiao's assertion that the local Communist cadres in Canton acted without the knowledge of the party center seems rather untenable. What remains unclear, however, is the precise role of the Comintern and Lominadze, and in particular that of agent Heinz Neumann (who arrived in China in December 1927 and was in Canton during the revolt). It is uncertain whether Lominadze and Neumann were simply messengers for Stalin, or were involved in the planning or the execution of the uprising out of their own predilections. It should perhaps be noted that, in the words of Bernard Thomas, "the decision to seize Canton accorded generally with the much more 'leftist' insurrectionary policy guidelines adopted by the Chinese Communist leadership, under the close scrutiny and guidance of Comintern representatives, during the second half of 1927" (*"Proletarian Hegemony"*, 2). In his memoir, Zhang Guotao put the blame for the disaster on Neumann's dogmatic insistence on the significance of holding an urban center (*Wo de huiyi*, vol. 2, 755–56). A detailed study by a Chinese historian, while stressing the responsibility of Stalin and the Comintern for the "failures" of the period, largely sidesteps the issue of who actually initiated the uprising in Canton (Huang Xiurong, *Gongchan guoji yu Zhongguo geming guanxishi*, vol. 1, esp. 364–400).

154. "Shengwei dui zhongyang zhengzhiju huiyi tongguo zhi 'Guangzhou baodong zhi yiyi yu jiaoxun' de jueyian, 1928/1/16," 280.

155. Ibid., 281–83.

156. "Nie Rongzhen dui Guangzhou baodong de yijian, 1927/12/15," 357. Nie also maintained in his memoir that in November 1927 he had already argued against the idea of staging an uprising. Nie, *Nie Rongzhen huiyilu*, 79.

157. "Shengwei dui zhongyang zhengzhiju huiyi tongguo zhi 'Guangzhou baodong zhi yiyi yu jiaoxun' de jueyian, 1928/1/16," 283–84.

158. See, for example, "Guangdong shengwei tonggao (nos. 1 and 2), 1928/1." It is perhaps somewhat ironic that in the official annals of the Communist Party Li's name was later associated with "left adventurism"—carrying out insurrections in the absence of the appropriate objective conditions, that is to say, with precisely the kind of mistakes with which he charged some of the old party cadres of Canton in early

1928. The so-called Li Lisan Line was formally condemned by the Comintern and the Chinese Communist Party in 1930. See Huang Xiurong, *Gongchan guoji yu Zhongguo geming guanxishi*, vol. 2, 60–94. Also Thornton, *The Comintern and the Chinese Communists, 1928–1931*, 103–86.

159. Apart from the report by Nie Rongzhen, see other submissions by Chen Geng, Cai Shengxi, Zeng Ganting, Liu Chujie in *GQZ*, vol. 1, 362–72.

160. "Zhongyang gao Guangdong tongzhi shu, 1928/1/18," 287–301; "Zhongyang zhi shengwei xin, 1928/1/25," 306–18.

161. "Zhongyang zhi shengwei xin, 1928/1/25," 310, 316–17.

162. "Zhongyang tonggao, no. 35: 'Guangzhou baodong zhi yiyi yu jiaoxun' jueyian de buchong, 1928/2/26," 329–30.

Bibliography

Abend, Hallett. *My Life in China, 1926–1941*. New York: Harcourt Brace, 1943.

Anderson, Benedict. *Imagined Communities: Reflections on the Origin and Spread of Nationalism*. Rev. ed. London: Verso, 1991.

Annual Trade Reports and Returns. The Maritime Customs, China.

Arendt, Hannah. *The Human Condition*. Chicago: University of Chicago Press, 1958.

Asad, Talal. "Conscripts of Western Civilization." In *Civilization in Crisis*, ed. Christine Ward Gailey, Vol. 1, 333–51. Gainesville: University of Florida Press, 1992.

Baker, Keith Michael. *Inventing the French Revolution*. Cambridge: Cambridge University Press, 1990.

Bakulin, A. V. *Zhongguo dageming Wuhan shiqi jianwenlu* (What I know about the Great Chinese Revolution during the Wuhan period). Trans. Zheng Houan, Liu Gongxun, and Liu Zuohan. Beijing: Shehui Kexue, 1985.

Balazs, Etienne. *Chinese Civilization and Bureaucracy*. Trans. H. M. Wright. New Haven: Yale University Press, 1964.

Bechhofer, Frank and Brian Elliott, eds. *The Petite Bourgeoisie: Comparative Studies of the Uneasy Stratum*. New York: St. Martin's, 1981.

Befu, Harumi, ed. *Cultural Nationalism in East Asia: Representation and Identity*. Berkeley: Institute of East Asian Studies, 1993.

Bendix, Reinhard. *Force, Fate and Freedom*. Berkeley and Los Angeles: University of California Press, 1984.

Benedict, Carol. *Bubonic Plague in Nineteenth-Century China*. Stanford: Stanford University Press, 1996.

Bergère, Marie-Claire. *The Golden Age of the Chinese Bourgeoisie, 1911–1937*. Trans. Janet Lloyd. Cambridge: Cambridge University Press, 1989.

———. "The Role of the Bourgeoisie." In *China in Revolution: The First Phase, 1900–1913*, ed. Mary Wright, 229–95. New Haven: Yale University Press, 1968.

———. *Sun Yat-sen*. Trans. Janet Lloyd. Stanford: Stanford University Press, 1998.

Bernal, Martin. *Chinese Socialism to 1907*. Ithaca: Cornell University Press, 1976.

Bhabha, Homi K. *The Location of Culture*. London: Routledge, 1994.

————, ed. *Nation and Narration*. London: Routledge, 1990.

Blagodstov, A.V. *Zhongguo geming zhaji, 1925–1927* (Notebook on the Chinese Revolution). Trans. Zhang Kai. Chongqing: Xinhua, 1985.

Bourdieu, Pierre. *In Other Words*. Trans. Matthew Adamson. Stanford: Stanford University Press, 1990.

————. *Language and Symbolic Power*. Trans. Gino Raymond and Matthew Adamson. Cambridge: Harvard University Press, 1991.

————. *Outline of a Theory of Practice*. Trans. Richard Nice. Cambridge: Cambridge University Press, 1977.

Breuilly, John. *Nationalism and the State*. New York: St. Martin's, 1982.

Burke, Peter and Roy Porter. *The Social History of Language*. Cambridge: Cambridge University Press, 1987.

Cai Luo and Lu Quan. *Shenggang dabagong* (The Great Canton-Hongkong Strike). Guangzhou: Renmin, 1980.

Calhoun, Craig. "Civil Society and the Public Sphere." *Public Culture* 5, no. 2 (1993): 267–80.

————, ed. *Habermas and the Public Sphere*. Cambridge: MIT Press, 1992.

Calinescu, Matei. *Five Faces of Modernity*. Durham: Duke University Press, 1987.

The Canton Incident of June 23rd: The Truth. Guangzhou, 1925.

Canton: Its Port, Industries and Trade. Guangzhou, 1932.

Castoriadis, Cornelius. "The Imaginary Institution of Society." In *The Structural Allegory: Reconstructive Encounters with the New French Thought*, ed. John Fekete, 6–45. Minneapolis: University of Minnesota Press, 1984.

Chakrabarty, Dipesh. "Conditions for Knowledge of Working Class Conditions." In *Selected Subaltern Studies*, ed. Ranajit Guha and Gayatri Chakravorty Spivak, 179–230. New York: Oxford University Press, 1988.

————. *Rethinking Working-Class History: Bengal 1890–1940*. Princeton: Princeton University Press, 1989.

————. "Postcoloniality and the Artifice of History: Who Speaks for 'Indian' Pasts?" *Representations*, no. 37 (1992): 1–26.

Chan, F. Gilbert and Thomas H. Etzold, eds. *China in the 1920s: Nationalism and Revolution*. New York: New Viewpoints, 1976.

Chan, Ming K. *Labor and Empire: The Chinese Labor Movement in the Canton Delta, 1895–1927*. Ph.D. diss., Stanford University, 1975.

————. "A Turning Point in the Modern Chinese Revolution: The Historical Significance of the Canton Decade, 1917–27." In *Remapping China: Fissures in Historical Terrain*, ed. Gail Hershatter, Emily Honig, Jonathan N. Lipman, and Randall Stross, 224–41. Stanford: Stanford University Press, 1996.

Chan, Wellington K. K. "Personal Styles, Cultural Values, and Management: The Sincere and Wing On companies in Shanghai and Hong Kong 1900–1941." In

Asian Department Stores, ed. Kerrie L. MacPherson, 66–89. Honolulu: University of Hawai'i Press, 1998.

Chang, Hao. *Liang Ch'i-ch'ao and Intellectual Transition in China*. Cambridge: Harvard University Press, 1971.

Chang P'eng-yuan [Zhang Pengyuan]. *Lixianpai yu xinhai geming* (The constitutionalists and the 1911 Revolution). Taipei: Zhongguo xueshu zhuzuo jiangzhu weiyuanhui, 1969.

Chartier, Roger. *Cultural History: Between Practice and Representations*. Trans. Lydia Cochrane. Ithaca: Cornell University Press, 1988.

———. *The Cultural Origins of the French Revolution*. Trans. Lydia Cochrane. Durham: Duke University Press, 1991.

———. *On the Edge of the Cliff: History, Language, and Practices*. Trans. Lydia Cochrane. Baltimore: Johns Hopkins University Press, 1997.

Chatterjee, Partha. *The Nation and Its Fragments*. Princeton: Princeton University Press, 1993.

———. *Nationalist Thought and the Colonial World: A Derivative Discourse*. London: Zed Books, 1986.

———, ed. *Texts of Power: Emerging Disciplines in Colonial Bengal*. Minneapolis: University of Minnesota Press, 1995.

Chen Gongbo. *Kuxiaolu: Chen Gongbo huiyi, 1925–1936* (Bitter smile: Memoirs of Chen Gongbo). Hong Kong: University of Hong Kong, 1979.

Chen Guo. "Guangzhou shangtuan panbianhou de Chen Lianbo" (Chen Lianbo in the aftermath of the Merchant Corps rebellion). In *GDWZ*. Vol. 19, 86–118. 1965.

Chen Jiongming. *Zhongguo tongyi chuyi* (My humble opinion on the unification of China). n.p., n.d.

"Chen Quan, Zu Yi zhi Su Ji xin, 1927/7/2" (A letter from Chen Quan and Zu Yi to Su Ji). In *GGLWH. Zhonggong Guangdong shengwei wenjian, 1927* (Documents of the Guangdong Provincial Committee of the CCP), 5–15. 1982.

Chen Ta [Chen Da]. "Analysis of Strikes in China from 1918 to 1926." Parts 1–3. *Chinese Economic Journal* 1, no. 10 (1927): 843–65; no. 11 (1927): 945–62; no. 12 (1927): 1077–88.

———. "The Labor Movement in China." *International Labor Review* 15, no.3 (1927): 339–63.

———. *Zhongguo laogong wenti* (The labor problem in China). Shanghai: Shangwu, 1929.

Chen Tianjie. "Wo suo zhidao Chen Lianbo de ji jian shi" (Several things I know about Chen Lianbo). In *GZWZ*. Vol. 10, 182–94. 1963.

Chen Xingwu. "Ma Yingbiao yu Xianshi gongsi" (Ma Yingbiao and the Sincere Company). In *GZWZ*. Vol. 36, *Guangzhou gongshang jingji shiliao* (Source materials on industries and commerce of Canton), 124–35. 1986.

Chen Zhen, ed. *Zhongguo jindai gongyeshi ziliao* (Source materials on the history of Chinese modern industries). 4 vols. Beijing: Sanlian, 1961.

Chen Zhiling. *Diyici guonei geming zhanzheng shigao* (A draft history of the first revolutionary civil war). Xi'an: Renmin, 1981.

Ch'en, Chieh-ju. *Chiang Kai-shek's Secret Past*. Ed. and with an introduction by Lloyd E. Eastman. Boulder: Westview Press, 1993.

Ch'en, Jerome. *China and the West*. London: Hutchinson, 1979.

Cheng Hao. *Guangzhou gangshi: jindai bufen* (The history of the port of Canton: The modern era). Beijing: Haiyang, 1985.

Cheng Tiangu. *Cheng Tiangu huiyilu* (The memoir of Cheng Tiangu). Hong Kong: Longmen, 1978.

Cherepanov, A. I. *As Military Adviser in China*. Trans. Sergei Sosinsky. Moscow: Progress, 1982.

Chesneaux, Jean. *The Chinese Labor Movement, 1919–1927*. Trans. H. M. Wright. Stanford: Stanford University Press, 1968.

———. "The Federalist Movement in China, 1920–3." In *Modern China's Search for a Political Form*, ed. Jack Gray, 96–137. London: Oxford University Press, 1969.

Ch'i, Hsi-sheng. *Warlord Politics in China 1916–1928*. Stanford: Stanford University Press, 1976.

China: State and Society. Moscow: USSR Academy of Sciences, 1985.

Chow, Tse-tsung. *The May 4th Movement*. Cambridge: Harvard University Press, 1960.

Clifford, Nicholas R. *Shanghai, 1925: Urban Nationalism and the Defense of Foreign Privilege*. Ann Arbor: Michigan Center for Chinese Studies, 1979.

Coble, Parks M. Jr. *The Shanghai Capitalists and the Nationalist Government, 1927–1937*. Cambridge: Harvard University Press, 1980.

Cochran, Sherman. *Big Business in China: Sino-Foreign Rivalry in the Cigarette Industry, 1890–1930*. Cambridge: Harvard University Press, 1980.

Cody, Jeffrey W. "American planning in republican China, 1911–1937." *Planning Perspectives*, no. 11 (1996): 339–77.

Crossick, Geoffrey. "La petite bourgeoisie brittanique au XIXe siècle" (The petite bourgeoisie in nineteenth-century Britain). *Le mouvement social*, no. 108 (1979): 21–61.

Dai Chuanxian [Dai Jitao]. "Geming! Hegu? Weihe?" (Revolution! Why? For What?). *Jianshe* 1, no. 3 (1919): 1–31.

de Certeau, Michel. *The Practice of Everyday Life*. Trans. Steven Rendall. Berkeley and Los Angeles: University of California Press, 1984.

Deng Duanben. *Guangzhou gangshi: gudai bufen* (The history of the port of Canton: The premodern era). Beijing: Haiyang, 1986.

Deng Yusheng. *Quanyue shehui shilu chubian* (A draft veritable record of Guangdong society). Guangzhou: Diaocha quanyue shehuichu, 1910.

Deng Zhongxia. *Zhongguo zhigong yundong jianshi, 1919–1926* (A brief history of the Chinese labor movement). Beijing: Renmin, 1953.

Derrida, Jacques. *Of Grammatology*. Trans. Gayatri Chakravorty Spivak. Baltimore: Johns Hopkins University Press, 1976.

Dikötter, Frank. *The Discourse of Race in Modern China*. Stanford: Stanford University Press, 1992.

———. *Sex, Culture and Modernity in China*. Honolulu: University of Hawai'i Press, 1995.

Ding Richu. "Xinhai geming qian de Shanghai zibenjia jieji" (The Shanghai capitalist classes before the 1911 Revolution). In *Jinian xinhai geming qishi zhounian xueshu taolunhui lunwenji* (Conference essays commemorating the seventieth anniversary of the 1911 Revolution). Vol. 1, 281–321. Beijing: Zhonghua, 1983.

Ding You. "Yijiulingwunian Guangdong fanmei yundong" (The 1905 anti-American movement in Guangdong). In *Jindaishi ziliao* (Source materials on modern history), no. 5 (1958): 8–52.

Dirks, Nicholas B., ed. *Colonialism and Culture*. Ann Arbor: University of Michigan Press, 1992.

Dirlik, Arif. *Anarchism in the Chinese Revolution*. Berkeley and Los Angeles: University of California Press, 1991.

———. "Narrativizing Revolution: The Guangzhou Uprising (11-13 December 1927) in Workers' Perspective." *Modern China* 23, no. 4 (1997): 363–97.

———. *The Origins of Chinese Communism*. New York: Oxford University Press, 1989.

———. *Revolution and History*. Berkeley and Los Angeles: University of California Press, 1978.

Dittmer, Lowell and Samuel S. Kim, eds. *China's Quest for National Identity*. Ithaca: Cornell University Press, 1993.

Diyici guonei geming zhanzheng shiqi de gongren yundong (The labor movement during the first revolutionary civil war). Beijing: Renmin, 1980.

"Diyici guonei geming zhanzheng shiqi de Guangdong funü yundong" (The women's movement in Guangdong during the first revolutionary civil war). In *Guangdong dangshi ziliao* (Source materials on party history in Guangdong). Vol. 8, 152–91. 1986.

Dongfang zazhi (The Eastern Miscellany). Shanghai.

Dray-Novey, Alison. "Spatial Order and Police in Imperial Beijing." *Journal of Asian Studies* 52, no. 4 (1993): 885–922.

Duara, Prasenjit. "De-Constructing the Chinese Nation." *The Australian Journal of Chinese Affairs*, no. 30 (1993): 1–26.

———. *Rescuing History from the Nation*. Chicago: University of Chicago Press, 1995.

Durkheim, Emile. *The Division of Labor in Society*. Trans. W. D. Halls. New York: Free Press, 1984.

Elias, Norbert. *What Is Sociology?* Trans. Stephen Mennell and Grace Morrissey. New York: Columbia University Press, 1978.

Elvin, Mark. "The Gentry Democracy in Chinese Shanghai, 1905–1914." In *Modern China's Search for a Political Form*, ed. Jack Gray, 41–61. London: Oxford University Press, 1969.

Elvin, Mark and G. William Skinner, eds. *The Chinese City Between Two Worlds*. Stanford: Stanford University Press, 1974.

Eng, Robert. *Economic Imperialism in China: Silk Production and Exports, 1861–1932*. Berkeley: Institute of East Asian Studies, 1986.

"Erda" he "Sanda" (The Second Congress and the Third Congress). Beijing: Shehui kexue, 1985.

Esherick, Joseph W. *Reform and Revolution in China: The 1911 Revolution in Hunan and Hubei*. Berkeley and Los Angeles: University of California Press, 1976.

———. "Ten Theses on the Chinese Revolution." *Modern China* 21, no. 1 (1995): 45–76.

Eudin, Xenia J. and Robert C. North. *Soviet Russia and the East, 1920–1927: A Documentary Survey*. Stanford: Stanford University Press, 1957.

Fairbank, J. K., Katherine Frost Bruner, and Elizabeth Macleod Matheson, eds. *The I.G. in Peking: Letters of Robert Hart, Chinese Maritime Customs, 1868–1907*. 2 vols. Cambridge: Harvard University Press, 1975.

Fang Xiao, ed. *Zhonggong dangshi bianyilu* (An investigation of the history of the Chinese Communist Party). Taiyuan: Shanxi jiaoyu, 1991.

Faure, David. "What Made Foshan a Town? The Evolution of Rural-Urban Identities in Ming-Qing China." *Late Imperial China* 11, no. 2 (1990): 1–31.

Faure, David and Helen F. Siu, eds. *Down to Earth: The Territorial Bond in South China*. Stanford: Stanford University Press, 1995.

Felski, Rita. *The Gender of Modernity*. Cambridge: Harvard University Press, 1995.

Fewsmith, Joseph. *Party, State and Local Elites in Republican China: Merchant Organizations and Politics in Shanghai 1890–1930*. Honolulu: University of Hawai'i Press, 1985.

Fitzgerald, John. *Awakening China: Politics, Culture, and Class in the Nationalist Revolution*. Stanford: Stanford University Press, 1996.

———. "The Irony of the Chinese Revolution: The Nationalists and Chinese Society, 1924–1927." Paper presented at the Workshop on the Nationalists and Chinese Society, 1924–1949, Australian National University, Canberra, November 20–21, 1986.

———. "The Misconceived Revolution: State and Society in China's Nationalist Revolution, 1923–26." *Journal of Asian Studies* 49, no. 2 (1990): 323–43.

———. "The Nationless State: The Search for a Nation in Modern Chinese Nationalism." *The Australian Journal of Chinese Affairs*, no. 33 (1995): 75–104.

Foucault, Michel. *The Archaeology of Knowledge.* Trans. A. M. Sheridan Smith. New York: Pantheon, 1972.

———. *Discipline and Punish.* Trans. Alan Sheridan. New York: Vintage Books, 1979.

———. "Governmentality." In *The Foucault Effect,* ed. Graham Burchell, Colin Gordon, and Peter Miller, 87–104. Chicago: University of Chicago Press, 1991.

———. *Power/Knowledge: Selected Interviews and Writings, 1972–1977.* Trans. Colin Gordon, Leo Marshall, John Mepham, and Kate Soper. New York: Pantheon, 1980.

Friedman, Edward. *Backward toward Revolution: The Chinese Revolutionary Party.* Berkeley and Los Angeles: University of California Press, 1974.

———. *National Identity and Democratic Prospects in Socialist China.* Armonk, NY: M. E. Sharpe, 1995.

Fujitani, Takashi. *Splendid Monarchy: Power and Pageantry in Modern Japan.* Berkeley and Los Angeles: University of California Press, 1996.

Fuma Susumu. "Dōzenkai shōshi" (A short history of philanthropic associations). *Shirin* 65, no. 4 (1982): 37–76.

Fung, Edmund S. K. *The Military Dimension of the Chinese Revolution.* Vancouver: University of British Columbia Press, 1980.

Furet, François. *Interpreting the French Revolution.* Trans. Elborg Forster. Cambridge: Cambridge University Press, 1981.

Gao Yuhan. *Guangzhou jiyou* (A record of travel in Canton). Shanghai: Yadong, 1922.

Ge Gongzhen. *Zhongguo baoxueshi* (A history of Chinese newspapers). Beijing: Sanlian, 1955.

Geertz, Clifford. *The Interpretation of Cultures.* New York: Basic Books, 1973.

Gellner, Ernest. *Culture, Identity and Politics.* Cambridge: Cambridge University Press, 1987.

———. *Nations and Nationalism.* Ithaca: Cornell University Press, 1983.

Geming wenxian (Documents of the Revolution). Compiled by Zhongguo Guomindang zhongyang weiyuanhui dangshi shiliao bianzuan weiyuanhui (Committee on the compilation of materials on party history of the Central Executive Committee of the Chinese Nationalist Party). Multivolume. Taipei.

Giddens, Anthony. *Central Problems in Social Theory: Action, Structure and Contradiction in Social Analysis.* London: Macmillan, 1979.

———. *The Constitution of Society: Outline of the Theory of Structuration.* Berkeley and Los Angeles: University of California Press, 1984.

———, ed. *Positivism and Sociology.* London: Heinemann, 1974.

Gilmartin, Christina Kelley. *Engendering the Chinese Revolution.* Berkeley and Los Angeles: University of California Press, 1995.

Gong Zhiliu. "Guangzhou Xiguan shishen he Wenlan shuyuan" (The gentry of the western suburb of Canton and the Wenlan Academy). In *GZWZ*. Vol. 12, 162–67. 1964.

Gongchan guoji yu Zhongguo geming ziliao xuanji, 1926–1927 (Selected materials on the Communist International and the Chinese Revolution). Beijing: Renmin, 1985.

Goodman, Bryna. *Native Place, City, and Nation: Regional Networks and Identities in Shanghai, 1853–1937*. Berkeley and Los Angeles: University of California Press, 1995.

Gramsci, Antonio. *Selections from the Prison Notebooks*. Trans. Quintin Hoare and Geoffrey Nowell Smith. New York: International, 1971.

Gray, J. H. (Mrs.) *Fourteen Months in Canton*. London: Macmillan, 1880.

Gray, John Henry. *Walks in the City of Canton*. Hong Kong: De Souza, 1875.

Great Britain. Colonial Office. Archives, Public Record Office, London.

————. Foreign Office. Archives, Public Record Office, London.

Greenfeld, Liah. *Nationalism: Five Roads to Modernity*. Cambridge: Harvard University Press, 1992.

Guangdong caizheng jishi (Record of the financial administration of Guangdong). 3 vols. Guangzhou: Guangdongsheng caizhengting, 1934.

Guangdong dangshi ziliao (Source materials on party history in Guangdong). Compiled jointly by Zhonggong Guangdong shengwei dangshi ziliao zhengji weiyuanhui (Committee on the collection of materials on party history of the Guangdong Provincial Committee of the CCP) and Zhonggong Guangdong shengwei dangshi yanjiu weiyuanhui (Research committee on party history of the Guangdong Provincial Committee of the CCP). Multivolume. Guangzhou.

"Guangdong duliji" (A record of the independence of Guangdong). In *Guangdong xinhai geming shiliao* (Source materials on the 1911 Revolution in Guangdong), 111–52. Guangzhou: Renmin, 1981.

Guangdong gaixuan ziyiju yiyuan guize biaoce huibian (Rules on reselection of the members of the Provincial Assembly of Guangdong). Guangzhou, 1910.

Guangdong geming lishi wenjian huiji (Documents on the revolutionary history of Guangdong). Compiled by Zhongyang dang'anguan (the CCP Central Archives) and Guangdongsheng dang'anguan (the Guangdong Provincial Archives). Mimeographed. Multivolume.

Guangdong gongbao (Guangdong Government Gazette). Guangzhou.

Guangdong gongshang shiliao jilu (Source materials on industries and commerce in Guangdong). 6 vols. Guangzhou, 1987.

Guangdong jianshe yuekan: gongshang zhuanhao (Guangdong construction monthly: A special issue on industries and commerce) 2, no. 1 (1933).

Guangdong jingji nianjian (The Guangdong economic yearbook). Guangzhou: Guangdongsheng yinhang jingji yanjiushi, 1940.

Guangdong junfashi dashiji (Major events in the history of warlordism in Guangdong). Vol. 43 of *GDWZ*, 1984.

"Guangdong kouxiechao" (The turmoil caused by the seizure of weapons in
Guangdong). In *Yijiuersinian Guangzhou shangtuan shijian* (The 1924
Merchant Corps incident in Canton), 1–440. Hong Kong: Chongwen, 1974.

Guangdong qingdang xunkan (A tri-monthly journal on the party purge in Guangdong). Guangzhou, 1927.

Guangdong qishierhang shangbao (The Guangdong Seventy-two Guilds News).
Guangzhou.

Guangdong qishierhang shangbao nianwu zhounian jinianhao (Special issue commemorating the twenty-fifth anniversary of the *Guangdong Seventy-two Guilds
News*). Guangzhou, 1931.

"Guangdong shengwei tonggao (nos. 1 and 2), 1928/1" (Bulletins of the
Guangdong Provincial Committee of the CCP). In *GQZ*. Vol. 1, 259–65.

Guangdong wenshi ziliao (Source materials on the history and culture of
Guangdong). Compiled by Zhongguo renmin zhengzhi xieshang huiyi Guangdongsheng weiyuanhui wenshi ziliao yanjiu weiyuanhui (Research committee
on historical materials of the Guangdong Provincial Committee of the People's
Political Consultative Conference). Multivolume. Guangzhou: Renmin.

Guangdong xinhai geming shiliao (Source materials on the 1911 Revolution in
Guangdong). Guangzhou: Renmin, 1981.

Guangdong ziyiju choubanchu baogaoshu (Report of the planning office for the
Provincial Assembly of Guangdong). Guangzhou, 1909.

Guangdongqu dang, tuan yanjiu shiliao. (Research materials on the history of the
Party and Youth Corps in Guangdong). Compiled jointly by Guangdongsheng
dang'anguan (The Guangdong Provincial Archives) and Zhonggong Guangdong shengwei dangshi yanjiu weiyuanhui bangongshi (Office of the research
committee on party history of the Guangdong Provincial Committee of the
CCP). Vol. 1 (1921–1926), Guangzhou: Renmin, 1983; Vol. 2 (1927–1934),
Guangzhou: Renmin, 1986.

"Guangdongqu qunzhong yundong zhuangkuang, 1923/11" (The condition of the
mass movement in the Guangdong region). In *GDTYS*. Vol. 1, 55–58.
Guangzhou: Renmin, 1983.

Guangzhou bainian dashiji (Major events over a hundred years in Canton). 2 vols.
Guangzhou: Renmin, 1984.

"Guangzhou baodong zhi yiyi yu jiaoxun, 1928/1/3" (The meaning and lesson of
the Canton uprising). In *GQZ*. Vol. 1, 220–58.

"Guangzhou difang meiyue tuanyuan tongjibiao, 1922/1–7, 10–12" (Monthly statistical tables on members of the youth corps in the Canton area). In *GGLWH*.
Quntuan wenjian, 1922–1924 (Documents of mass organizations and youth
corps), 15–37. 1982.

"Guangzhou gonghui yundong de baogao, 1926 xia" (Report on the union movement in Canton, summer 1926). In *GGLWH. Zhonggong Guangdong quwei wenjian*, 1921–1926 (Documents of the Guangdong Provincial Committee of the CCP), 321–46. 1982.

"Guangzhou gongren daibiao dahui baogao, 1928/1" (Report of the meeting of the workers' deputies in Canton). In *GGLWH. Suweiai, gonghui, nonghui*, 1927–1934 (Soviets, worker associations, peasant associations), 221–41. 1982.

Guangzhou jinbainian jiaoyu shiliao (Source materials on education in Canton for the last hundred years). Guangzhou: Renmin, 1983.

Guangzhou minguo ribao (The Canton Republican Daily). Guangzhou.

Guangzhou nianjian (The Canton Yearbook). Guangzhou: Guangzhoushi zhengfu, 1935.

Guangzhou qiyi ziliao (Source materials on the Canton Uprising). Compiled by Guangdong geming lishi bowuguan (The museum of Guangdong revolutionary history). 2 vols. Beijing: Renmin, 1985.

Guangzhou Shaji cansha'an jiaoshe wenjian shoubian (Documents on the negotiations regarding the Shakee Massacre in Canton). Guangzhou, 1925.

Guangzhou wenshi ziliao (Source materials on the history and culture of Canton). Compiled by Zhongguo renmin zhengzhi xieshang huiyi Guangdongsheng Guangzhoushi weiyuanhui wenshi ziliao yanjiu weiyuanhui (Research committee on historical materials of the Guangzhou Municipal Committee [Guangdong province] of the People's Political Consultative Conference). Multivolume. Guangzhou: Renmin.

Guangzhou zhi miye (The rice trade of Canton). Guangzhou: Guangdongsheng yinhang jingji yanjiushi, 1938.

Guangzhou zhi xinxing gongye: xiangjiao ye (A new industry in Canton: The latex industry). Guangzhou: Guoli Zhongshan daxue jingji diaochachu, 1935.

Guangzhou zhinan (A guide to Canton). Guangzhou: Guangzhoushi zhengfu, 1934.

Guangzhoufu zhi (Gazetteer of Guangzhou Prefecture), 1879.

Guangzhoushi caizhengju renli shouche chezhan jiamubiao (The Finance Bureau's table of stops and fares for rickshaws in Canton). Guangzhou, 1927.

Guangzhoushi dang'anguan (Guangzhou Municipal Archives). Guangzhou.

Guangzhoushi dianli gongsi ershi nianlai zhi gaikuang (The Canton Electricity Company in the last twenty years). Guangzhou: Guangzhoushi shangban dianli gufen youxian gongsi, 1929.

Guangzhoushi nianyinian renkou diaocha baogao (Report of the 1932 census in Canton). Guangzhou: Guangzhoushi diaocha renkou weiyuanhui, 1932.

"Guangzhoushi shangban yinhang diaocha" (A survey of the commercial banks in Canton). *Xinshangmin*, no. 1 (1926): 20–22.

"Guangzhoushi shangdian gezhong de xiguan" (The various customs of the shopkeepers of Canton). *Xinshangmin*, no. 2 (1926): 38–44.

Guangzhoushi shehuiju yewu baogao (Reports of the Social Affairs Bureau of Canton). Guangzhou, 1934.

Guangzhoushi shizheng baogao huikan (Reports of the Canton Municipal Government). Guangzhou: Guangzhoushi shizhengting, 1924.

Guangzhoushi shizheng gongbao (The Canton Municipal Government Gazette). Guangzhou.

Guangzhoushi shizhengfu tongji nianjian (The statistical yearbook of the Canton Municipal Government), 1929.

Guangzhoushi shizhengting shehui diaochagu baogao (Report of the Social Survey Section of the Canton Municipal Government), 1926.

Guangzhoushi tudiju dengji ji zhengshui fali huiji (Registration and taxation laws of the Land Bureau of Canton). Guangzhou, 1926.

Guangzhoushi yan'ge shilüe (A brief history of Canton). Appended to *Guangzhoushi shizheng baogao huikan*. Guangzhou: Guangzhoushi shizhengting, 1924.

Guha, Ranajit. "Discipline and Mobilize." In *Subaltern Studies VII*, ed. Partha Chatterjee and Gyanendra Pandey, 69–120. Delhi: Oxford University Press, 1993.

———. *Dominance Without Hegemony: History and Power in Colonial India*. Cambridge: Harvard University Press, 1997.

———, ed. *A Subaltern Studies Reader, 1986–1995*. Minneapolis: University of Minnesota Press, 1997.

Guha, Ranajit and Gayatri Chakravorty Spivak, eds. *Selected Subaltern Studies*. New York: Oxford University Press, 1988.

Guo Zenong. "Guangdong sanjiangbang de xingqi, fanrong ji shuailuo" (The rise, prosperity and decline of the Sanjiangbang merchants of Guangdong). In *GDWZ*. Vol. 21, 56–70. 1965.

Habermas, Jürgen. *The Structural Transformation of the Public Sphere*. Trans. Thomas Burger. Cambridge: MIT Press, 1989.

Hall, Stuart, David Held, Don Hubert, and Kenneth Thompson, eds. *Modernity: An Introduction to Modern Societies*. Oxford: Blackwell, 1996.

Hao, Yen-p'ing. *The Commercial Revolution in Nineteenth-Century China*. Berkeley and Los Angeles: University of California Press, 1986.

———. *The Comprador in Nineteenth-Century China: Bridge Between East and West*. Cambridge: Harvard University Press, 1970.

Harvey, David. *The Condition of Postmodernity*. Cambridge: Blackwell, 1990.

Hazama Naoki. "'Sendai seisaku' to kōho gunkō" (The "Three Great Policies" and the Whampoa Academy). *Tōyōshi kenkyū* 46, no. 2 (1987): 126–51.

———, ed. *Chūgoku kokumin kakumei no kenkyū* (A study of the Chinese Nationalist Revolution). Kyōto: Kyōto daigaku jimbun kagaku kenkyūjo, 1992.

He Deming. *Zhongguo laogong wenti* (The labor problem in China). Shanghai: Shangwu, 1938.

He Huaimin. "Guangshao duan tielu yunshu hangye" (The transport industry along the Canton-Shaoguan railroad). In *GZWZ*. Vol. 14, 62–66. 1965.

He Yuefu. "Guangdong shishen zai Qingmo xianzheng zhong de zhengzhi dongxiang" (Political trends of the Guangdong gentry during constitutional rule in the late Qing). *Jindaishi yanjiu* 34, no. 4 (1986): 31–54.

———. *Wanqing shishen yu jindai shehui bianqian* (Late Qing gentry and the transformation of society in the modern period). Guangzhou: Renmin, 1994.

Held, David and John Thompson, eds. *Social Theory of Modern Societies: Anthony Giddens and His Critics*. Cambridge: Cambridge University Press, 1989.

Henriot, Christian. *Shanghai, 1927–1937*. Trans. Noël Castelino. Berkeley and Los Angeles: University of California Press, 1993.

Hershatter, Gail. *The Workers of Tianjin, 1900–1949*. Stanford: Stanford University Press, 1986.

Historical and Statistical Abstract of the Colony of Hong Kong, 1841–1932. 3rd ed. Hong Kong Government, 1932.

Ho Ping-ti [He Bingdi]. *Zhongguo huiguanshi lun* (A historical survey of *Landmannschaften* in China). Taipei: Xuesheng, 1966.

Hobsbawm, Eric. *The Age of Empire, 1875–1914*. New York: Vintage, 1989.

———. *Nations and Nationalism Since 1780*. Cambridge: Cambridge University Press, 1990.

Hobsbawm, Eric and Terence Ranger, eds. *The Invention of Tradition*. Cambridge: Cambridge University Press, 1983.

Honig, Emily. *Creating Chinese Ethnicity*. New Haven: Yale University Press, 1992.

———. *Sisters and Strangers: Women in the Shanghai Cotton Mills, 1919–1949*. Stanford: Stanford University Press, 1986.

The Hong Kong Daily Press. Hong Kong.

Hou Guiping. "Dageming shiqi Guangzhou youye gongren de douzheng he Huaxian nongmin yundong" (The struggle of the oil-processing workers in Canton and the peasant movement in Hua County during the Great Revolution). In *Guangdong dangshi ziliao* (Source materials on party history in Guangdong). Vol. 2, 144–53. 1984.

Hsiao, Tso-liang. "Chinese Communism and the Canton Soviet of 1927." *China Quarterly*, no. 30 (1967): 49–78.

———. *Chinese Communism in 1927, City vs. Countryside*. Hong Kong: The Chinese University of Hong Kong, 1970.

Hsieh, Winston. "The Ideas and Ideals of a Warlord: Ch'en Chiung-Ming (1878–1933)." *Papers on China* 16 (1962): 198–252.

Hu Guangming. "Lun zaoqi Tianjin shanghui de xingzhi yu zuoyong" (A discussion of the nature and functions of the early chamber of commerce in Tianjin). *Jindaishi yanjiu* 34, no. 4 (1986): 182–223.

Hu Hanmin. *Hu Hanmin zizhuan* (The autobiography of Hu Hanmin). Taipei: Zhuanji wenxue, 1969.

―――. "Hu Hanmin zizhuan xubian" (Supplement to the autobiography of Hu Hanmin). *Jindaishi ziliao* (Source materials on modern history), no. 52 (1983): 30–79.

―――. "Jieji yu daode xueshuo" (Class and Moral Theories). *Jianshe* 1, no. 6 (1920): 1–43.

Hu Shi. "Women de zhengzhi zhuzhang" (Our political views). Vol. 2, part 3 of *Hu Shi wencun* (Works of Hu Shi). Taipei: Yuanliu, 1986.

Hu Weixi, ed. *Xinhai geming yu Zhongguo jindai sixiang wenhua* (The 1911 Revolution and modern Chinese thought and culture). Beijing: Renmin daxue, 1991.

Hua Gang. *Zhongguo dageming shi, 1925–1927* (A history of the Great Revolution in China). Beijing: Wenshi, 1982.

"Huanan gongren yundong zhong de Gongchandang ren, 1925/1/9" (Report on the Communists in the labor movement of south China). In *Jialun zai Zhongguo, 1924–1927* (Jialun [V. K. Blyukher] in China), trans. Zhongguo shehui kexueyuan, 96–104. Beijing: Shehui kexue, 1983.

Huang Dingsan and Zhu Liyu. "Yijiuersinian qianhou Jiangmen shangtuan huodong jianwen huiyi" (Recollections of the activities of the Jiangmen Merchant Corps around 1924). In *Wenshi ziliao xuanji* (Selected source materials on history and culture). Vol. 2, 128–35. 1961.

Huang Fushan. "Jiefang qian Guangdong huochai gongye gaimao" (A sketch of the match industry in Guangdong before Liberation). In *GDWZ*. Vol. 28, 160–86. 1980.

Huang Jianxin and Luo Yixing. "Lun Ming Qing shiqi Foshan chengshi jingji de fazhan" (A discussion of the economic development of urban Foshan during the Ming-Qing period). In *Ming Qing Guangdong shehui jingji yanjiu* (A study of the economy and society of Guangdong during the Ming-Qing period), ed. Ye Xian'en and Jiang Zuyuan, 26–56. Guangzhou: Renmin, 1987.

Huang Shaosheng. "Wusi yundong zai Guangzhou" (The May Fourth Movement in Canton). In *GDWZ*. Vol. 24, 17–32. 1979.

Huang Xihui. "Guangzhoushi gongshangye xinhai geming hou fazhan shili" (Examples of the development of industries and commerce in Canton after the 1911 Revolution). In *Jinian xinhai geming qishi zhounian shiliao zhuanji* (Source materials commemorating the seventieth anniversary of the 1911 Revolution). Vol. 1, 157–85. Guangzhou: Renmin, 1981.

―――. "Guangzhoushi xiangjiao hangye shihua" (A history of the latex industry in Canton). In *Guangdong gongshang shiliao jilu* (Source materials on industries and commerce in Guangdong). Vol. 2, 346–86. 1987.

Huang Xiurong. *Gongchan guoji yu Zhongguo geming guanxishi* (A history of the relationship between the Communist International and the Chinese Revolution). 2 vols. Beijing: Zhonggong zhongyang dangxiao, 1989.

Huang Yan and Li Boxin, eds. *Sun Zhongshan cangdang xuanbian* (Selected archival materials on Sun Yat-sen). Beijing: Zhonghua, 1986.

Huang Yanpei. *Yisui zhi Guangzhoushi* (Canton at one year old). Shanghai: Shangwu, 1921.

Huang Yibo. *Guangdong zhi jiqi gongren* (The machinists of Guangdong). Guangzhou: Guangdong jiqi zonggonghui, 1929.

Huangpu junxiao shiliao, 1924–1927 (Source materials on the Whampoa Academy). Guangzhou: Renmin, 1982.

Hunt, Lynn. *Politics, Culture and Class in the French Revolution*. Berkeley and Los Angeles: University of California Press, 1984.

——, ed. *The New Cultural History*. Berkeley and Los Angeles: University of California Press, 1989.

Hunter, W. C. *The "Fan Kwae" at Canton*. London: Kegan Paul and Trench, 1882.

Jacobs, Dan N. *Borodin: Stalin's Man in China*. Cambridge: Harvard University Press, 1981.

Jameson, Frederic. *The Political Unconscious*. Ithaca: Cornell University Press, 1981.

Jansen, Marius B. *The Japanese and Sun Yat-sen*. Cambridge: Harvard University Press, 1954.

Jiang Jieshi nianpu chugao (A draft chronological biography of Jiang Jieshi [Chiang Kai-shek]). Beijing: Dang'an, 1992.

Jianshe (Construction). Shanghai.

"Jieji zhidulun" (A discussion of the class system). In *Dongfang zazhi* 9, no. 1 (neiwai shibao [domestic and foreign current affairs]) (1912): 24–27.

Jindai Zhongguo zichan jieji yanjiu (A study of the modern Chinese bourgeoisie). Shanghai: Fudan daxue, 1983.

Jones, Gareth Stedman. *Languages of Class: Studies in English Working Class History, 1832–1982*. Cambridge: Cambridge University Press, 1983.

Jordan, David P. *Transforming Paris: The Life and Labors of Baron Haussmann*. New York: Free Press, 1995.

Jordan, Donald A. *The Northern Expedition: China's National Revolution of 1926–1928*. Honolulu: University of Hawai'i Press, 1976.

Judge, Joan. *Print and Politics: "Shibao" and the Culture of Reform in Late Qing China*. Stanford: Stanford University Press, 1996.

Kedourie, Elie, ed. *Nationalism in Asia and Africa*. New York: New American Library, 1970.

Kelly, Michael, ed. *Critique and Power*. Cambridge: MIT Press, 1994.

Kerr, J. G. *The Canton Guide*. 5th ed. Hong Kong: Kelly and Walsh [Canton: A. S. Watson], 1891.

Kimura Ikujirō. *Chūgoku rōdō undō shi nempyō* (A chronological history of the Chinese labor movement). Tokyo: Kyūko, 1978.

Kitamura Minoru. "Dai-ichiji kokkyō-gassaku no tenkai ni tsuite" (The development of the First United Front). *Shirin* 66, no. 4 (1983): 62–101.

——. "Kanton kokumin seifu ni okeru seiji kōsō to Shō Kaiseki no taitō"

(Political struggle in the Nationalist government in Guangdong and the rise of Chiang Kai-shek). *Shirin* 68, no. 5 (1985): 113–51.

Kuhn, Philip A. "Chinese Views of Social Classification." In *Class and Social Stratification in Post-Revolutionary China*, ed. James L. Watson, 16–28. Cambridge: Cambridge University Press, 1984.

———. "Local Self-Government under the Republic: Problems of Control, Autonomy, and Mobilization." In *Conflict and Control in Late Imperial China*, ed. Frederic Wakeman and Carolyn Grant, 257–98. Berkeley and Los Angeles: University of California Press, 1975.

Kwan, Daniel Y. K. *Marxist Intellectuals and the Chinese Labor Movement: A Study of Deng Zhongxia (1894–1933)*. Seattle: University of Washington Press, 1997.

"Labor Conditions in Canton: A Statistical Study." *Chinese Economic Journal* 4, no. 6 (1929): 516–21.

LaCapra, Dominick. *Soundings in Critical Theory*. Ithaca: Cornell University Press, 1989.

Laclau, Ernesto. *New Reflections on the Revolution of Our Time*. London: Verso, 1990.

Lai Zehan. "Sun Fo yu Guangzhoushi de jindaihua" (Sun Fo [Sun Ke] and the modernization of Canton). In *Zhongguo xiandaishi lunji* (Essays on contemporary Chinese history), ed. Zhang Yufa. Vol. 7, 83–102. Taipei: Lianjing, 1982.

Landis, Richard B. "Training and Indoctrination at the Whampoa Academy." In *China in the 1920s: Nationalism and Revolution*, ed. F. Gilbert Chan and Thomas H. Etzold, 73–93. New York: New Viewpoints, 1976.

Lary, Diana. *Region and Nation: The Kwangsi Clique in Chinese Politics, 1925–1937*. Cambridge: Cambridge University Press, 1974.

Lee, Edward Bing-shuey. *Modern Canton*. Shanghai: Mercury Press, 1936.

Lee, Leo Ou-fan. "In Search of Modernity: Some Reflections on a New Mode of Consciousness in Twentieth-Century Chinese History and Literature." In *Ideas Across Cultures: Essays on Chinese Thought in Honor of Benjamin I. Schwartz*, ed. Paul A. Cohen and Merle Goldman, 109–35. Cambridge: Harvard University Press, 1990.

Lee, Leo Ou-fan and Andrew Nathan. "The Beginnings of Mass Culture: Journalism and Fiction in the Late Ch'ing and Beyond." In *Popular Culture in Late Imperial China*, ed. David Johnson, Andrew J. Nathan and Evelyn S. Rawski, 360–95. Berkeley and Los Angeles: University of California Press, 1985.

Lefebvre, Henri. *Introduction to Modernity*. Trans. John Moore. London: Verso, 1995.

———. *The Production of Space*. Trans. Donald Nicholson-Smith. Oxford: Blackwell, 1991.

Leong, S. T. "The Hakka Chinese of Lingnan: Ethnicity and Social Change in Modern Times." In *Ideal and Reality: Social and Political Change in Modern*

China, ed. David Pong and Edmund S. K. Fung, 287–326. Lanham: University Press of America, 1985.

Levenson, Joseph. *Confucian China and Its Modern Fate: The Problem of Intellectual Continuity*. Berkeley and Los Angeles: University of California Press, 1958.

Li Benli. "Shunde cansiye de lishi gaikuang" (A historical outline of the silk industry in Shunde County). In *GDWZ*. Vol. 15, 102–31. 1964.

Li Boyuan and Ren Gongtan. *Guangdong jiqi gongren fendoushi* (A history of the struggle of the Guangdong machinists). Taipei: Laogong fulishe, 1955.

Li Dazhao. *Li Dazhao wenji* (Selected works of Li Dazhao). 2 vols. Beijing: Renmin, 1984.

Li Fu. "Huiyi Guangzhou tielu gongren de geming douzheng" (Recollections of the revolutionary struggle of the railroad workers in Canton). In *GZWZ*. Vol. 25, 1–18. 1982.

Li Guoqi. *Minguoshi lunji* (Essays on republican history). Taipei: Nantian, 1990.

Li Henggao and Yu Shaoshan. "Yueshang zizhihui yu yueshang weichi gonganhui" (The Merchant Self-Government Association and the Merchant Association for the Maintenance of Public Order). In *GZWZ*. Vol. 7, 21–36. 1963.

Li Huichan. "Guangzhou ge gongyi shetuan gaikuang" (The general conditions of the philanthropic organizations in Canton). In *GZWZ*. Vol. 22, 195–210. 1978.

Li Jiannong. *Zhongguo jinbainian zhengzhishi* (A political history of China in the last hundred years). 2 vols. Taipei: Shangwu, 1974.

Li Shoukong. *Minchu zhi guohui* (The parliament of the early Republic). Taipei: Zhongguo xueshu zhuzuo jiangzhu weiyuanhui, 1964.

Li Taichu. *Guangdong siye maoyi gaikuang* (The general conditions of the silk trade in Guangdong). Guangzhou: Zhonghua bianyi, 1930.

Li Weishi. "Guangdongsheng cansiye de maoyi ji qi shuailuo" (The silk trade of Guangdong and its decline). In *GZWZ*. Vol. 16, 70–80. 1965.

Li Xianheng, Lin Hongnuan, and Yang Shaolian. *Chen Yannian*. Guangzhou: Renmin, 1985.

Li Xiaoti. *Qingmo de xiaceng shehui qimeng yundong* (The enlightenment movement of the lower stratum of society in the late Qing). Taipei: Zhongyang yanjiuyuan jindaishi yanjiusuo, 1992.

Li Xin, ed. *Guomin geming de xingqi* (The rise of the Nationalist Revolution). Shanghai: Renmin, 1991.

Li Xinkui. "Guangdong min fangyan yingcheng de lishi guocheng" (The history of the formation of the Guangdong Min dialect). *Guangdong shehui kexue*, no. 3 (1987): 119–24; no. 4 (1987): 142–50.

Li Xixian. "Wei Bangping ren Guangdong shenghui jingcha tingzhang jian Guangdong quansheng jingwu chuzhang shi de jingcha, 1917–1920" (The police during Wei Bangping's tenure as the head of both the municipal and provincial departments of police). In *GZWZ*. Vol. 14, 1–26. 1965.

Li Yaofeng. "Huiyi sishi nianjian Guangzhou diqu de huochai gongye" (Recollections of forty years of the match industry in the Canton region). In *GZWZ*. Vol. 14, 1–26. 1965.

———. "Wo shi zenyang canjia shangtuan de" (How I joined the Merchant Corps). In *GZWZ*. Vol. 7, 95–96. 1963.

Li Yunhan. *Cong ronggong dao qingdang* (From accomodating the Communists to the purge in the [Chinese Nationalist] Party). 2 vols. Taipei: Zhongguo xueshu zhuzuo jiangzhu weiyuanhui, 1966.

Li Zonghuang. *Xin Guangdong guanchaji* (Observations in new Guangdong). Shanghai: Shangwu, 1922.

Li Zongren. *Li Zongren huiyi* (The memoir of Li Zongren). Hong Kong: Nanyue, 1987.

Liang Jiabin. *Guangdong shisanhang kao* (A study of the thirteen guilds of Guangdong). Shanghai: Guoli bianyi, 1937.

Liang Langqiu. *Guangzhou shangyun yan'geshi* (A history of the merchant movement in Canton). Guangzhou, 1934.

Liang Moyuan and Xue Zemin. "Xietonghe jiqichang huigu" (Reminiscences of the Xietonghe Machine-Tool Factory). In *GZWZ*. Vol. 9, 1–17. 1963.

Liang Qichao. "Xinminshuo" (On New People). In *Yinbingshi quanji* (Works from the Yinbing Studio), 1–133. Taipei: Wenhua, 1989.

———. *Yinbingshi wenji* (Collected essays from the Yinbing Studio). 45 *juan* [16 volumes]. Taipei: Zhonghua, 1960.

Liang Shuming. *Zhongguo wenhua yaoyi* (The main themes of Chinese culture). Hong Kong: Sanlian, 1989.

Liang Sicheng. *Zhongguo jianzhushi* (A history of Chinese architecture). Taipei: Mingwen, 1981.

Liang Tingnan. *Yuehaiguan zhi* (Annals of the Guangdong Maritime Customs). Taipei: Chengwen, 1968.

Liao Zhongkai. *Shuangqing wenji* (Selected Works of Shuangqing [Liao Zhongkai and He Xiangning]). Vol. 1. Beijing: Renmin, 1985.

Lin Fang. "Wo canjia shangtuan de jingguo" (My experience of joining the Merchant Corps). In *GZWZ*. Vol. 7, 97–100. 1963.

Lin, Yu-sheng. *The Crisis of Chinese Consciousness: Radical Anti-Traditionalism in the May Fourth Era.* Madison: University of Wisconsin Press, 1979.

Lin Yungai. "Jieji douzheng zhi yanjiu" (A study of class struggle). *Jianshe* 2, no. 6 (1920): 1–16.

———. "Wanguo lianmeng yu diguo zhuyi" (The League of Nations and imperialism). *Jianshe* 2, no. 2 (1920): 1–11.

Lin Zhijun et al. "Chen Jiongming pan Sun, liansheng zizhi ji minxuan xianzhang" (Chen Jiongming's revolt against Sun Yat-sen, his federalism and electoral scheme for county heads). In *GZWZ*. Vol. 9, 168–95. 1963.

Ling Hongxun [H. H. Ling]. *Zhongguo tieluzhi* (A comprehensive survey of railway development in China). Taipei: Changliu, 1954.

Liu, Lydia H. *Translingual Practice: Literature, National Culture, and Translated Modernity—China, 1900–1937*. Stanford: Stanford University Press, 1995.

Liu Mingkui, ed. *Zhongguo gongren jieji lishi zhuangkuang, 1840–1949* (Historical conditions of the Chinese working class). Vol. 1, part 1. Beijing: Zhonggong zhongyang dangxiao, 1985.

Liu Yongming. *Guomindang ren yu wusi yundong* (Guomindang [Nationalist Party] members and the May Fourth Movement). Beijing: Shehui kexue, 1990.

Liuda yiqian (Before the Sixth Congress). Beijing: Renmin, 1980.

Loewe, Michael. *Imperial China: The Historical Background of the Modern Age*. London: George Allen and Unwin, 1966.

Lu Yu. "Guangzhou de fangbian yiyuan" (The Fangbian Hospital of Canton). In *GDWZ*. Vol. 8, 139–50. 1963.

Luhaijun dayuanshuai dabenying gongbao xuanbian, 1923/2–1924/4 (Selected bulletins from the headquarters of the Generalissimo). Beijing: Shehui kexue, 1981.

"Lun diguo zhuyi fada ji ershi shiji shijie zhi qiantu" (A discussion of the growth of imperialism and the prospects of the world in the twentieth century). In *Xinhai geming qian shinianjian shilun xuanji* (Selected essays of current opinions from the decade prior to the 1911 Revolution), ed. Zhang Nan and Wang Renzhi. Vol. 1, 53–58. Beijing: Sanlian, 1978.

Luo Daming, Sun Lüxi, Liang Furan, Tan Zhushan, and Ma Shaofang. "Dageming shiqi Guangdong gongyun qingkuang de huiyi" (Recollections of the conditions of the labor movement in Guangdong during the Great Revolution). In *GDWZ*. Vol. 42, 144–75. 1984.

Luo Hequn and He Jinzhou. *Liu Ersong*. Guangzhou: Renmin, 1986.

Luo Xing. "Diyici guogong hezuo shiqi Guangzhou gongren daibiaohui de yan'ge" (A history of the Council of Workers' Deputies during the First United Front). In *GDWZ*. Vol. 42, 123–43. 1984.

Ma Chaojun, ed. *Zhongguo laogong yundongshi* (A history of the Chinese labor movement). Vols. 1 and 2. Taipei: Laogong fulishe, 1959.

Ma Min and Zhu Ying. *Chuantong yu jindai de erchong bianzou* (The dual transformation of tradition and modernity). Chengdu: Bashu, 1993.

———. "Qiantan wanqing Suzhou shanghui yu hanghui de qubie ji qi lianxi" (Exploring the differences and relations between the Suzhou Chamber of Commerce and the guilds of the late Qing). *Zhongguo jingjishi yanjiu*, no. 3 (1988): 78–89.

Mann, Susan. *Local Merchants and the Chinese Bureaucracy, 1750–1950*. Stanford: Stanford University Press, 1987.

Mao Sicheng, ed. *Minguo shiwunian yiqian zhi Jiang Jieshi xiansheng* (Mr. Jiang Jieshi [Chiang Kai-shek] before 1926). Hong Kong: Longmen, 1965.

Mayer, Arno J. "The Lower Middle Class as Historical Problem." *Journal of Modern History* 47, no. 3 (1975): 409–36.

McCord, Edward A. "Militia and Local Militarization in Late Qing and Early Republican China: The Case of Hunan." *Modern China* 14, no. 2 (1988): 156–87.

———. *The Power of the Gun: The Emergence of Modern Chinese Warlordism.* Berkeley and Los Angeles: University of California Press, 1993.

Meisner, Maurice. *Li Ta-chao and the Origins of Chinese Marxism.* New York: Atheneum, 1979.

Miller, Michael. *The Bon-Marché: Bourgeois Culture and the Department Store: 1869–1920.* Princeton: Princeton University Press, 1981.

Mingqing Guangdong shehui jingji xingtai yanjiu (A study of the state of economy and society in Guangdong during the Ming-Qing period). Guangzhou: Renmin, 1985.

Minsheng ribao (The People's Livelihood Daily). Guangzhou.

Mitchell, Timothy. *Colonising Egypt.* Berkeley and Los Angeles: University of California Press, 1991.

Mizoguchi Yūzō. "Chūgoku no kō, shi" (Chinese concepts of public and private). *Bungaku*, no. 9 (1988): 88–102; no. 10 (1988): 73–84.

Nanhai xianzhi (Gazetteer of Nanhai County), 1872 and 1910.

Naquin, Susan and Evelyn Rawski. *Chinese Society in the Eighteenth Century.* New Haven: Yale University Press, 1987.

Nathan, Andrew J. *Chinese Democracy.* Berkeley and Los Angeles: University of California Press, 1985.

"Native Banks in Canton". *Chinese Economic Journal* 11, no. 3 (1932): 187–200.

Negishi Tadashi. *Baiban seido no kenkyū* (A study of the compradorial system). Tokyo: Nihon tosho, 1948.

Ni Xiying. *Guangzhou* (Canton). Guangzhou: Zhonghua, 1936.

"Nie Rongzhen dui Guangzhou baodong de yijian, 1927/12/15" (Nie Rongzhen's comments on the Canton Uprising). In *GQZ*. Vol. 1, 354–59.

Nie Rongzhen. *Nie Rongzhen huiyilu* (The memoir of Nie Rongzhen). Beijing: Jiefangjun, 1984.

Nord, Philip. *Paris Shopkeepers and the Politics of Resentment.* Princeton: Princeton University Press, 1986.

Nozawa, Yutaka, ed. *Chūgoku kokumin kakumeishi no kenkyū* (A study of the Chinese Nationalist Revolution). Tokyo: Aoki, 1974.

Osborne, Peter. *The Politics of Time.* London: Verso, 1995.

Ou Jiluan. *Guangdong zhi diandangye* (The pawn shops of Guangdong). Guangzhou: Guoli Zhongshan daxue jingji diaochachu, 1934.

———. *Guangdong zhi yinye* (The native banks of Guangdong). Guangzhou: Guoli Zhongshan daxue jingji diaochachu, 1932.

———. *Guangdong zhibishi* (A history of paper currency in Guangdong). 2 vols. Guangzhou: Guoli Zhongshan daxue jingji diaochachu, 1934 and 1936.

Ozouf, Mona. *Festivals and the French Revolution*. Trans. Alan Sheridan. Cambridge: Harvard University Press, 1988.

Pan Jueqiu. "Wo suo zhi de Guangzhoushi minchan baozhengju" (What I know about the Bureau of Guarantee of People's Properties in Canton). In *GZWZ*. Vol. 9, 137–46. 1963.

Pan Lupeng. "Huifeng yinhang yu Chen Lianbo caozong yinye de huodong" (How the Hongkong and Shanghai Bank and Chen Lianbo controlled the banking sector). In *GZWZ*. Vol. 7, 17–20. 1963.

Panyuxian xuzhi (Supplement to the Gazetteer of Panyu County), 1931.

Peng Zeyi. "Guangzhou shisanhang xutan" (Further investigation of the thirteen guilds of Canton). *Lishi yanjiu*, no. 4 (1981): 110–25.

———. "Qingdai Guangdong yanghang zhidu de qiyuan" (The origins of the Guangdong yanghang system during the Qing). *Lishi yanjiu*, no. 1 (1957): 1–24.

———. "Yapian zhanzheng qian Guangzhou xinxing de qingfang gongye" (The new light industries in Canton before the Opium War). *Lishi yanjiu*, no. 3 (1983): 109–16.

Perrot, Philippe. *Fashioning the Bourgeoisie: A History of Clothing in the Nineteenth Century*. Trans. Richard Bienvenu. Princeton: Princeton University Press, 1994.

Perry, Elizabeth J. *Shanghai on Strike: The Politics of Chinese Labor*. Stanford: Stanford University Press, 1993.

Prakash, Gyan. "Postcolonial Criticism and Indian Historiography." *Social Text*, no. 31/32 (1992): 8–19.

———. "Subaltern Studies as Postcolonial Criticism." *American Historical Review* 99, no. 5 (1994): 1475–90.

———. "Writing Post-Orientalist Histories of the Third World: Perspectives from Indian Historiography." *Comparative Studies of Society and History* 32, no. 2 (1990): 383–408.

Qian Mu. *Zhongguo lidai zhengzhi deshi* (An appraisal of the Chinese political system through imperial times). Hong Kong: Rensheng, 1952.

———. *Zhongguo lishi yanjiufa* (Research methodologies on Chinese history). Taipei: Dongda, 1991.

Qian Yizhang. *Shaji tongshi* (The bitter history of Shaji [Shakee]). Guangzhou, 1925.

Qin Qingjun. "Beifa zhanzheng shiqi de Guangdongsheng caizheng" (The financial administration of Guangdong Province during the Northern Expedition). In *GZWZ*. Vol. 27, 161–93. 1982.

———. "Minguo shiqi Guangdong caizheng shiliao" (Source materials on the financial administration of Guangdong during the Republic). In *GZWZ*. Vol. 29, 1–115. 1983.

Qiu Jie. "Guangdong junzhengfu chuqi de caizheng zhuangkuang" (The financial conditions of the Guangdong military government in the early Republic). In

Jinian xinhai geming qishi zhounian shiliao zhuanji (Source materials commemorating the seventieth anniversary of the 1911 Revolution). Vol. 1, 191–217. Guangzhou: Renmin, 1981.

———. "Guangdong shangren yu xinhai geming" (The Guangdong merchants and the 1911 Revolution). In *Jinian xinhai geming qishi zhounian xueshu taolunhui lunwenji* (Conference essays commemorating the seventieth anniversary of the 1911 Revolution). Vol. 1, 362–96. Beijing: Zhonghua, 1983.

———. "Xinhai geming shiqi de yueshang zizhihui" (The Merchant Self-Government Association and the 1911 Revolution). In *Jinian xinhai geming qishi zhounian qingnian xueshu taolunhui lunwenxuan* (Selected conference essays by younger scholars commemorating the seventieth anniversary of the 1911 Revolution). Vol. 2, 373–400. Beijing: Zhonghua, 1983.

Qu Dajun. *Guangdong xinyu* (New notes on Guangdong). 2 vols. Beijing: Zhonghua, 1985.

Quan Hansheng. *Zhongguo hanghui zhidushi* (A history of the Chinese guild system). Taipei: Shihuo, 1978.

Rankin, Mary Backus. *Elite Activism and Political Transformation in China.* Stanford: Stanford University Press, 1986.

———. "The Origins of a Chinese Public Sphere." *Études chinoises* 9, no. 2 (1990): 13–60.

———. "Some Observations on a Chinese Public Sphere." *Modern China* 19, no. 2 (1993): 158–82.

Rawski, Thomas G. *Economic Growth in Prewar China.* Berkeley and Los Angeles: University of California Press, 1989.

Rea, Kenneth W., ed. *Canton in Revolution: The Collected Papers of Earl Swisher, 1925–1928.* Boulder: Westview Press, 1977.

Remer, C. F. *A Study of Chinese Boycotts (With Special Reference to Their Economic Effectiveness).* Baltimore: Johns Hopkins Press, 1933.

The Report of the Commission for the Investigation of the Shakee Massacre, June 23, 1925, Canton, China. Guangzhou, 1925.

"Report on the Communistic Movement of Youth in China (to November 1926)." In *Missionaries of Revolution*, ed. C. Martin Wilbur and Julie Lien-ying How, 472–78. Cambridge: Harvard University Press, 1989.

Rhoads, Edward. *China's Republican Revolution: The Case of Kwangtung, 1895–1913.* Cambridge: Harvard University Press, 1975.

———. "Merchant Associations in Canton, 1895–1911." In *The Chinese City Between Two Worlds*, ed. Mark Elvin and G. William Skinner, 97–117. Stanford: Stanford University Press, 1974.

———. "Nationalism and Xenophobia in Kwangtung (1905–1906): The Canton Anti-American Boycott and the Lienchow Anti-Missionary Uprising." *Papers on China* 16 (1962): 154–97.

Rigby, Richard W. *The May 30 Movement: Events and Themes*. Canberra: Australian National University Press, 1980.

Ristaino, Marcia R. *China's Art of Revolution: The Mobilization of Discontent, 1927 and 1928*. Durham: Duke University Press, 1987.

Rowe, William T. *Hankow: Commerce and Society in a Chinese City, 1796–1889*. Stanford: Stanford University Press, 1984.

———. *Hankow: Conflict and Community in a Chinese City, 1796–1895*. Stanford: Stanford University Press, 1989.

———. "The Problem of 'Civil Society' in Late Imperial China." *Modern China* 19, no. 2 (1993): 139–57.

———. "The Public Sphere in Modern China." *Modern China* 16, no. 3 (1990): 309–29.

Rozman, Gilbert. *Population and Marketing Settlements in Ch'ing China*. Cambridge: Cambridge University Press, 1982.

Ruan Xiaoxian. *Ruan Xiaoxian wenji* (Selected works of Ruan Xiaoxian). Guangzhou: Renmin, 1984.

Schafer, Edward H. *The Golden Peaches of Samarkand*. Berkeley and Los Angeles: University of California Press, 1963.

Schiffrin, Harold Z. *Sun Yat-sen and the Origins of the Chinese Revolution*. Berkeley and Los Angeles: University of California Press, 1968.

Schoppa, R. Keith. "Local Self-Government in Zhejiang, 1909–1927." *Modern China* 2, no. 4 (1976): 503–30.

———. "Province and Nation: The Chekiang Provincial Autonomy Movement, 1917–1927." *Journal of Asian Studies* 36, no. 4 (1977): 661–74.

Schwarcz, Vera. *The Chinese Enlightenment: Intellectuals and the Legacy of the May Fourth Movement of 1919*. Berkeley and Los Angeles: University of California Press, 1986.

Schwartz, Benjamin I. *Chinese Communism and the Rise of Mao*. Cambridge: Harvard University Press, 1951.

———. "Culture, Modernity, and Nationalism—Further Reflections." *Daedalus* 122, no. 3 (1993): 207–26.

———. *In Search of Wealth and Power: Yen Fu and the West*. Cambridge: Harvard University Press, 1964.

Scott, David. "Colonial Governmentality." *Social Text*, no. 43 (1995): 191–220.

Scott, Joan Wallach. *Gender and the Politics of History*. New York: Columbia University Press, 1988.

Seligman, Adam. *The Idea of Civil Society*. New York: Free Press, 1992.

"Shanghai shangtuan xiaoshi" (A brief history of the Shanghai Merchant Corps). In *Xinhai geming* (The 1911 Revolution). Vol. 7, 86–90. Shanghai: Renmin, 1957.

Shanghai Yongan gongsi de chansheng, fazhan he gaizao (The establishment, devel-

opment and transformation of the Shanghai Yongan [Wing On] Company).
Shanghai: Renmin, 1981.

Shangmin yundong (Merchant movement). Guangzhou.

Shen Qionglou. "Guangzhoushi Haopanjie he Datongjie de bianqian" (The transformation of Haopan Street and Datong Street of Canton). In *GZWZ*. Vol. 7,
1–16. 1963. [Supplement in Vol. 8, 207–10. 1963.]

———. "Qingmo minchu Guangzhou baoye zayi" (Miscellaneous recollections of
the newspaper industry in Canton during the late Qing and the early Republic). In *Zhongguo jindai baokan fazhan gaikuang* (The general development of
newspapers and periodicals in modern China), ed. Yang Guanghui, Xiong
Shanghou, Lü Lianhai, and Li Zhongming, 226–57. Beijing: Xinhua, 1986.

Shen Qionglou and Lu Dunweng. "Cong Qingmo dao kangzhan qian de
Guangzhou baoye" (The Canton newspaper industry from the late Qing to
1937). In *GZWZ*. Vol. 18, 1–32. 1965.

Shen Weibin and Yang Liqiang. "Shanghai shangtuan yu xinhai geming" (The
Shanghai Merchant Corps and the 1911 Revolution). In *Jindai zhongguo zichan
jieji yanjiu* (A study of the modern Chinese bourgeoisie), 400–29. Shanghai:
Fudan daxue, 1983.

Shenggang dabagong ziliao (Source materials on the Great Canton-Hongkong
Strike). Guangzhou: Renmin, 1980.

"Shengwei dui zhongyang zhengzhiju huiyi tongguo zhi 'Guangzhou baodong zhi
yiyi yu jiaoxun' de jueyian, 1928/1/16" (Resolutions of the Guangdong Provincial Committee regarding the passage of 'The meaning and lesson of the Canton Uprising' by the Central Politburo [of the CCP]). In *GQZ*. Vol. 1, 280–84.

"Shengwei duiyu Guangzhou baodong jueyian, 1928/1–5" (Resolutions of the
Guangdong Provincial Committee [of the CCP] regarding the Canton Uprising). In *GQZ*. Vol. 1, 206–13.

Shuangshi: Guangzhou fan'gemingpai shangtuan tusha shiminji (Double tenth: A
chronicle of the massacre by the counterrevolutionary Merchant Corps of
Canton). Guangzhou: Nonggong xunkan, 1924.

Smith, Anthony D. *National Identity*. Reno: University of Nevada Press, 1991.

Smith, Joanna Handlin. "Benevolent Societies: The Reshaping of Charity during
the Late Ming and Early Ch'ing." *Journal of Asian Studies* 46, no. 2 (1987):
309–33.

Soja, Edward W. *Postmodern Geographies: The Reassertion of Space in Critical Social
Theory*. London: Verso, 1989.

———. "The Spatiality of Social Life: Towards a Transformative Retheorisation."
In *Social Relations and Spatial Structures*, ed. David Gregory and John Urry,
90–127. London: Macmillan, 1985.

"Stepanov's Report to a Meeting of the Soviet Group at Canton (Before April 16,
1926)." In *Missionaries of Revolution*, ed. C. Martin Wilbur and Julie Lien-ying
How, 708–16. Cambridge: Harvard University Press, 1989.

Storch, Robert D. "The Policeman as Domestic Missionary: Urban Discipline and Popular Culture in Northern England, 1850–1880." *Journal of Social History* 9, no. 4 (1976): 481–509.

Strand, David. "Community, Society, and History in Sun Yat-sen's *Sanmin zhuyi.*" In *Culture and State in Chinese History: Conventions, Accommodations, and Critiques,* ed. Theodore Huters, R. Bin Wong, and Pauline Yu, 326–45. Stanford: Stanford University Press, 1997.

———. *Rickshaw Beijing: City People and Politics in the 1920s.* Berkeley and Los Angeles: University of California Press, 1989.

Su Yunfeng. "Minchu zhi shangren" (The merchants of the early Republic). *Zhongyang yanjiuyuan jindaishi yanjiusuo jikan,* no. 11 (1982): 47–82.

Sun Benwen. *Dangdai Zhongguo shehuixue* (Contemporary Chinese sociology). Taipei: Liren, 1984.

Sun dazongtong Guangzhou mengnanji (A chronicle of President Sun [Yat-sen]'s mishaps in Canton). Shanghai: Minzhi, 1922.

Sun Fo [Sun Ke]. "Dushi guihualun" (On urban planning). *Jianshe* 1, no. 5 (1919): 1–17.

Sun Yat-sen. *Sanmin zhuyi* (The Three People's Principles). Taipei: Wenhua, 1979.

Sun Zhongshan quanji (Collected works of Sun Zhongshan [Sun Yat-sen]). 11 vols. Beijing: Zhonghua, 1981–86.

Sun Zhongshan xuanji (Selected works of Sun Zhongshan [Sun Yat-sen]). Beijing: Renmin, 1981.

"Symposium: 'Public Sphere'/'Civil Society' in China?" *Modern China* 19, no. 2 (1993).

Taipingyang (The Pacific). Shanghai. 3, no. 7 (Liansheng zizhihao [Special issue on federalism]) (1922).

Takatsuna Hirofumi. "Chūgoku tetsudō rōdō undō no hatten to sono kōzō" (The development and organization of the Chinese railroad labor movement). *Rekishi hyōron,* no. 8 (1977): 26–42.

"Tan Liting de huiyi" (The reminiscences of Tan Liting). In *GZWZ.* Vol. 7, 57–60. 1963.

Tang, Xiaobing. *Global Space and the Nationalist Discourse of Modernity.* Stanford: Stanford University Press, 1996.

Tang Zhijun, ed. *Zhang Taiyan zhenglun xuanji* (Selected political writings of Zhang Taiyan [Zhang Binglin]). 2 vols. Beijing: Zhonghua, 1977.

Tao Lügong. "Shehui" (Society). *Xinqingnian* 3, no. 2 (1917): 1–5.

Thomas, S. Bernard. *"Proletarian Hegemony" in the Chinese Revolution and the Canton Commune of 1927.* Ann Arbor: Michigan Center for Chinese Studies, 1975.

Thompson, E. P. "Eighteenth-century English Society: Class Struggle without Class?" *Social History* 3, no. 2 (1978): 133–65.

———. *The Making of the English Working Class.* London: Pelican, 1968.

Thongchai, Winichakul. *Siam Mapped: A History of the Geo-Body of a Nation*. Honolulu: University of Hawai'i Press, 1994.

Thornton, Richard C. *The Comintern and the Chinese Communists, 1928–1931*. Seattle: University of Washington Press, 1969.

Tochigi Toshio. "Kokumin kakumeiki no Kanton seifu" (The Guangdong Government during the Nationalist Revolution). In *Chūgoku kokumin kakumeishi no kenkyū* (A study of the Chinese Nationalist Revolution), ed. Nozawa Yutaka, 32–78. Tokyo: Aoki, 1974.

Touraine, Alain. *Critique of Modernity*. Trans. David Macey. Oxford: Blackwell, 1995.

"Trade Conditions in Canton." *The Chinese Economic Bulletin* 8, no. 254 (1926): 3–5.

Tsin, Michael. "Canton Remapped." In *Remaking the Chinese City: Modernity and National Identity, 1900–1950*, ed. Joseph W. Esherick. Honolulu: University of Hawai'i Press, forthcoming.

———. "Imagining 'Society' in Early Twentieth-Century China." In *Imagining The People: Chinese Intellectuals and the Concept of Citizenship, 1890–1920*, ed. Joshua A. Fogel and Peter G. Zarrow, 212–31. Armonk, NY: M. E. Sharpe, 1997.

"Tuan Guangzhou diwei gongnongbu baogao, 1925/7/21" (Report of the worker-peasant bureau of the Canton Regional Committee of the Youth Corps). In *GGLWH*. Quntuan wenjian, 1925 (Documents of mass organizations and youth corps), 308–19. 1982.

"Tuan yue quwei guanyu Guangdong gongnong zhuangkuang de baogao 1924/3/6" (Report on the conditions of Guangdong workers and peasants by the Provincial Committee of the Youth Corps). In *GGLWH*. Quntuan wenjian, 1922–1924 (Documents of mass organizations and youth corps), 350–57. 1982.

Turner, John A. *Kwang Tung or Five Years in South China*. London: S. W. Partridge, 1894.

Unger, Jonathan, ed. *Chinese Nationalism*. Armonk, NY: M. E. Sharpe, 1996.

Van de Ven, Hans J. *From Friend to Comrade: The Founding of the Chinese Communist Party, 1920–1927*. Berkeley and Los Angeles: University of California Press, 1991.

Vishnyakova-Akimova, V. V. *Two Years in Revolutionary China, 1925–1927*. Trans. Steven I. Levine. Cambridge: Harvard University Press, 1971.

Wakeman, Frederic, Jr. "The Civil Society and Public Sphere Debate." *Modern China* 19, no. 2 (1993): 108–38.

———. *Policing Shanghai, 1927–1937*. Berkeley and Los Angeles: University of California Press, 1995.

———. *Strangers at the Gate: Social Disorder in South China, 1839–1861*. Berkeley and Los Angeles: University of California Press, 1966.

Waldron, Arthur N. *From War to Nationalism.* Cambridge: Cambridge University Press, 1995.

———. "Theories of Nationalism and Historical Explanation." *World Politics* 37, no. 3 (1984): 416–33.

Wang Jianchu and Sun Maosheng. *Zhongguo gongren yundongshi* (A history of the Chinese labor movement). Shengyang: Renmin, 1987.

Wang Jingwei yanjianglu (Speeches of Wang Jingwei II). Zhongguo yinshuguan, 1926.

Wang Jingwei yanshuoji (Speeches of Wang Jingwei I). Zhongguo yinshuguan, 1926.

Wang Jingyu, ed. *Zhongguo jindai gongyeshi ziliao* (Source materials on the history of modern Chinese industries). Vol. 2, parts 1 and 2 [1895–1914]. Beijing: Kexue, 1957.

Wang Ping. "Guangdongsheng de difang zizhi: minguo ershi niandai" (Local self-government in Guangdong during the 1930s). *Zhongyang yanjiuyuan jindaishi yanjiusuo jikan* 7 (1978): 485–508.

Wang Qingbin, Wang Shuxun, Lin Songhe, and Fan Hong, eds. *Diyici Zhongguo laodong nianjian* (The first Chinese labor yearbook). Beiping: Shehui diaochabu, 1928.

Wang Yunsheng. *Liushinianlai Zhongguo yu Riben* (Sixty years of relationship between China and Japan). Vol. 5. Beijing: Sanlian, 1980.

Wang Zhenghua. "Guangzhou shiqi guomin zhengfu de caizheng" (The financial administration of the Nationalist government during its Canton years). In *Zhongguo jindai xiandai shi lunji* (Essays on modern and contemporary Chinese history). Vol. 24, 511–44. Taipei: Zhonghua wenhua fuxing yundong tuixing weiyuanhui, 1986.

Wang Zongyan. *Guangdong wenwu congtan* (Miscellaneous writings on the culture of Guangdong). Hong Kong: Zhonghua, 1974.

Wasserstrom, Jeffrey N. *Student Protests in Twentieth-Century China.* Stanford: Stanford University Press, 1991.

White, Hayden. *Tropics of Discourse: Essays in Cultural Criticism.* Baltimore: Johns Hopkins University Press, 1978.

Who's Who in China. 3rd ed. Shanghai: The China Weekly Review, 1925.

Wilbur, C. Martin. *Forging the Weapons: Sun Yat-sen and the Kuomintang in Canton, 1924.* Mimeographed. New York: East Asian Institute of Columbia University, 1966.

———. *The Nationalist Revolution in China, 1923–1928.* Cambridge: Cambridge University Press, 1983.

———. "Problems of Starting a Revolutionary Base: Sun Yat-sen and Canton, 1923." *Bulletin of the Institute of Modern History, Academia Sinica,* no. 4, part 2 (1974): 665–727.

———. *Sun Yat-sen: Frustrated Patriot*. New York: Columbia University Press, 1976.

Wilbur, C. Martin and Julie Lien-ying How, eds. *Missionaries of Revolution: Soviet Advisers and Nationalist China, 1920–27*. Cambridge: Harvard University Press, 1989.

Williams, Raymond. *Key Words: A Vocabulary of Culture and Society*. Rev. ed. New York: Oxford University Press, 1985.

Wolf, Eric R. "Inventing Society." *American Ethnologist* 15, no. 4 (1988): 752–61.

Wong, Siu-lun. *Sociology and Socialism in Contemporary China*. London: Routledge & Kegan Paul, 1979.

Woodside, Alexander B. *Community and Revolution in Modern Vietnam*. Boston: Houghton Mifflin, 1976.

Wou, Odoric Y. K. *Mobilizing the Masses*. Stanford: Stanford University Press, 1994.

Wu Guilong. "Qingmo Shanghai difang zizhi yundong shulun" (An account of the local self-government movement in late Qing Shanghai). In *Jinian xinhai geming qishi zhounian qingnian xueshu taolunhui lunwenxuan* (Selected conference essays by younger scholars commemorating the seventieth anniversary of the 1911 Revolution). Vol. 2, 401–46. Beijing: Zhonghua, 1983.

Wu Jin. "Jiefang qian Guangzhoushi siying jiqi gongye gaikuang" (The general conditions of the machine-tool industry in the private sector of Canton before Liberation). In *GZWZ*. Vol. 23, 73–106. 1981.

Wu Tiecheng. *Wu Tiecheng huiyilu* (The memoir of Wu Tiecheng). Taipei: Sanmin, 1968.

Wu, Tien-wei. "Chiang Kai-shek's April 12th Coup of 1927." In *China in the 1920s: Nationalism and Revolution*, ed. F. Gilbert Chan and Thomas H. Etzold, 147–159. New York: New Viewpoints, 1976.

———. "Chiang Kai-shek's March Twentieth Coup d'etat of 1926." *Journal of Asian Studies* 27, no. 3 (1968): 585–602.

Wu Weiyong. "Guangdong bingqi zhizaochang gailüe" (A sketch of the Guangdong arsenal). In *GDWZ*. Vol. 9, 18–28. 1963.

Wu Yannan, Feng Zuyi, and Su Zhongli, eds. *Qingmo shehui sichao* (Currents of ideas in late Qing society). Fuzhou: Renmin, 1990.

Wusa yundong shiliao (Source materials on the May Thirtieth Movement). 2 vols. Shanghai: Renmin, 1981 and 1986.

Wusi aiguo yundong dang'an ziliao (Archival materials on the patriotic May Fourth Movement). Beijing: Shehui kexue, 1980.

Wusi shiqi de shetuan (Social organizations during the May Fourth period). 4 vols. Beijing: Sanlian, 1979.

Xian Yuqing. "Qingdai liusheng xiban zai Guangdong" (Theatrical troupes from six provinces in Qing Guangdong). *Zhongshan daxue xuebao*, no. 3 (1963): 105–20.

Xiao Fanbo. "Guangzhou Xianshi gongsi saduonian de shengshuai" (The rise and decline of the Xianshi [Sincere] Company in thirty-plus years). In *GZWZ*. Vol. 23, 126–52. 1981.

Xing Bixin, Wu Duo, Lin Songhe, and Zhang Tiezheng, eds. *Dierci Zhongguo laodong nianjian* (The second Chinese labor yearbook). Beiping: Shehui diaochabu, 1932.

Xinqingnian (New Youth). Shanghai and Guangzhou.

Xinshangmin (New Merchant). Guangzhou.

Xu Junming, Guo Peizhong, and Xu Xiaomei. *Guangzhou shihua* (A history of Canton). Shanghai: Renmin, 1984.

Yan Fu. *Yan Fu juan* (Selected works of Yan Fu). Ed. and with an introduction by Liu Mengxi. Hebei: Jiaoyu, 1996.

———. "Yuanqiang" (On the source of strength). In *Zhongguo zhexueshi ziliao xuanji: jindai zhi buxia* (Selected source materials on the history of philosophy in China: Part II of the modern period), 357–89. Beijing: Zhonghua, 1953.

Yang Guanghui, Xiong Shanghou, Lü Lianghai, and Li Zhongming, eds. *Zhongguo jindai baokan fazhan gaikuang* (The general development of newspapers and periodicals in modern China). Beijing: Xinhua, 1986.

Ye Xian'en and Jiang Zuyuan, eds. *Ming Qing Guangdong shehui jingji yanjiu* (A study of the economy and society of Guangdong during the Ming-Qing period). Guangzhou: Renmin, 1987.

Yeh, Wen-hsin. *The Alienated Academy: Culture and Politics in Republican China, 1919–1937*. Cambridge: Harvard University Press, 1990.

———. *Provincial Passages: Culture, Space, and the Origins of Chinese Communism*. Berkeley and Los Angeles: University of California Press, 1996.

"Yida" qianhou (Around the First Congress). 2 vols. Beijing: Renmin, 1980.

"Yida" qianhou de Guangdong dang zuzhi (The organization of the Guangdong party around the First Congress). Compiled jointly by Zhonggong Guangdongsheng shengwei dangshi yanjiu weiyuanhui bangongshi (Office of the research committee on party history of the Guangdong Provincial Committee of the CCP) and Guangdongsheng dang'anguan (The Guangdong Provincial Archives), 1981.

Yijiuersinian Guangzhou shangtuan shijian (The 1924 Merchant Corps incident in Canton). Hong Kong: Chongwen, 1974.

Yokoyama Hiroaki. "Kanton seiken no zaisei hippaku to Son Bun seiji" (Sun Wen [Sun Yat-sen]'s government and the financial crisis of the Guangdong administration). *Shakai keizai shigaku* 42, no. 5 (1977): 22–43.

———. *Son Chūzan no kakumei to seiji shidō* (The revolutionary and political leadership of Sun Zhongshan [Sun Yat-sen]). Tokyo: Kembun, 1983.

Yokoyama Suguru. *Chūgoku no kindaika to chihō seiji* (Local government and the modernization of China). Tokyo: Keisō, 1985.

Youguan Chen Jiongming ziliao (Source materials on Chen Jiongming). Mimeographed. Guangzhou: Guangdongsheng shehui kexueyuan, 1965.

Young, Ernest P. *The Presidency of Yuan Shih-k'ai*. Ann Arbor: University of Michigan Press, 1977.

Young, John D. "Sun Yatsen and the Department Store: An aspect of national reconstruction." In *Asian Department Stores*, ed. Kerrie L. MacPherson, 33–45. Honolulu: University of Hawai'i Press, 1998.

Young, Robert. *Colonial Desire: Hybridity in Theory, Culture and Race*. London: Routledge, 1995.

———. *White Mythologies: Writing History and the West*. London: Routledge, 1990.

Yu Qizhong, ed. *Guangzhou gongren jiating zhi yanjiu* (Research on workers' families in Canton). Guangzhou: Guoli Zhongshan daxue jingji diaochachu, 1934.

———, ed. *Guangzhou laozi zhengyi de fenxi* (An analysis of capital-labor disputes in Canton). Guangzhou: Guoli Zhongshan daxue jingji diaochachu, 1934.

Yueshang weichi gonganhui tongrenlu (The membership roster of the Guangdong Merchant Association for the Maintenance of Public Order). Guangzhou, 1912.

Yueshang zizhihui hanjian chubian (Correspondence of the Guangdong Merchant Self-Government Association). Guangzhou, 1908.

Yuesheng shangtuan yuebao (The Guangdong Merchant Corps Monthly). Guangzhou.

Zeng Yangfu. *Guangzhou zhi gongye* (The industries of Canton). Guangzhou: Guangzhou shili yinhang jingji diaochashi, 1937.

Zeng Zhongmou. *Guangdong jingji fazhanshi* (A history of the economic development of Guangdong). Guangzhou: Guangdongsheng yinhang jingji yanjiushi, 1942.

Zhang Guotao. *Wo de huiyi* (My recollections). 2nd ed. 3 vols. Hong Kong: Mingbao, 1971–74.

Zhang Hong. *Xianggang haiyuan dabagong* (The Great Hongkong Seamen's Strike). Guangzhou: Renmin, 1979.

Zhang Jingru and Liu Zhiqiang, eds. *Beiyang junfa tongzhi shiqi Zhongguo shehui zhi bianqian* (The transformation of Chinese society during the rule of the northern warlords). Beijing: Renmin daxue, 1992.

Zhang Junqian and Chen Guo. "Foshan shangtuan jianwen" (What I know about the Foshan Merchant Corps). In *Foshan wenshi ziliao* (Source materials on the history and culture of Foshan), 43–46. 1982.

Zhang Lei. "Sun Zhongshan yu yijiuersinian Guangzhou shangtuan panluan" (Sun Zhongshan [Sun Yat-sen] and the 1924 Merchant Corps rebellion). In *Shixue lunwenji* (Essays on historical studies), 167–92. Guangzhou: Renmin, 1980.

Zhang Nan and Wang Renzhi, eds. *Xinhai geming qian shinianjian shilun xuanji*

(Selected essays of current opinions from the decade prior to the 1911 Revolution). 3 vols. Beijing: Sanlian, 1978.

Zhang Songnian. "Shehui" (Society). *Xinqingnian* 9, no. 3 (suiganlu [record of miscellaneous thoughts]) (1921): 1–2.

Zhang Yuanfeng, ed. *Guangzhoushi shehui tongji huikan* (Statistics on Canton society). Guangzhou: Guangdongsheng diaocha tongjiju, 1935.

Zhang Yufa, ed. *Zhongguo xiandaishi lunji: hufa yu beifa* (Essays on contemporary Chinese history: The protect-the-constitution movement and the Northern Expedition). Vol. 7. Taipei: Lianjing, 1982.

Zheng Yanfan. "Wo zai wusi yundong zhong de yixie jingli" (Some of my experiences during the May Fourth Movement). In *GDWZ*. Vol. 24, 33–37. 1979.

Zheng Yifang. *Shanghai qianzhuang, 1843–1937* (The native banks of Shanghai). Taipei: Zhongyang yanjiuyuan sanmin zhuyi yanjiusuo, 1981.

"Zhonggong Guangdong quwei guanyu gongren yundong de baogao, 1925/10/10" (Report on the labor movement by the Guangdong Provincial Committee of the CCP). In *GGLWH*. Zhonggong Guangdong quwei wenjian, 1921–1926 (Documents of the Guangdong Provincial Committee of the CCP), 45–79. 1982.

"Zhonggong Guangdong quwei guanyu shenggang bagong qingkuang de baogao, 1925/7" ([First] report on the conditions of the Canton-Hongkong Strike by the Guangdong Provincial Committee of the CCP). In *GGLWH*. Zhonggong Guangdong quwei wenjian, 1921–1926 (Documents of the Guangdong Provincial Committee of the CCP), 25–37. 1982.

"Zhonggong Guangdong quwei guanyu shenggang bagong qingkuang de baogao, 1925/10" ([Second] report on the conditions of the Canton-Hongkong Strike by the Guangdong Provincial Committee of the CCP). In *GGLWH*. Zhonggong Guangdong quwei wenjian, 1921–1926 (Documents of the Guangdong Provincial Committee of the CCP), 81–91. 1982.

"Zhonggong Guangdong shengwei gei zhongyang de baogao, 1927/12/8" (Report from the Guangdong Provincial Committee to the Party [CCP] Center). In *GGLWH*. Zhonggong Guangdong quwei wenjian, 1921–1926 (Documents of the Guangdong Provincial Committee of the CCP), 185–86. 1982.

Zhongguo Guomindang diyierci quanguo daibiao dahui huiyi shiliao (Source materials on the First and Second Party Congresses of the Chinese Nationalist Party). Compiled by Zhongguo dier lishi dang'anguan (The no. 2 archives). 2 vols. Jiangsu guji, 1986.

Zhongguo jindai jinrongshi (A history of modern Chinese finance). Beijing: Jinrong, 1985.

Zhongguo jindai xiandaishi lunji [hufa yu beifa] (Essays on modern and contemporary Chinese history [The protect-the-constitution movement and the Northern Expedition]). Vol. 24. Taipei: Zhonghua wenhua fuxing yundong tuixing weiyuanhui, 1986.

Zhonghua minguo huobishi ziliao, Vol. 1 [1912–1927] (Source materials on the history of currencies in the Republic). Shanghai: Renmin, 1986.

Zhonghua minguo kaiguo wushinian wenxian [geming yuanliu yu geming yundong] (Documents from the first fifty years of the Republic [The sources of revolution and the revolutionary movement]). Vol. 16, part 1. Taipei: Zhonghua minguo kaiguo wushinian wenxian weiyuanhui, 1965.

Zhonghua minguoshi dang'an ziliao huibian [cong Guangzhou junzhengfu zhi Wuhan guomin zhengfu] (Archival materials on republican history [From the Canton Military Government to the Wuhan Nationalist Government]). Compiled by Zhongguo dier lishi dang'anguan (The no. 2 archives). Vol. 4, parts 1 and 2. Jiangsu guji, 1986.

"Zhongyang gao Guangdong tongzhi shu, 1928/1/18" (Correspondence from the Party [CCP] Center to the comrades in Guangdong). In *GQZ*. Vol. 1, 287–301.

"Zhongyang tonggao, No. 35: 'Guangzhou baodong zhi yiyi yu jiaoxun' jueyian de buchong, 1928/2/26" (Bulletin from the Party [CCP] Center, No. 35: Supplement to the resolution on "The meaning and lesson of the Canton Uprising"). In *GQZ*. Vol. 1, 325–32.

"Zhongyang zhi shengwei xin, 1928/1/25" (Letter from the Party [CCP] Center to the Provincial Committee). In *GQZ*. Vol. 1, 306–18.

Zhou Ruisong. "Yijiuersinian Guangzhou de minchan baozheng" (Guaranteeing people's properties in Canton in 1924). In *GZWZ*. Vol. 9, 132–36. 1963.

Zhou Siming. "Wushinianlai de Guangdong jinrong gaikuang" (The general conditions of the Guangdong financial market over fifty years). In *Wenshi ziliao xuanji* (Selected source materials on history and culture). Vol. 5, 20–43. Guangzhou: Renmin, 1962.

Zhou Xiuluan. *Diyici shijie dazhan shiqi Zhongguo minzu gongye de fazhan* (The development of Chinese native industries during the First World War). Shanghai: Renmin, 1958.

Zhou Yumin and Shao Yong. *Zhongguo banghuishi* (A history of secret societies, fraternal organizations and gangs in China). Shanghai: Renmin, 1993.

Zhu Ying. "Xinhai geming shiqi de Suzhou shangtuan" (The Suzhou Merchant Corps during the 1911 Revolution). *Jindaishi yanjiu*, no. 35 (1986): 109–23.

Zou Lu. *Zhongguo Guomindang shigao* (A draft history of the Chinese Nationalist Party). Taipei: Shangwu, 1970.

Index

Abend, Hallett, 143, 146, 167
Academy of Law and Government, Guangdong, 43, 56
Addresses to the German Nation, 53
Aiyu, the, 25–26, 27, 28, 35, 45, 105
American China Development Company, 134
Anderson, Benedict, 4
anti-American boycott of 1905, 34, 41
anti-Japanese boycott of 1908, 39, 40
Anti-Opium Association, Guangdong, 29, 35–36, 38
Association of Chambers of Commerce, Guangdong, 93, 105
Association for the Maintenance of Trade, Guangdong, 105–6

banks: Hongkong and Shanghai Bank, 22, 89, 95, 109; during late Qing period, 22, 29, 33, 37; during republican period, 47, 70, 89, 95, 97, 106, 109, 158, 159, 198n25, 216n76
Beijing Road, 61, 62
Bi Changyan, 35
Blyukher, V. K., 126
Borodin, Michael, 98
boycotts, 34, 39, 40, 154–55, 169, 171
Bund, the, 58–60, 62, 106, 124, 125, 151, 152
Bureau of Guarantee of People's Properties, 97, 149

Cai Chang, 106
Canton, during late Qing period: banks in, 22, 29, 33, 37, 47; Chamber of Commerce in, 18–19, 28–29, 34, 37, 41, 43; city walls, 17–18, 26, 27; commerce in, 16–23, 59; descriptions, 16–21; end of Qing government

in, 44–47; and foreign trade, 20, 21–22, 37, 40–41; gentry/gentry-merchants in, 18–19, 24, 25–26, 27, 29, 33, 34, 35, 36, 37, 40, 41, 42, 43, 44; Haopanjie (Moatside Street) in, 19–20, 21; imperial officials in, 17, 18–19, 21, 25, 27, 29, 32, 33–34, 44; industrialists in, 40–41, 65–66; merchant militias in, 24, 25, 44; merchants in, 16–23, 24, 25, 27–29, 31, 31–32, 33–34, 35–36, 37–38, 40, 42, 43, 44, 47–50, 91; municipal government in, 17, 18, 60; Nine Charitable Halls in, 10, 24–31, 32, 33, 34, 35, 39, 200n58; opposition to republicans in, 44–45; political importance of, 17; as port city, 21, 22–23; relations with Hong Kong, 21–22, 23, 28, 45, 134; Seventy-two Guilds of, 28–29, 41; urban reconstruction in, 57–58, 119; Wenlan Academy, 21, 35; Western presence in, 21–22; Xiguan (Western Suburb) in, 20–21, 25, 26, 27, 29. *See also* Canton, during republican period; Guangdong Anti-Opium Association; Guangdong Merchant Self-Government Association; Guangdong Province
Canton, during republican period: banks in, 70, 89, 97, 106, 158, 159, 198n25, 216n76; the Bund in, 58–60, 62, 106, 124, 125, 151, 152; Chamber of Commerce in, 89, 93–94, 100–101, 102, 103, 105, 113; Changdi section in, 58–60; Communist uprising in, 172–73, 174–76, 234n153; department stores in, 58–60, 62, 64–65, 74, 106; descriptions, 143, 146, 167, 171; dual ownership of shops in, 98–102; Honam section in, 65, 66, 69, 71, 106–7; industrialists in, 11, 65–72, 88, 102; May Day Riot of 1926, 115–16, 119,

269

Library of Congress Cataloging-in-Publication Data

Tsin, Michael Tsang-Woon.
    Nation, governance, and modernity: Canton, 1900–1927 / Michael Tsin
        p.   cm. — (Studies of the East Asian Institute, Columbia University)
    Includes bibliographical references and index.
    ISBN 0-8047-4820-9 (pbk. : alk. paper)
        1. Guangzhou (China)—Social policy. 2. Guangzhou (China)—Social
conditions—20th century.
        I. Title.   II. Series: Studies of the East Asian Institute.
HN740.G83T75 1999
306'.0951'275—dc21   99-16648

Original printing 1999

Last figure below indicates year of this printing:
08   07   06   05   04   03   02

Typeset by BookMatters in 11/14 Adobe Garamond